Praise for *Neuroscience for Leadership*

"*Neuroscience for Leadership* is a must-read for any leader, not just business leaders. The authors take the complicated world of brain function and emotions and map them to those critical decision moments all leaders face – making it clear that the inside factors are just as important, if not more so, as the outside ones!"

–Glenn A. Youngkin, Co-President and Co-Chief Operating
Officer, The Carlyle Group

"Where science meets leadership, for aspiring leaders in the new and dynamic tech world. This fascinating book takes over where other 'how to' books leave off."

–Ned Spieker, Former Chairman, CEO, Spieker Properties NYSE
(New York Stock Exchange); Chairman, Continuing Life

"In absolute contrast with the typically lightweight fare found in books on leadership, *Neuroscience for Leadership* really educates, informs, and gives actionable advice. It's not tediously academic nor riddled with airport bookstore clichés. Food for the mind. Highly recommended."

–Raymond van Niekerk, CMO, Investec

"In all of the dozen or more businesses I have created, the towering issue has been enabling people to do simple things they find difficult to do. The neuroscience of this is the missing link in management training. The authors provide a hugely valuable insight."

–Brian Kingham, Chairman, Reliance Security Group Ltd.

"The authors blend neuroscience, brain chemistry, psychology, and business to better understand what leaders do, why they do it, and most importantly how they can change to be more effective. The book is infinitely readable and pragmatic, with fun facts about the brain and practical steps to creating sustainable behavioral change. Covering topics from emotional intelligence to goal setting, values and purpose to self-confidence, risk to inertia, this book is wide in reach and application."

–Deborah L Ancona, Seley Distinguished Professor of Management,
Faculty Director of the MIT Leadership Center

"Thoroughly researched and finely written, the real brilliance of *Neuroscience for Leadership* is how it links scientific brain network research with solid advice on decision-making, employee motivation, and organizational growth! Perceptive and brilliant!"
    –Marshall Goldsmith, author or editor of 34 books including the global bestsellers *MOJO* and *What Got You Here Won't Get You There*

"If you have ever wondered what could be going on in the brain of individuals you are managing – or in your brain – this book provides a clear, easy to understand, and entertaining neuroscience explanation. More importantly, it shows how to use these neurochemical processes to develop your leadership capacity to full potential and to inspire and motivate others to innovate and achieve common organizational goals."
    –Dr William A Ribich, Director, Physical Sciences Inc; Former President, CEO Foster-Miller Inc (one of the 100 most innovative companies in the USA, *INC Magazine*)

"If you are jaded by the torrent of books on leadership and organizational behavior, read this one for a refreshing change! The authors distil the conclusions from neuroscience research and apply them to leadership, governance, management, administration, and personal development in a most readable way. Each chapter presents fascinating vignettes on a wide range of topics."
    –Sir John Daniel, O.C., Former Assistant Director-General, UNESCO for Education; Former Vice-Chancellor, The Open University

"This stimulating book brims with useful insights and sage advice on practically every page. Managing emotions, communication, decision-making, and intuition are just some of the topics that it illuminates. Highly recommended!"
    –Dennis Tourish, Professor of Leadership and Organisation Studies, Royal Holloway; author of *The Dark Side of Transformational Leadership!*

The Neuroscience of Business series

Neuroscience is changing our understanding of how the human brain works and how and why people behave the way they do. Properly understood, many of these insights could lead to profound changes in the way businesses interact with their employees and customers. The problem is that, until now, most of this research has been published in specialist journals and has not made its way to managers' desks. At the same time, however, business leaders and managers are faced with a plethora of extravagant claims based on misunderstood, or exaggerated, neuroscientific research.

Palgrave's The Neuroscience of Business series seeks to bridge the gap between rigorous science and the practical needs of business. For the first time this series will describe the practical managerial applications of this science in an accessible, but in-depth, way that is firmly underpinned by a clear explanation of the science behind the management actions proposed.

Series editors: Peter Chadwick and Roderick Millar

Series ISBN 9781137478320

Neuroscience for Leadership

Tara Swart
CEO, The Unlimited Mind, UK

Kitty Chisholm
Director, Boardwalk Leadership, UK

Paul Brown
Senior Advisor, Vietnam Veterans of America Foundation, Vietnam. Faculty Professor – Organisational Neuroscience, Monarch Business School, Switzerland

First published 2015 by
PALGRAVE MACMILLAN

Palgrave Macmillan in the UK is an imprint of Macmillan Publishers Limited, registered in England, company number 785998, of Houndsmills, Basingstoke, Hampshire, RG21 6XS.

Palgrave Macmillan in the US is a division of St Martin's Press LLC, 175 Fifth Avenue, New York, NY 10010.

Palgrave is the global academic imprint of the above companies and has companies and representatives throughout the world.

Palgrave® and Macmillan® are registered trademarks in the United States, the United Kingdom, Europe and other countries.

ISBN 978–1–137–46685–3

This book is printed on paper suitable for recycling and made from fully managed and sustained forest sources. Logging, pulping and manufacturing processes are expected to conform to the environmental regulations of the country of origin.

A catalogue record for this book is available from the British Library.

Library of Congress Cataloging-in-Publication Data
Swart, Tara.
Neuroscience for leadership : harnessing the brain gain advantage / Tara Swart, CEO, The Unlimited Mind, UK, Kitty Chisholm, Director, Boardwalk Leadership, UK, Paul Brown, Senior Advisor, Vietnam Veterans of America Foundation, Vietnam.
pages cm. — (The neuroscience of business)
ISBN 978–1–137–46685–3 (hardback)
1. Leadership—Psychological aspects.   I. Chisholm, Kitty.   II. Brown, Paul.   III. Title.
BF637.L4S93 2015
158'.4—dc23   2014038811

Typeset by MPS Limited, Chennai, India.

Dedications

Tara: In their memory – my grandmother Amiya Kana Ganguli, a true leader as matriarch, and my grandfather Narendranath Banerjee, who nurtured my developing brain with unconditional love.

Kitty: For Aleca and Jacey (the but for whom), Alexandra and Roderick, with my love and gratitude.

Paul: To Tara, who made this book come alive for me; and to Jane Meyler who made the introduction to Tara.

Contents

Boxes and Figures / x
Acknowledgments / xiii
Preface / xiv

1   There is Chemistry and Then There is *Chemistry* / 1

2   Brains, Bodies and Businesses: A Systems Approach / 18

3   The New Model Leader / 40

4   Testosterone, Risk and Entrepreneurship / 60

5   Why is the Soft Stuff so Hard? / 76

6   The Challenge of Decisions / 93

7   Changing Yourself – Changing Others / 111

8   Elite Performance, Brain Agility and Engagement / 126

9   Stress, Resilience and Confidence / 150

10   Creating the Spark, Lighting the Fire / 173

11   Difference, Diversity and Gender / 192

12   Whole Person, Vibrant Organization / 211

Glossary / 224
Notes / 233
Index / 247

Boxes and Figures

Boxes

1.1   Neurotransmitters / 5

1.2   Neurotransmitters and hormones / 5

1.3   Hormones / 6

1.4   Adaptive behavior / 10

1.5   Oxytocin / 15

2.1   Executive functions / 19

2.2   Evolutionary responses / 20

2.3   Maintaining success / 21

2.4   Studies on neuroplasticity / 22

2.5   Dealing with distractions / 29

2.6   Don: a case study / 33

2.7   Body scan exercise / 35

3.1   Self-control and marshmallows / 47

4.1   Risk and culture / 64

4.2   Carter: a case study / 70

5.1   Your brain creates the world / 77

5.2   Theory of Mind / 79

6.1   Decisions are hard work / 95

6.2   The Zeigarnik effect / 99

7.1   Neuronal connections / 111

7.2   Marina: a case study / 113
7.3   Pruning connections / 115
7.4   Free will or free won't / 120
8.1   Brain and body challenges / 127
8.2   Art: a lavender case study / 128
8.3   Aaron: a case study / 131
8.4   Engagement / 144
8.5   The amygdala response / 146
9.1   Cortisol / 154
9.2   Cortisol contagion / 157
9.3   Cognitive behavioral stress management (CBSM) / 159
9.4   Nate: a case study / 160
9.5   Contested and uncontested leadership and stress / 163
9.6   Scarcity effect / 164
9.7   Cognitive bias modification (CBM) / 165
10.1   Andy: a case study / 177
10.2   Flow / 180
10.3   Cui bono? / 183
10.4   A walk in the woods / 189
10.5   Chris: a case study / 190
11.1   Creativity from adversity / 196
11.2   Attitudes to uncertainty / 202
11.3   Imposter syndrome / 206
12.1   Memes / 213
12.2   Making memes virulent / 216

Figures

1.1   Eight basic emotions spectrum / 12
3.1   A new neuroscience-based leadership model / 58
4.1   Neural Tethering Model© / 69
8.1   Bodily maps of emotions / 130
8.2   Brain agility model / 137
8.3   Brain agility model© percentages / 140
11.1   Differential wiring of male (upper) versus female (lower) brains / 199
11.2   Barriers to women achieving board-level leadership roles / 204

Acknowledgments

We would all like to thank Roddy Millar and Peter Chadwick for their belief in us, their support and for publishing Paul Brown's *Brain Gain* series in IEDP's *Developing Leaders* since 2012. Our profound gratitude to Tamsine O'Riordan, Josie Taylor and Stephen Partridge for their enthusiasm for the book, and for their hard work and patience that saw us through.

Very special thanks to those who inspired us and those who read and commented on the book at various stages.

Kitty:

Thanks to John Chisholm whose critical comments, experience and examples helped enormously and Shaheena Janjuha-Jivraj, who went well beyond the call of duty, to Shamus and Ella Foster and Diana Theodores. Thanks to all the participants in the Cisco ADP program for their challenges and insights, and thanks also to the Henley MSc In Coaching and Behavioural Change duo, Patricia Bossons and Alison Hardingham for their inspirational teaching and introduction of Tara and Kitty. To my fellow MSc cohort and especially our Supervision group, you know how much I owe you! And finally my gratitude to all the leaders I have worked with and for, for teaching me so much.

Paul and Tara:

To Jane Meyler for introducing us to each other and encouraging us on to the path of applying neuroscience to business. Also to all the patients and clients who have sculpted our brains over the years.

Preface

If those leading-edge institutions, the Royal Society, the Royal Society of Arts and the Royal Institution all independently set up programs about modern neuroscience,[1] as they have done since 2010, then something must be stirring in the scientific community. When US President Obama committed 100 million dollars a year for ten years to this specific area of research, as he did in 2013, then doubled it the next year; and the European Union also committed 100 million euros a year for the same period to a slightly different approach to brain research; and when, in 2013, the US National Institute for Mental Health (NIMH) said the latest edition of psychiatry's "bible", the *Diagnostic and Statistical Manual of Mental Disorders* (DSM-5) needed to be torn up and the whole exercise started again based on what was going on in the brain, then it might reasonably be assumed that something is more than stirring – especially when it is realized that private funding in this area is far outstripping public funding. When Muse released their sixth album *The 2nd Law* with a colorful image of the white matter fibers in the brain obtained with diffusion MRI (Diffusion Tensor Imaging), an image obtained from the Human Connectome project, a five year project funded by the National Institutes of Health (NIH) to find the networks of the human brain, then neuroscience is also creeping into popular culture.

This area feels like the final great frontier of knowledge. It is the systematic, scientific exploration of the most complex known structure, the human brain. How do 86 billion brain cells, triggered by electrical discharges that create chemical messengers travelling at a little short of 300 miles an hour within the spongy tissues that fill the small space of the skull, and that we call "the brain" make us conscious and (arguably) rational human beings – able, indeed, to let us think we can inspect our own thinking? How do they create "a person"?

Transplant a liver from one person to another it functions like the liver that was lost. Transplant a brain from one person to another – a medical advance not yet accomplished, but within the realm of imagination, if not possibility – and do you think it would express the same personality as it did when it resided in its original owner's skull or take on the embodied mind of the new owner?

Our brains are us but through experience and especially through relationship, we also shape our brains. So though the overall *structure* of any one person's brain is largely the same as any other person's, the precise *function* is unique to the individual. Towns are the same the world over, and yet every one is different. So it is with human beings. The elements of all brains are the same but the way they have been organized within any one particular person is unique to that person. No wonder human beings are difficult to manage! Think if, in every dealing room in the world, each computer's system operated just a little differently from every other one. What chaos! But that's how people are and what management contends with. What a relief to know more about how to contend successfully.

In 2004 Greene and Cohen argued persuasively that, so far as the law was concerned, "neuroscience changes nothing and everything".[2] We are of a similar view with regard to the application of neuroscience in organizations. What we are fascinated by is how the research that is going on in laboratories around the world can be responsibly put into organizational use. Driven essentially by genetics and medicine, the research findings in modern neuroscience also have huge implications for both ordinary and extraordinary human behavior. In the way that thirty years ago medicine moved from repairing sports injuries to finding ways of enhancing sporting performance, so applied neuroscience has that possibility too. We want to help move it from medicine to the management of both the organization and the individual. This book is about that.

So the neurobiology (the study of the biology of nervous systems, including the brain) of behavior is going to be the defining science of the first half of the twenty-first century, in the way that genetics and information sciences were in the second half of the twentieth century. If profit comes from the way that human behavior – and especially energy – is directed towards the strategic and operational goals of the organization, then improving leadership's understanding of how that works has huge implications for organizational sustainability. Human beings are energy resources and have boundless supplies if properly managed. Badly managed, they react like a car driven with one foot on the accelerator and one on the brake. They shudder to a halt or burn out. It is called executive stress, and is largely unnecessary. This book explains why.

It is no longer disputed that every thought, action, feeling that goes on in every one of us millisecond by millisecond is underpinned by its own neurochemistry (the study of the chemistry of nervous systems, including the brain) within the cells that make up the brain. In 2009[3] Paul and Tara, together with their colleague Jane Meyler, argued for an approach to using neuroscience in organizations that started from what the new findings in neuroscience were telling us. In particular they called for more work on what leaders need to know about the functioning of their own brains so that they might understand and influence the decision-making organs of their colleagues more by intention than by chance. This book is that work.

As authors we came together from three different areas of expertise to channel our sense that neuroscience was changing the way we could understand some of the "why" people behave as they do, and why some ways of leading in organizations work and others don't, into something that could be used by leaders across different kinds and sizes of organizations globally. We brought with us a passionate enthusiasm for this subject, and deep knowledge and experience in different fields; medicine and neuroscience (Tara), leadership and organizational learning (Kitty), and clinical and organizational psychology (Paul). All three of us are also experienced executive coaches, working at senior levels across different countries, cultures and industries, in both the private and public sectors.

So you will hear three voices as you read this book. We have not tried to homogenize them. Sometimes these voices will be telling their stories in harmony, sometimes provoking dissonance by looking at the same issue from a very different angle, elaborating along specialist paths. We hope that you will enjoy the individual differences and that the variety will make the book more useful to you as well as more readable. We felt very strongly that we needed not only to make the neuroscience of behavior widely available but to do it in a way that avoided some of the overpromises in various media. "Neuro-" has become a very sexy prefix, often not backed up by sufficient evidence in whatever field it is being used. By and large neuroscientists are interested in the brain and the nervous system as a whole. But people who have a profound interest in human behavior – everyone involved in managing organizations included – do not have easy access to knowledge about the brain.

Applied neuroscience is a relatively new field that aims to bridge that gap. It is about the way the brain makes people behave as they do and, building on our capacity to change our brains, what they can do to change themselves when change would be adaptively useful. The brain is an amazingly complex process of parallel systems that can combine together to represent themselves in a productive and sustainable fashion – which is also, interestingly, the goal of all good organizations.

Although with attention and effort a brain can be changed throughout life, there are some things that cannot change, some things that will be harder after a certain age and some that will be easier or quicker than others. Brains also require the right environment both internally (lack of stress, appropriate levels of energy) and externally (calm, light and conducive to learning or concentrating).

Imagine if you could pro-actively guide your neural activity along pathways that made you naturally more able to ignore distractions and interference (the infernal email alerts), regulate emotional responses to achieve your desired behaviors, solve problems and integrate "data" from the external environment and your inner world to reach your goals.

This book will help you move towards that, borne of rigorous neuroscience, with tips for what you can do with that science presented in bite sized chunks that will help to sculpt and shape your brain by the time you have finished reading.

We have endeavored, as much as possible, to focus on areas where there is sufficient clustering of evidence and scientific consensus for us to be able to say, "well, here is a direction that looks right". We have tried very hard to find a language that does not imply absolute proof, but gives pointers. We have tried to give you, wherever we can, references to where you can find out more, so that you can dynamically add to what is emerging for you from the research.

We trust that much of this book will cause you to say, "Of course! I knew this all along" and also "it helps to know that there is some sound backing for my intuition". We hope that other parts will give you an "aha!" moment. Above all we hope that you will enjoy and make the most of the knowledge of the brain's capacity to change and grow, even into old age, for yourself and for others. And that, if you are one of the skeptics who cannot believe that people are capable of profound and lasting change, or that leadership doesn't really matter to an organization's success, we will give you at least pause for thought.

Because this is still such an emerging field it is changing even as we write and proofread. We very much hope that you will engage critically with this book and let us know about your own relevant experiences and knowledge, what you think about what we say and how we say it and especially where and how you found it useful. We are still at the stage of trying to understand how much we don't know as well as what we do. We are enjoying the finding out enormously and we hope that you will share your "whys" and "hows" with your networks with just as much pleasure.

Tara Swart
CEO of The Unlimited Mind
TaraSwart@the-unlimited-mind.com
Faculty at MIT Sloan Swart@mit.edu TBC

Kitty Chisholm
kitty@boardwalkleadership.com

Paul Brown
ptbpsychol@aol.com

chapter 1

There is Chemistry and Then There is Chemistry

"Wetware: Human brain cells or thought processes regarded as analogous to, or in contrast with, computer systems."

Oxford English Dictionary

Wetware drives human behavior – the chemistry of the brain and body. It is popular these days to talk about the brain being hardwired. Immediately an image of circuits in the brain, fixed connections and messages being shunted around comes to mind – as if the brain were a complex railway network or road system; stimulus in, response out, and clever switchgear organizing it all. But not so; the whole process is much more fluid and complex than such a metaphor suggests.

Think of the most complex flavors in the most delicious food you have ever tasted and the subtleties with which the chemistry of cooking can please your palate. Those are the chemicals of delight. They are also the chemicals that create effective human relationships. Then think what would happen if the most delicious food got suddenly swamped with salt. Its corrosive qualities are like the chemicals that flood the brain under constant stress.

Think then of the most standardized fast food you can imagine swamped by brown sauce or tomato ketchup – no subtlety of flavor there, created just for satisfying immediate hunger and designed, perhaps, to encourage an addictive longing for more. No exploring of complex sensations here – like many organizations, where the human processes are boringly familiar and exist within a very narrow range of possibility.

So it is in the brain. One person's brain and decision-making processes can be organized around subtle, highly-developed and refined feelings generated by the complexities of the chemistry that underlie the emotions that combine to make feelings. Another person's brain can be organized around a very limited range of feelings that define all situations – like living next door to a fish-and-chip shop and never being able to escape the smells of frying. Let's shift the metaphor a bit.

Chemistry

Despite the extraordinary sophistication of modern cars, there are two vital fluids that must be in there for the car to run at all. One is some refined volatile substance – petrol or diesel. The other is oil. The volatile substance needs a spark to create the explosion that releases energy to drive a piston or spin the jet blades. Oil doesn't need a spark, but its capacity to lubricate is vital in making the systems work well.

Then there are some more fluids that make the car function well – coolant, hydraulic fluids for brakes and steering, screen-wash water, and so on – a surprising number that most days we take for granted.

So it is with the brain and body. There are two major chemical systems that control our behavior and wellbeing. One predominates in the brain and, just like petrol in an engine, requires electricity to make it work. It is the neurochemistry of the brain. The other, more like oil, predominates in the rest of the body, circulates in the blood, is managed by the endocrine glands and is called the endocrine system. Adrenalin is one endocrine chemical or, because it affects the brain, is also referred to as a neuroendocrine (nerves and hormones) chemical. In all kinds of ways endocrines oil the works and make the body efficient for whatever the task is that is in hand. They are vital to making the system work. They send messages around the body, telling it what to do.

The two systems interact in humans in ways which are so complex and multi-layered that we are not even close to fully understanding them. Although our basic system of electrical signaling might be recognizably akin to that of a simple animal like the squid, the evolutionary demands that led to the growth in number of neurons and connections and dense folding of the mammalian, then human, brain also led to more signaling mechanisms and much more nuanced relationships between them.

The two systems interact together, of course, not only in times of ordinary demand but also when unusual stress, load or demand is placed upon the system – just as in a car going continuously uphill in excessively hot and dusty conditions. If the systems have been geared to withstand extreme stress then, well prepared, they will. But if the demands are too great, some part of the system will break down.

It is exactly the same in modern executive life.

This book is designed to help you accumulate sufficient knowledge about how some of the major systems of your brain and body work so that you may be able to take better care of the machinery, understand it when it becomes distressed, and enjoy the power of it when, properly cared for, it is working smoothly and well.

It is by no means all plain sailing, though. Take the case of Dr Alen Salerian, who wrote a controversial book on the subject called *Viagra for Your Brain*.[1] Reported as being a psychiatrist used by the FBI and founder of the Salerian Center for Neuroscience and Pain, on 23 April 2012 the medical authorities of Washington DC banned him from prescribing a particular class of painkillers, to the distress of many of his patients. Dr Salerian challenged the ban immediately. As of April 2014 he has been adjudged incompetent to assist in the preparation of his own defense and awaits committal to some place where his competency may be restored.[2]

Perhaps he found the boundaries between the potency of what he could prescribe and responding to the demands of patients more fluid than conventional medical practice might propose. But underlying his practice is the fact that the second half of the twentieth century produced enormous amounts of information about how we are each affected by the neurochemistry of the body that we have and, increasingly, the power of medicine to intervene.

Dr Salerian's book is especially good on depression, worry and stress – reactions to demand on the system that can destroy brain cells, shorten life and cause suicide. It is extraordinary that a living system can decide to end its own capacity to live, and that to the person taking that decision it seems a completely logical and proper act despite its illogicality to others and the pain and distress it will almost inevitably cause them. The Stoics of ancient Rome saw suicide as the final act of a rational person. Suicide is a stark way of observing that the chemicals in our brain are very powerful indeed in controlling our behavior. And the opposite to suicide is equally powerful. The capacity of an energetic, life-enhancing, engaged and engaging person to stimulate life, energy and activity in others is also remarkable. It is the quality of a good leader to do so. The chemistry that can operate at both ends of this spectrum, and right across the range, is one of the core messages of this book.

So now that science knows there is no behavior of any kind at all without some chemistry in the brain and body behind it, what are the chemicals that might reduce the confusion?

How it comes about that all behavior has, behind it, a specific neurochemistry, is not entirely understood. It is as true for the most primitive single cell organisms as it is for Nobel Prize winners. Chemistry creates (and is structured by) our behavior – and raises fascinating questions of whether each of us is in charge of our brain or our brain is in charge of us.

Neurochemistry – the specialism in science that is concerned with the chemistry of the nervous system – knows that there are over 100 different chemicals at work in the brain. For our purposes, though, it is useful to know that the main chemicals that control behavior are either neurotransmitters or hormones (see Boxes 1.1 and 1.2).

BOX 1.1   NEUROTRANSMITTERS

Neurotransmitters are of two kinds. They stimulate or they calm. They relay signals between nerve cells (neurons). The brain uses neurotransmitters to trigger hormones to tell your heart to beat, your lungs to breathe, and your stomach to digest. They can also affect mood, sleep, concentration, weight, and can cause adverse symptoms when they are out of balance. Neurotransmitter levels can be depleted in many ways. Stress, poor diet, neurotoxins, genetic predisposition, drugs (prescription and recreational), including alcohol, nicotine and caffeine usage can cause these levels to be out of optimal range. It is estimated that 86 per cent of Americans have suboptimal neurotransmitter levels.

BOX 1.2   NEUROTRANSMITTERS AND HORMONES

The main neurotransmitters are:

Dopamine   Serotonin

Oxytocin   Noradrenalin

The main hormones are:

Cortisol   Adrenalin

Testosterone   Estrogen/progesterone

They work together. Earlier we likened neurotransmitters to petrol in an engine and hormones to oil and the other crucial fluids that make brakes work or power-assist the moving parts. Neurotransmitters need a spark – an electrical current generated in a nerve cell – to make them effective. Hormones (Box 1.3) are released by the demands of neurochemical signals directly into the bloodstream from ductless glands around the body and, like all the fluids in a car, are necessary in the right quantities and in the right places to make things work effectively.

One way of thinking about the neurotransmitters is that they act directly on the emotions and trigger the hormones: whilst the hormones act directly on the body. Of course in practice both are integrated. That might be a bit simplistic, but it is not a bad starting point.

In the following pages we shall start sorting out what each one does, how they function together, what the motivational system is really about, and how eight emotions underpin every conscious and non-conscious decision we make and every purposeful action that we take. If learning more about the brain as a whole really engages you, then Professor Bruce Hood's Royal Institution Christmas lectures of 2011[3] are well worth the time it will take to view them. Equally Lord Winston has an engaging and short video,[4] which shows how brain cells develop while a person is learning – perhaps it's tidier and more elegant than in real life, but it's an energetic metaphor he works out, showing how to bridge a ravine as a way of demonstrating how brain pathways are created.

BOX 1.3   HORMONES

Hormones are chemicals that carry messages from glands to cells within tissues or organs in the body. They also maintain chemical levels in the bloodstream to help achieve *homeostasis*, which is a state of stability or balance within the body. They are part of the endocrine ("within the secreting") system. Glands manufacture hormones. These chemicals circulate freely in the bloodstream, waiting to be recognized by a target cell responding to an instruction from a neurotransmitter signal. The target cell has a receptor that can be activated only by a specific type of hormone, after which the cell knows to start a certain function within its walls. Genes might get activated, for example, or energy production resumed.

Systems

In writing about "the brain", we should never forget that there are 11 major systems in the body[5] and they are part of a whole system. That's not unlike any organization, in which there are specialized and highly differentiated functions like the following – to name just some – that need to work well together for the whole system to achieve maximum performance:

- Marketing
- Leadership
- Strategy
- Sales
- Production management.

The brain is the master controller for integrating all the systems in the body including the main components of heart and gut too. The leader is the master controller for that in the organization. How the leader's brain manages to do that is what we shall be working towards understanding in this book. But the leader can only manage the brains of others well by managing his or her own so that followers' brains want to tune themselves to the leader's brain. When that happens, endless possibilities arise. That is why it is important that, now we have increasing knowledge about the brain, leaders learn how to manage their own brains well in order to engage the brains of others most effectively.

So, among many matters we shall touch on, we are certainly going to explore the neurobiology of which system is really in charge:

- Head, heart or gut?
- What the difference really is between mind and body.
- Why a leader needs intelligent emotions rather than worrying about emotional intelligence.
- The neurological make-up of the leader who others see as authentic and want to follow.

We shall explore the fact of starting out life being female, which all men as well as all women do, and what happens in becoming male or staying female. And we shall look at keeping risk and relationships properly connected and how decision making happens.

The simple purpose of this book is to give leaders the modern knowledge they need so that they can think more clearly and productively about the complexity of not only being a human being but also being human in relation to others.

Due to increasing knowledge about the workings of the brain there is a revolution taking place in understanding human behavior and, we are certain, organizations are not extracting enough from that new knowledge yet. As this book develops we hope readers will become better informed and get the chance to catch up on a science that is opening a door into the future of human behavior in organizations.

> *"When soldiers know their leaders care for them as they care for their own children, then the soldiers love their leaders as they do their own fathers."*
>
> Liu Ji (1310–75) *Lessons of War*

We are in an age when we can, with some scientific certainty, begin to understand how we have evolved as people, as organizations and in business cultures: how fast-moving and emerging markets and a global economy mean we have to be brain-wise to interact with more varied cultures, as well as being sensitive to hierarchies in mergers and acquisitions: and how the Western world knows that the old extractive model of seeking profit at any price for personal enrichment really won't do any more but a new paradigm has not yet emerged.

It is our view that a new paradigm will only emerge when there is a much deeper understanding in organizations of the forces that connect human beings together in complex enterprises. That new model will be about the subtleties of relationships – something Liu Ji saw in his army 700 years ago.

In this developing account of the neurobiology of leadership, what we also want to explore is a new action model for organizations. Our focus is on integrating the attachment emotions of excitement, joy, trust and even love into organizational cultures – embedding new ways of being and working together. The defensive, survival emotions of fear, anger, disgust, shame and sadness are much more easily triggered, though; and most organizations trigger them most of the time in simplistic stick-and-carrot motivational systems.

Emotions

What leaders applying stick-and-carrot systems usually fail to recognize is that the carrot only feeds the recipient enough to wait for the next application of the stick. The brain remembers the stick very much more strongly than the carrot. A stick in many forms can force a person forwards but not make them joyous in achieving anything. One of the great accomplishments of Nelson as a commander of men under the terrifying conditions of the sea battles of his time was that his sailors trusted and loved him. The appearance of Wellington on the field of battle, exhorting his men at moments of great danger, was said to be worth a whole regiment of guards in his effect upon individual performance. Those were leaders who could wield the stick of summary punishment and death. But the attachment of their followers overrode any fear.

When the attachment emotions are properly engaged not only do people work willingly but they stretch themselves in the company's interest. So we explore what the neurochemistry of the body is that supports such capacity or, alternatively, finds itself destructively threatened.

Arguably the most successful and least self-publicizing entrepreneur of recent times, Sir Terry Leahy, bit-by-intuitive-bit, worked out for Tesco that focusing on *attracting* customers is not a clever strategy. Focusing on *attaching* the customers you have is, though. It was the old adage writ new: "The best customer is the one you already have".

Organizations need customers and the cost of finding new ones is huge – in some financial services groups it consumes nearly 50 per cent of observable costs. At such a level it soon becomes too expensive to attract new customers. That is not much of a business model.

So focusing on attraction and ignoring attachment only leads to promiscuous customer behavior – looking for the next good deal. Sir Terry saw that relationship was the key to success and did everything he could to instill that at the center of Tesco's remarkable growth. The index to *Management in 10 Words*, Sir Terry's first book on retiring, does not mention neuroscience, the brain or biology once; but pragmatically, as a marketing man first and foremost, Sir Terry worked out how the attachment mechanisms of the brain work – to his customers' and Tesco's huge mutual advantage.

Sir Terry went for what he knew *kept* customers. He trusted them in the way he developed stores and they reciprocated. Mutual trust is what good relationships are about, together with having sufficient resilience to sort things out when they are wrong. Mutual trust is immensely powerful but also very fragile. That is why it scares so many organizations, whose systems are essentially based on fear; and really terrifies politicians, who know they make false promises.

BOX 1.4 ADAPTIVE BEHAVIOR

Some years ago a television program set up a competition between two native Aboriginal Australians and two of Australia's toughest but non-native army survival experts. The task was to make a journey of five days' duration to a defined end point across seriously hostile territory, living off the land. The hook in the program was to see which team got where and when and how in the allotted time.

After four days the native Aboriginals were in sight of their goal, but something off to the side attracted them. So they entirely ignored the TV company's goal, winning, and went off to explore something that intrigued them. It turned out to be a new water source – an immensely valuable commodity in context and much more important than winning, which in any event was not a construct that made much Aboriginal sense.

After five grueling and exhausting days the two soldiers arrived just in time. They had done what they were highly trained to do – survive. But they had no life left in them for going on exploring. The native Aboriginals did what they had to do their way. The soldiers did what they were trained to do and had trained many others to do.

If we shift the story in Box 1.4 to complex project management, the difference between ending a project exhausted and ending it with a sense of alert excitement about other possibilities is huge. We all contain the chemistry that makes both possible. Though we can't have both functioning at the same time we can switch from one state to the other with remarkable speed. What is it that triggers one or the other?

> *Tzu-kung asked, "What is kingcraft?"*
>
> *The Master said: "Food enough, troops enough, and a trusting people."*
>
> *Tzu-kung said: "Were there no help for it, which could best be spared of the three?"*
>
> *"Troops," said the Master.*
>
> *"And were there no help for it, which could better be spared of the other two?"*
>
> *"Food," said the Master. "From of old all men die, but without trust a people cannot stand."*
>
> *The Sayings of Confucius*, XII, 7. The Harvard Classics (1909–14)

Emotions are the irreducible basics of making sense of anything. Combined together, they create feelings. Although there is a good deal of debate as to how many emotions there actually are, the accumulated evidence (based on Goleman's *Emotional Intelligence*[6]) favors eight. Think of them like primary colors. Three primary colors make the whole of the color spectrum. Eight primary emotions make the whole emotional spectrum of the feeling system.[7]

Of the eight primary emotions, the five survival emotions (fear, anger, disgust, shame and sadness) involve the release of cortisol. They are likely to be represented in the autonomic nervous system (ANS) that is functioning largely below the conscious level, and are all escape/avoidance/survival emotions, generating complex behaviors.

The two attachment emotion spectrums (love/trust and joy/excitement) are mediated by the effects of oxytocin, dopamine and noradrenalin on brain receptors.

One emotion, surprise, is a "potentiator" that can flip response states from attachment to survival or survival to attachment. Noradrenalin intensifies the effects of many other neurochemicals and probably underlies surprise.

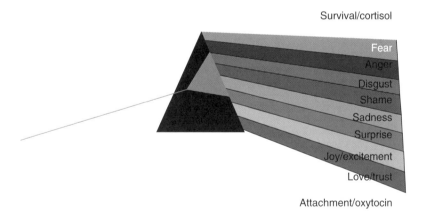

FIGURE 1.1 / **Eight basic emotions spectrum**

Source: © Swart 2011.

Sometimes, of course, all eight emotions can be firing simultaneously. In intense jealousy, for example, love and anger can be equally strong. When firing in competition with each other the distress can often only be relieved by violent action. It changes the emotional context, sometimes catastrophically, when the emotions themselves are in such intense opposition as they are when jealousy is raging.

It is becoming more and more widely accepted that an emotionally intelligent leader's ability to build and sustain trust leads to a business's long-term survival and success. Much as the attachment emotions build the neural architecture of our children, inspiring trust in the workplace encourages team bonding, learning and innovation. These are higher functions in the brain that demand a large proportion of its precious resources, and these resources get used up in self-preservation where the brain perceives any potential threat.

Trust

Although humans are capable of transmitting ideas and adopting innovations faster than any other species, the human brain is still shaped by evolutionary development that adapts structures rather than destroying them to build new ones. Tomorrow looks uncertain and risky and hence the brain reacts as if the future is a physical threat. The ambiguity inherent in decisions about the future can lead to "safe" decisions, or, more worryingly, delay them. Creativity is constrained by fear of uncertainty.

In modern organizations, where it is primarily the quality of thinking and innovation that matter and where relationships with customers, suppliers and partners are key success factors, just giving orders cannot deliver the kind of performance needed. Leaders can no longer rely on hierarchical position for their power. More than ever, they need to persuade, inspire and motivate. In any case, leadership is required at all levels in an organization, not just top-down. Intelligent, highly educated, intrinsically motivated people require goals they can believe in and subscribe to. The leader nevertheless sets the cultural DNA of the organization. It's there where essential trust has to reside.

So in order for a leader to inspire and motivate, he or she has to be trusted. Trust creates an environment in which threats are reduced, and thinking and creativity are liberated. A trusted leader will be believed when they tell stories about what the future will be like, thus reducing fear and anxiety. A trusted leader with a strong emotional commitment to a cause or goal will be able to engender commitment in others. A trusted leader who takes risks and persists through difficulties will continue to be followed even when the journey seems dangerous.

Why does trust work?

Trust is a keystone of human society. It is the basis of our concept of money, our institutions of government, law and of the professions. It is trust in our social environment and institutions that permits us to expect to be fairly rewarded for our ideas and labor, to engage in commerce, to leave money in a will. Without trust, there is fear. Without trust, our basic human rights and responsibilities cannot be robust.

The reasons for the importance of trust to human societies are likely to be rooted in our need of others in order to survive. Trust is a multilayered and multidimensional concept. What most scholars seem to agree on however is that it is a mental action or state. We would further suggest that trust is the mental state of expecting fairness from the trusted.

Fairness seems to be almost instinctively available to humans as a working concept – evidenced from arguments with three-year-olds. It seems that fairness, like affiliation (social contact), is a primary need for humans. The brain responds strongly both to perceived fair and unfair actions and situations. In the first case positively, with the reward centers firing; in the latter case aversively, with those parts of the brain that respond to threats. We humans have such strong aversion to unfair behavior towards us that it overwhelms more rational assessments of the balance between gain and loss.

Trust and attachment

One chemical underlying trust is the neuropeptide oxytocin (Box 1.5). Oxytocin levels rise significantly during childbirth and breast feeding. It is implicated in bonding between mothers and infants in mammals. It has recently been shown to be more prevalent also in new fathers, thus presumably encouraging them to develop a relationship with their baby. It underlies a wide range of human social affiliations and is popularly known as the love hormone, as it floods the brain when people fall in love and when they behave lovingly towards each other.

It has been shown experimentally that oxytocin might also increase the level of trust in the truster. Administered via a nasal spray, it caused a significant change in behavior during a game played with real money, (apparently not linked to lowering risk aversion). Trust, social affiliation and love are not the same, but an increase in oxytocin levels is implicated in all three. It is possible therefore that an increase in oxytocin in a relationship where trust was developed, would also increase affiliation.

BOX 1.5 OXYTOCIN

Produced by the hypothalamus and stored and secreted by the posterior pituitary gland, oxytocin acts primarily as a neuromodulator in the brain and is known as the bonding hormone. In an experiment where men were asked to rate pictures of 100 women on attractiveness, they rated them as more attractive after one nasal spray of oxytocin with the pictures being presented for a second time in a different order to the first time. So oxytocin underpins trust and "bonding" behavior in real life and in simulated tasks by inducing a calm, warm mood that increases tender feelings and attachment and may lead us to lower our guard.

Trust is not only restricted to relationships between people, or between people and animals. It can arise with objects such as clocks or tools, or organizations and their brands – I trust Amazon to deliver my goods, I trust Audi to have a car which keeps my family safe. It can be broken, but, with good management, it can overcome mistakes and even crises. Trust then becomes the basis of a strong emotional relationship, between people, things and concepts, in which there is a sense of safety and a reduction of fear and risk and perhaps even an increase in liking. This facilitates influence and enables creativity and innovation. Trust develops over time and is not absolute, but needs continuous care and maintenance.

Summary

Brain chemicals, and other inputs such as chemicals and electrical impulses generated in the heart and the gut, underlie every single action of everyday life. All thoughts, feelings and moods are emergent. In the way that experience shapes the growing brain, so experience also makes chemical patterns and in turn the chemical patterns define our behavior and expectations. As humans we have our own unique chemical patterning in just the same way that we have our own individual way of walking, speaking, laughing and everything else that makes us the individual that we are. Knowing the effect of the neurochemicals on behavior may make it possible for a leader to consider his or her own behavior and what impact it is having on others: and consider what chemistry he or she wishes to trigger in reports. The neurochemistry of others' brains is being triggered in any event by what a leader does and doesn't do. Knowledge might make that a more efficient and deliberate process. Throughout the book are ways of recognizing the physiology, managing it and creating the conditions for success in the environment we operate and interact in.

Actions and reflections

If you are a parent, have you ever thought about using the emotions that underlie the values that guide your parenting style to inform your leadership style at work? Not the actual parenting behaviors, but if you think about how you would like to raise your children to be secure, independent, emotionally intelligent adults, or whatever your aspirations for them are, which three values guide you most strongly when choosing how to behave with them? How might these concepts, such as generosity, compassion or discipline, be applied in your work context?

- What did people do before we could speak? Ask for feedback on the gestures, mannerisms and noises you may make without even realizing it. You can do this with an executive coach or someone else that you trust. Things as subtle as throat-clearing, an overly firm handshake or shrugging could be perceived negatively by others. Knowing how others perceive you will give you some material for evolving your emotional intelligence and physicality positively.
- Work on empathy by imagining – mentally and physically – how it would feel to be in another person's shoes. We respond to micro-muscular changes in other people's faces and simulating these ourselves can help us to imagine how they may be feeling. Pay closer attention to people's eyes narrowing, jaw clenching or flinching.
- Whilst looking in the mirror each morning, pause and consider the face looking back at you. Pause, and ask:
  - Are these the facial expressions I want to represent me today?
  - What emotions or states is your face conveying: confidence, fear, interest, indifference?
  - People will pick up on micro-muscular changes in your face. What impact will it have upon them?

chapter 2

Brains, Bodies and Business: A Systems Approach

"I cannot trust a man to control others, who cannot control himself."

Robert E. Lee

The idea for this systems approach to applied neuroscience was sparked when Tara and Dr Peter Hirst MBE, executive director of executive education at the MIT Sloan School of Management, went to a meeting with four researchers from the Brain and Cognitive Science Unit at MIT. It was discussed that what neuroscientists refer to as executive functions (see Box 2.1) and what business people think of as the functions of an executive are two quite different things. There is growing interest in applying neuroscience to leadership and many laboratories publishing fascinating neuroscience research but not enough people, forums or environments in which the crucial information can be simply and pragmatically translated for practical use in businesses. The impact of technology on neuroscience is also striking in that it has allowed tangible, physical data on what is going on in the brain to distinguish neuroscience from psychology, with the focus in this book being on using that data on applications to business and leadership. The tangible nature of that data makes the premise more compelling for some and strengthens the argument for others on the importance of both cognitive science and physiology and the interplay between them.

BOX 2.1 EXECUTIVE FUNCTIONS

The terms selective attention and cognitive control, and supervisory attentional system, tend to be used interchangeably with executive functions. The supervisory attentional system can override the automatic response system to allow for plans and intentions – for example, to ignore interruptions that might mean missing a project deadline – and it has an 'executive' branch for focusing attention, a skill we will emphasize the importance of many times throughout this book.

In a paradigm similar to the "Structural Balance in Teams" chapter of the book *Exploring Positive Relationships at Work*,[1] we strive towards a system that learns to reflect on its own functioning and focuses on health and generativity, integration, structure and systems thinking, towards what the authors refer to as dynamic wholeness. Here we apply those concepts to how the brain works in individuals, and how individuals work in businesses.

Executive functions

What if there was less focus on the kind of subjects and language neuroscientists use, like structures of the brain or even the functional systems of the brain and what they do in everyday life? What if concepts started with what leaders need to do, focusing on the capabilities and competencies that leaders would pick to be best at or improve upon so as to be able to do their job superbly, influence teams to perform at their best and improve the bottom line of their business? Those functions of an executive are not so disconnected from executive functions in the brain but they have not been articulated clearly with business and leadership as the starting point and science as the explanatory rather than just the descriptive element. Also, neuroscientific language can sometimes have the effect of bamboozling rather than clarifying in applications for business and it is one of the aims of this book to demystify the topic. In this chapter we will go through some of those terms as they underlie many of the concepts later in the book.

If you ask people about the functions of a leader you will hear things that include:

- Create a vision
- Set the strategic direction
- Find talent and other resources
- Make decisions
- Build relationships and trust
- Motivate and influence.

BOX 2.2   EVOLUTIONARY RESPONSES

Responding to dangerous events is a great example of how our brain is still defined by what it did to protect us when we were cave people – these days we would more likely refer to dealing with something technically or socially difficult rather than physically life-threatening.

If you ask a neuroscientist or psychologist what the executive functions are, they are likely to say things that include the following:

- Controlling and managing thought processes such as attention, motivation, working memory (the contents of our present awareness, which is limited to about nine pieces of information our brain can actively keep track of) and reasoning.
- Task flexibility (a speedy switch in what you are doing).
- Planning and execution – usually of movement.
- Managing "higher" cognitive processes like flexibility of thinking, impulse control, concept formation, abstract thinking and creativity.
- Decision making, error correction or troubleshooting.

- Dealing with new situations or ones you are not well rehearsed at, that is, ones that are not habits or automatic responses underpinned by default pathways in your brain.
- Responding to dangerous events and overcoming ingrained behavior patterns or resisting temptation, for example, anticipating that difficult interview making your heart beat faster, or spending too much time on routine emails when you have an important deadline looming.

Popular neuroscience literature tends to associate these executive functions with the frontal lobes of the brain and particularly the pre-frontal cortex (PFC). We will talk about the PFC throughout this book but it is worth noting that while the pre-frontal areas are pivotal for executive functions they are not the only part of the brain involved.

Executive functions are shaped by physical and hormonal changes in the brain as well as life experiences – at work, on training programs and in life generally. We know a lot about how the core executive functions develop from childhood through adolescence into early adulthood, and there is a growing mass of research into successful aging focused on the over 65s, but here we are interested in what you can do to maximize your potential by boosting your cognitive power in order to improve performance as a leader, whatever your age.

BOX 2.3 MAINTAINING SUCCESS

"Successful" aging is associated with good nutrition, cardiovascular exercise, cognitive stimulation and positive/rewarding relationships, but these are not things you can turn on all of a sudden and expect a new change in behavior to shield you from the effects of aging. It begs the question, to what extent does lifelong personality (conscientiousness) predict health in later years or indeed prevent cognitive decline or even reverse the aging process? And why shouldn't leaders be focusing on those factors now?

The lifelong challenge of changing brain and behavior

In this book we will work on the understanding of these four steps for creating sustainable behavior change (see further Chapter 7):

- Raising awareness – any reading you do, all personal development work, self-reflection, psychometrics and 360 degree feedback etc.
- Focused attention – being present, focusing on what is important and looking out for examples in your everyday life of the behaviors you no longer want, or opportunities to try out new ways of being.
- Deliberate practice – the saying goes "practice makes permanent in the brain" or "act it until you are it". This may seem controversial given the buzz around neuroplasticity (the ability of the brain to change itself). We describe mechanisms for neuroplasticity in this chapter as the mode of forging new, stronger pathways in your brain. Plasticity means you can create new links between neurons, new pathways, which with each practice grow stronger. Also, each time you practice your new behavior or attitude, you are NOT using the old one, which means that those links weaken.
- Therapeutic relationship – all these things are easier if something or someone else is supporting you and holding you accountable. The therapeutic relationship can be with a coach, mentor, buddy, personal trainer, nutritionist, partner or even an online tracking system or wearable technology connected to a smart device app.[2]

> *"If you have a simple consistent message – and you keep repeating it, eventually that's what happens – that's how you get through."*
>
> Jack Welch

BOX 2.4 STUDIES ON NEUROPLASTICITY

1 Nuclear bomb tests carried out during the cold war have had an unexpected benefit. A radioactive carbon isotope expelled by the blasts has been used to date the age of adult human brain cells, providing the first definitive evidence that we humans generate new brain cells throughout our lives. The

study also provided the first model of the dynamics of the process, showing that the regeneration of neurons does not drop off with age as sharply as expected.

In mammals, most types of brain cell are created at or soon after birth and are never renewed. But studies in rodents and monkeys have shown that in two regions new neurons continue to be created even in adulthood – the hippocampus, which is involved in learning and the formation of new memories, and the olfactory bulb, which processes smell.

However, there has been some controversy over whether the same is true for humans. Fifteen years ago a study found evidence for such neurogenesis (the creation of new neurons) in adults up to the age of 72 (*Nature Medicine*, doi.org/b7hjfz), but the research relied on a chemical called bromodeoxyuridine (BrdU) to label neurons. BrdU was used at the time to track the spread of tumors in people with cancer, but it was banned shortly after and so the study was never repeated, leading some researchers to question the results.

2 Another study on London taxi drivers suggested that the hippocampus grows with increasing knowledge of the city but this, too, has been controversial. The new study settles the debate. "The existence of adult hippocampal neurogenesis in humans is not arguable this time", says Sandrine Thuret at King's College London, who was not involved in the work.

3 Instead of chemical labeling, Jonas Frisén at the Karolinska Institute in Stockholm, Sweden, and colleagues used a by-product of the above-ground nuclear bomb tests carried out by the US, UK and Soviet Union between 1945 and 1963. As a result of these detonations, atmospheric levels of the radioactive isotope carbon-14 increased dramatically during this period. It has decreased steadily since. Carbon-14 enters the food chain and eventually finds its way into our cells, which integrate carbon-14 atoms into their DNA when a parent cell splits into two new daughter cells. The amount of carbon-14 in the atmosphere is therefore mirrored in the cells at the time they are born.

Concepts that come later in the book, like loss aversion, bias signals and stress levels leading to diversion of resources (oxygen and glucose) within the brain, can mean that you may struggle to achieve your goals alone as your brain may trick you into feeling tired or demotivated as a way of ensuring your "survival". So how do you override your "cave man brain" to achieve what you want in the sophisticated modern world?

Neuroplasticity

What we know now about the brain's ability to change itself is that, within limits, you can change yourself; that is, you can learn to be a leader – at all levels, as a self-authoring person, respected husband, role-model mother, successful entrepreneur or CEO of an iconic brand. Neuroplasticity occurs through three main mechanisms:

- Myelination
- Synaptic connection
- Neurogenesis.

The most obvious clinical example of neuroplasticity is in recovery from stroke through rehabilitation training. If one scrutinizes what the therapists do it boils down to raising awareness, focusing attention and repetitive practice in a therapeutic environment with physiotherapists, occupational therapists, psychologists, doctors and nurses – so essentially the four step process described at the beginning of this chapter. The physiological changes that then occur are:

- Myelination – the wrapping of a white coating around neurons to speed up transmission along them. In the business setting this is most akin to becoming even better at something you are already good at.
- Synaptic connection and growth in critical areas – making more and/ or new connections between existing neurons, and allowing the map in the brain for that particular skill to grow (like when you use one

language more than another, the disused one takes up less space in the brain and the more used one takes over some of its space). The best example of this is London cab drivers that do "the Knowledge". The navigation part of their memory centers (the hippocampus) actually grows. This is applicable to the workplace in terms of improving a skill you are already good at and have remaining potential to grow.

• Neurogenesis – we know much less about this, and have only relatively recently discovered that it can occur in the central nervous system (brain and spinal cord) not just the peripheral nervous system (nerves throughout the rest of your body). Neurogenesis involves actually growing new neurons from embryonic nerve cells (progenitor cells) and is most likely linked to developing a skill that you don't have a natural talent for or have never practiced before. Therefore this one is probably the hardest to achieve. As far as we know it does not happen a lot in the adult brain. Growth of new neurons is only evidenced in a few parts of the brain, such as the hippocampus, and we believe that it is possible to develop an entirely new skill by linking existing neurons in new networks elsewhere.

Mindset

The fascinating work of Carol Dweck at Stanford University on Mindsets[3] is gathering even more momentum based on the mechanisms of neuro-plasticity, because it will mean leaders can move along the spectrum from having a Type 1 mindset to a Type 2 mindset. That is, leaders can move away from being:

"Fixed" – fearful of making mistakes; feeling that failure is shameful and painful; achieving only incremental innovation.

And nurture their people to become more focused on:

"Growth" – fearful only of losing out on opportunities; seeing failure as exciting; ashamed by sitting on the sidelines whilst others run away with great ideas; unleashing insights that lead to step changes in innovation.

All these forms of neuroplasticity and behavior change are created by the four-step process outlined already coupled with an understanding of the four brain networks described later in this chapter.

Standing on the brink of the cutting edge

The *Harvard Business Review* article "Your Brain at Work" by Adam Waytz and Malia Mason (July/August 2013) is cutting edge.[4] They present it as an "interim report" because as so much is changing in our understanding of applied neuroscience what is postulated now may turn out to be understood very differently in ten years time – but that is the nature of science and research and part of dealing with ambiguity.

Waytz and Mason focus on four of about 15 brain networks rather than regions of the brain, and they separate fact from fiction when it comes to understanding how neurological processes affect management and leadership. Associate Professor of Business Mason starts by raising the issue that there is no clear agreement around what leadership even is. The complexity of human thinking and behavior are such that they do not map onto brain regions one to one, so you cannot scan two CEOs' brains and tell which person is the better leader or provide a blueprint for what a leader's brain might be like. However most leaders would agree about what they would like their brains to be capable of doing and new scanning technologies have given us a better idea of some of the underlying brain areas and activities.

Given the massive amount of funding that has been put into brain research in the US and Switzerland, we get asked all the time what the outcomes might be. The only thing neuroscientists can say is that there is going to be more change in the next ten years than there has been in our lives so far, hence agility of thinking, adaptability and tolerance for ambiguity will be more highly valued than strong technical skills alone.

"We now accept the fact that learning is a lifelong process of keeping abreast of change."

Peter Drucker

The contribution of brain scanning is liberating in that we no longer have to look at brains where something has gone wrong (illness or physical injury) and extrapolate the functions of those parts of the brain that are damaged through, for example, tumors or strokes, but we can actually look at what is going on when brains are functioning ably or even expertly. The new tools and approaches have already produced insights into the physiology of thinking and revolutionized our thinking of concepts crucial to business such as:

- How to enable creativity.
- How to structure reward.
- The role of emotions in decision making.
- The pros and cons of multitasking.

Brain networks

The four key networks Waytz and Mason describe within their more sophisticated framework of the brain at work are the:

- DEFAULT network, which is engaged in introspection and in imagining a different time, place or reality.
- REWARD network, which activates in response to pleasure.
- AFFECT network, which plays a central role in emotions.
- CONTROL network, which is involved in understanding consequences, impulse control and selective attention.

These networks are pivotal individually and in interplay because they moderate the capabilities and competencies that we have already described as functions of a leader.

Default network

The default network allows creative thought to flourish by transcending the present moment and environment, to "think outside the box". How often does your default network really get free reign? That means an email free holiday or being able to switch your phone off and not feel like you need to obsessively check what is going on at work.

Being "in your body" rather than the endless thoughts crammed into your mind, is a form of meditating – by which we don't mean sitting crossed legged and engaging in something mystical or spiritual, but anything that gets you into the feeling of being "in the zone" like running, swimming, yoga, getting lost in music, art, playing with your kids and really listening to them, really being there, or just "being".

Really detaching in whatever way is right for you can generate off-the-scale innovation. Anything less and you can hope for a bit of incremental change without much hope that it will be sustainable. And by this we do not mean only good business ideas, leadership skills or talent development, we mean seeing the wood for the trees when it comes to what you really want to do with your life.

- What do you want to stand for?
- What is the meaning and purpose of YOU being on this planet?
- What will be your legacy?

That is potentially what you are cheating yourself, your family and your employees of, if the default system doesn't get the resources (time or prioritization) to fire up at least periodically. See the fascinating article "Fast time and the aging mind" in the *New York Times*[5] and Ellen Langer's book *Counterclockwise*,[6] which poses the question: "If we could turn back the clock psychologically could we also turn it back physically?" (see Box 2.5).

BOX 2.5 DEALING WITH DISTRACTIONS

In modern life we are much more distracted than ever before and our attention is stretched to encompass and maintain many more "things" in life. Although our brains have evolved to be better at doing this, the increased engagement of our attentional resources may cause time to appear to be passing faster. And because we were not paying attention all along, we may not get a chance to sit down and reflect until we retire. Because children have fewer emotional "data points" in their life, they feel like time goes more slowly *ergo* an argument for bringing mindfulness into your life to trick your brain into feeling younger and responding accordingly.

The Google "20% time policy" where employees get one day a week to work on a project of personal interest is cited. Google are huge ambassadors of neuroscience in business with their sleep pods for napping and other initiatives, but we all know the feeling that it takes the first week of your holiday to just wind down from work and that it is towards the end of the second week that you actually start to get new ideas or space in your head.

Reward network

The basic human drives are for hunger/thirst, sleep/wake and sex. Pleasure and rewards are contextual and can vary for any given situation. Recent neuromarketing research has shown that people will primarily be stimulated by food or sex. Brain scans may be able to differentiate customers based on whether pictures of food or attractive members of the opposite sex lead to certain responses. There is an obvious reason for these being such fundamental drivers of behavior, integral to our survival. But the executive functions also have an evolutionary purpose. Things like creativity, emotional intelligence and being able to plan for the future probably improve your chances of surviving and passing on your genetic material more today than they did a million years ago. It is said that in humans the reward network is also sensitive to secondary rewards, not directly related to physical survival or reproduction, such as money. However in this day and age it could be argued that money is directly related to survival both physical and psychological, and that may indeed explain many workplace behaviors both positive and negative.

The important and complex issue here is that money registers a reward (dopamine) in the brain, but things like fairness, sharing, learning and enjoyment of work can release dopamine equally, if not more, depending on the circumstances. A lot of the consulting work we do, particularly in financial services, is around equitable pay and motivation. In short, offering coaching, interesting seminars, praise for performance and engendering a culture of transparency and trust reap unimaginable rewards through the effect of oxytocin and dopamine on the reward system but are greatly underused and undervalued.

This is understandable considering that functional brain scanning has only recently given backbone to what we have intuitively known – that these things seem fluffy but are important. It just goes to show how long it takes to overcome a legacy of carrot-and-stick motivation and thinking you can drive people to an early grave if you pay them enough. People just are not willing to endure this anymore. Generations X and Y are simply motivated differently and we have heard too many coaching clients at chief executive level (usually aged 40 plus) articulate that this job is not worth their life. Too many are living with the constant angst that they will keel over with a heart attack (caused by cortisol) if they keep going at this pace and not live to see their children grow up. Neuroscience now backs up that this is not the way to get the best out of people anyway.

Affect network

The debate around intuition or gut instinct over logical thinking is an interesting one. We know now that all decisions are biased by emotions and that you ignore this at your peril. Even if you admit that you can get emotional at home with the kids or when it comes to sport but that you are totally logical at work, think again. There is an inordinately large nerve supply between the gut and the limbic (deeper, emotional) part of the brain so a "gut feeling" is a neurological occurrence that generates a physical response. Within this system a part called the hippocampus stores memories associated with certain emotions. Certain events or experiences are made more memorable by association by the following:

- Intensity of emotion – highly charged situations tend to make people feel more bonded even to strangers or remember an incident with laser like clarity.
- Repetition of event – the more something happens the more ingrained it becomes in our brain.
- Time elapsed – are childhood memories more formative because we are more impressionable at a young age?

Hebbian theory is often summarized as "cells that wire together fire together" but it is specifically the adaptation of neurons in the brain during the process of learning. It describes a mechanism for synaptic plasticity where changes occur in the postsynaptic cell due to repeated and persistent firing of neurons. These memories of experiences then move from our modern logical cortex into our ancient neural architecture through Hebbian learning. This may be due to efficiency over storage space as well as the fact that something experienced enough times becomes a habit or pattern and therefore part of our instinctive system not our more thoughtful or calculated one. Eventually patterns can move from our limbic system into our brainstem and body such that certain events can trigger changes in our body like sweating, blushing, goose bumps, increased breathing and heart rate. These are all data that can be used to inform our decision making.

If you have read *Thinking Fast and Slow*,[7] *The Chimp Paradox*[8] or seen Simon Sinek[9] speak then you will recognize the concepts of System 1 and System 2, the chimp and the human, or the Golden circle made up of three concentric circles representing the cortex, limbic system and brainstem and why these are important to business and leadership.

The four-step process, which we've mentioned a few times, consists of:

- Raising awareness
- Focused attention
- Deliberate practice
- Therapeutic relationship.

This process lies behind the golden circle idea in that it eventually moves data from the cortex to the limbic system (this is the stage at which something moves from being effortful to becoming a habit) and eventually through the brainstem to the body (meaning that the action becomes involuntary – you don't even think about it, just like you beat your heart and breathe).

This is permanent and sustainable behavior change that is transformational. You are no longer doing something because that is how you think you should behave to get a promotion, get married or get fit. It is who you ARE now. And you fully contemplate and embody why you do what you do.

Intuition

When coaching leaders we will look out for things like this as far as we can see, as well as jaw clenching, flinching muscles and level of eye contact to ascertain the neuropsychological state. We may even use physical data from our own bodies (little hairs standing on end, butterflies in our stomach, a physical feeling of discomfort or disengagement) to inform the coaching process. But this is a skill that needs to be honed or hunches can mislead you because of connotations leading to biases, both positive and negative, that is, instinctive rather than intuitive.

For example, being overly optimistic about investing in something because it warmly reminds you of childhood holidays in some indefinable way – for instance, your red Ferrari has the same orangey tones as the poppy fields in France where you used to go camping with your cousins when you dreamt of being a successful business owner one day. Another example could be that you are not consciously aware of this but you screw your nose up every time you see your CFO because something about his aftershave distantly reminds you of a food you hated as a seven year old. That action signals something to your brain because smell and taste are closely associated and meetings with him always leave a bad taste in your mouth literally and metaphorically. That is how much every smell, every relationship and every experience you have ever had affects all that you do today.

So these feelings are worth exploring and monitoring to decide how much you want to include in your decision-making process – they should be seen as stemming from valuable experiences and integral to being a leader who is not totally dispassionate. These feelings should also to be treated with caution at least until the process of pre-frontal regulation (regulating your emotions) has become stronger.

We like to talk about this as distinguishing between instinct (could be misleading) and intuition (probably based on valuable experience), discussed further in Chapter 6. One of our coaching clients calls this "the Jedi mind trick" and another says his brain hurts when he tries to do it – which only means that he has to try harder!

A famous quote, often attributed to Victor Frankl's *Man's Search for Meaning*, is a beautiful expression of the theory that it is our pre-frontal regulation, or executive control, over our instinctive, intuitive, System 1, chimp reactions that gives us "free will":

> "Between stimulus and response, there is a space. In that space is our power to choose our response. In our response lies our growth and our freedom … Forces beyond your control can take away everything you possess except one thing, your freedom to choose how you will respond to the situation."

As leaders, that is the space that enables us to set genuine strategic directions, to create plans that deliver transformation, true innovation and change.

BOX 2.6 DON: A CASE STUDY

Don was getting coaching to improve his emotional intelligence as a CFO and motivate and inspire his team better. But he was also morbidly obese and expressed a desire to live long enough to see his teenage children reach adulthood, so we worked on weight loss alongside the executive coaching. I had known that coaching was quite intangible and that he had never managed to lose the weight before. The HRD and CEO said he would be the first case I would not "crack". So Don and I rose to the challenge and when he lost 28lbs that was the first time it really hit me that when people see their leader put his or her mind to something and achieve it in a demonstrable way it has a wonderful and far-reaching impact on them. He got so much positive feedback and people were talking about it even outside the business. I think it actually made him want to be a nicer person and gave him the energy to do so. It was a case of coaching the body and thereby promoting new behaviors in the brain that were also related to focus and discipline.

Using intuition better starts to come naturally with age, experience, expertise and gathering wisdom. It can be practiced using reflection, for example:

- Simply recording in a journal your feelings and their connections to successful or regrettable decisions.
- More modern methods, such as behavioral finance software for financial decision making and risk taking.
- Apps that remind you to stop and reflect every so often.
- Guided mindfulness practice.

Increasingly we are hearing people say they used to dismiss their gut instinct most of the time but now realize that had not necessarily been the best thing to do. You then have to start taking some risks and this can feel scary. Threats to the brain include:

- Learning or trying something new.
- Feeling uncertain.
- Not being at your most resilient.
- Lack of control of a situation.

One starts to see why letting go of logical, analytical thinking and technical skills, which you have been trained in and praised for over many years, is not easy.

Interoception

We all know about the five senses and we will delve into them a little more with the Leadership Brain Agility© model in Chapter 9, where we also look at the sixth sense. But there is another sense, a very real neurological sense that is little discussed and massively underused in common parlance. This is interoception or the sense of the physiological condition of the body. The answer to the question "How do you feel?" that you get by doing a "body scan" (see Box 2.7).

BOX 2.7   BODY SCAN EXERCISE

Sustained practice is a way of honing your skills. Having read this far you might have an intellectual understanding of the benefits of self-reflection, intuition and interoception, but how do you make these a part of your leadership armory? Try the following exercise – on interoception – at least once a day for a week or two. Make a brief note of how you feel each time, using language that is as accurate as possible. At the end, ask yourself what you now know about yourself and your physical reactions that you did not know before.

This will increase your ability to recognize and use data that come from your body – the physical axis of the brain–body connection. For instance, knowing that our adrenal glands register before our conscious minds do, would you want to know how it feels in your body when you have higher levels of adrenalin? Regularly practicing a body scan will make you more aware of changes in your heart rate, breathing rate and depth, sweating, blushing and butterflies in your stomach. All signs that can signal your body is heightened to risk.

Close your eyes and take note of how you feel from top to toe by scanning down your body and focusing on one area at a time. Try this in different contexts at different times of the day.

Or try a guided version on YouTube such as: https://www.youtube.com/watch?v=obYJRmgrqOU.

Interoception is particularly honed in those who practice yoga, mindfulness, meditation or work with biofeedback, for example in sports. In terms of neuroplasticity we often get asked how long it takes to form a new habit or unlearn an existing behavior and we have to say: "How long is a piece of string?" Things like getting back to the gym regularly can take just a few weeks but moving along the spectrum from relying on our logic to taking the chance on our intuition or interoception could be closer to the 10,000 hours of practice popularly quoted to be required for becoming an expert at anything. It is beginning to sink in that soft skills may really be harder to master than getting an MBA.

Neuroscientist A D Craig states that "as humans we perceive feelings from our bodies that relate to our state of well-being, our energy and stress levels, our mood and disposition".[10] The neural system that represents the "material me" to us might provide a foundation for subjective feelings, emotion and self-awareness. This is a neural system as real as proprioception for joint position sense, nociception for pain and others like thermoception (temperature) and equilibrioception (balance).

Volition

This physical basis and explanation thereof holds a lot of comfort for executives who struggle with the validity of concepts like emotional intelligence and mindfulness. It gives leaders somewhere to start from that is tangible, practical and interesting. The plasticity of your neurons and your own commitment will determine how far you go with it. As with anything, this correlates with how much you practice and how much you care. Volition is part of the learning process in the brain. The emotional significance that your brain associates with a certain process correlates to its success.

The emotional significance that your brain associates with a certain process correlates to its success.

In an experiment with three groups of rats, those in the first group were kept in a relatively confined space; the rats in the second group were allowed to roam free and get on a running wheel whenever they wanted; and those in the third group were forced to stay on a running wheel for a certain number of hours per day. Only the rats in the second group grew new brain cells (neurogenesis) in response to exercise. This would have been through a combination of oxygenation and brain derived neurotrophic factor (BDNF) but only in the presence of *desire* to carry out that activity. This illustrates again the effect of the mind on the body. That is the explanation for things like:

- People having to buy into a process such as coaching.
- Winning hearts and minds with a new vision for the business.
- Why people are more likely to achieve goals they have set for themselves, even if they are harder goals than you would have set as their leader.
- Why McKinsey write about increasing the "meaning quotient" by engaging people with a story that they care about and giving them a sense of choice.[11]

Control network

The ability to create achievable goals is one of the things that separates us from other animals. The control network and default network (the two bookends of the four networks described earlier – control for task focus and default for creativity or imagination) operate in a see-saw relationship by diverting blood flow to regions that produce the relevant neural firing so they cannot be active at the same time.

The control network allows us to override some of our instincts and impulses from all the other networks to achieve our goals, prioritize and focus without losing track of what is going on around us.

Just as we advise leaders to limit the number of habits they are trying to change at any one time to one or two, on a macro level businesses need to streamline change processes to a manageable number. The brain pays most attention to unfinished tasks and cannot do any of them well if the resources are too divided. This can in fact lead to burnout and there is a slippery slope to this state, which we will discuss in Chapter 9.

In a way the CEO is like the PFC regulating gratification (reward), clarifying competing priorities, diverting resources accordingly for multiple tasks and seeing what is not important. Towards the end of the book we will talk about the organization in terms of being as complex and elegant as the brain. This brings to mind one of our favorite quotes: "if the brain were so simple that we could understand it, we would be so simple that we couldn't." By this we mean: it will not be easy but it is a good aspiration.

Summary

What can we do with this knowledge and what do we want to do with our executive functions? Much of the functions of these systems and networks are genetic in basis but with huge epigenetic influencers, and relatively stable through life unless intelligent effort is applied, but we already know that there is potential to boost our ability to update, inhibit and shift the way we think.

More research is required to establish how information flows between the PFC and the rest of the brain where executive functions are used. The funding into brain research pledged for the next decade will bring in at exponential rate new insights into how we can maximize the potential of our brains.

We know there is an advantage of being bilingual from infancy especially in terms of inhibitory control, task switching and conflict processing and that this advantage persists throughout life. It may be too late for us to change that now, but how can we improve our ability to identify situations where conflict may arise, make decisions in uncertainty or when a decreased chance of a favorable outcome is detected?

Our brains have an unfortunate tendency to seek out negative memories and sense danger where there is none once it perceives it is under threat. Consciously we need to continuously monitor our thoughts, quickly add or remove the things we need to remember, supersede the sorts of impulsive responses we become hijacked by from certain triggers (know what they are) and have the flexibility to switch between different tasks or mental states. If you would like to be able to more dynamically co-ordinate your cognitive resources in the pursuit of personal and organizational leadership please read on.

Actions and reflections

- Meditation (including a body scan like in the video link in Box 2.7). There is more on different types of meditation in Chapter 9. Download an app, audiobook or find videos on YouTube.
- Yoga practice to improve interoception. Use www.yogadownload.com at home or join a class or course to experience the benefits of yoga.
- If you are really struggling with the interoception piece then try any form of wearable technology (app, wristband, heart rate monitor) to give you some data you can actually work with perhaps on an online platform like tictrac.com.
- Try the "intuition" or "decisions" diary.

Whatever you do, do not think you have to clear your mind of all thoughts or sit in an uncomfortable position for hours. The brain is designed to think. Make it as easy as possible for yourself to reach a calm place of relaxed alertness – that is what meditation yoga and introspection are all about.

chapter 3

The New Model Leader

"You must be the change you wish to see in the world."
Mahatma Gandhi

Leadership training has become a huge industry, with an apparently insatiable market. Millions of books and articles, thousands of courses and training programs from hundreds of academic and other organizations all offer theories on what leadership is, what leaders do, as well as advice on becoming an effective leader. The demand for good leadership drives this market, but there is little hard evidence that any of the existing products work, or that we know why something works when it does. There is, on the other hand, plenty of evidence that complex organizations in global market economies do not have enough of the kind of leaders they need. There has not been enough in all this activity that has a robust base in science. Where can we start in order to begin to sift what really works, what might deliver sustainable, long-term results, from all the noise and fashionable fads?

We have seen organizations model themselves on their leaders, leaders change outcomes and a change of leader leading to a change of fortune. We have seen a new leader deliver increased morale and dramatically improved performance, with a combination of an ambitious vision, laser-sharp clarity on what matters to clients and stakeholders and support for existing good people, before the new corporate strategy was even put on paper.

We have spent a lot of our careers in listening and talking to leaders who can see the need for change, in themselves and in others, but want more evidence for how best to go about making beneficial changes that last, in people and organizations. We have worked with boards looking to improve themselves and their executives. We have worked with people who are new in leadership positions, or who can see that this is something they want to do, and feel they have real potential, but want to improve their capabilities and impact. We have seen excellent leaders in one context floundering in another. We have found many brilliantly able women and men who have been overlooked for senior positions. We have heard many stories about expensive, impressive leadership development programs that provoke great insights, excitement and motivation, but fizzle out within a week of ending. Uniquely we have looked at leaders and leadership holistically and systemically: looking at human cognition, emotion and behavior in brain, body and environment, and how they change.

Neuroscience is beginning to shed some light on how the brain works and the neural correlates of behaviors, beliefs and attitudes. For the first time, there is evidence that challenges, confirms or questions some of the experiential and common sense knowledge we have about leaders and leadership. There are now some findings relevant to leadership that are like signposts, giving us directions if not proof, and sufficiently agreed on to be worth looking at. Together with knowledge of business and organizations, these directions give a sound basis for understanding how leadership works and how it can be learned and developed throughout a career.

A new science of leadership: what's in a leader?

There are many more or less valid definitions, but for the purposes of this book, ours is minimalist, because leadership is dynamic and adaptable and depends on a wide range of contexts and the perceptions of those who are led, not just on the characteristics of the leader. Leaders are individuals who have sufficient

- Status
- Power
- Dominance
- Influence.

in a group to be able to achieve innovatory goals with and through others. In our view, leaders go beyond the status quo to forge new and different directions: they deliver success where others have failed, even in established market conditions. Groups can be small or large, formal or informal, multinational, multicultural, from families through corporations to tribes, states and nations. Can science tell us anything usable about leadership? We will look at this question from two perspectives: that of the leaders themselves and of the people they lead.

Leaders are less stressed

For years, conventional wisdom held that leaders were highly stressed and needed support to deal with that. However, it was also known that people at the top of organizations or professions were healthier and lived longer than those lower down – the initial assumption being that this was a result of socioeconomic differences. The famous Whitehall studies of UK civil servants in the late 1960s and 1980s, looking at a relatively narrow socioeconomic band also found that, when other risk factors were accounted for, work related stress correlated much more with bad health at lower levels than at senior levels. These studies did not look at biological markers (the presence or absence of biological parameters such as hormone levels) for stress, but looked at a small number of other factors: for example, the combination of high demand and low control, conflicting demands between home and work responsibilities, effort/reward imbalance and job insecurity.

They found that people with intermediate or low job control had over twice the incidence of coronary heart disease as people with high job control, that supportive managers and social networks had a positive effect and that the combination of high effort and low reward increased the risk of heart disease.[1]

More recently, a small number of studies have concluded that leaders have lower levels of cortisol, (the hormone that the body produces in response to stress) than those in subordinate positions.[2] Earlier research with primate groups[3] had shown similar results: in hierarchical groups, when status is not under threat, those at the top have less stress than those lower down. You will recall that cortisol prepares the body to deal with stressors and threats, enabling the brain to focus resources on responding appropriately. Low levels of cortisol are not harmful, but high levels, especially sustained over time, are damaging to the immune system and can destroy neurons: those in the hippocampus (related to memory) appear especially vulnerable. Chronic stress can indeed be a significant factor in higher levels of heart disease (see also Chapter 9).

It is not yet possible to say whether lower stress is a cause or effect of status, whether leaders get to the top because they are less affected by stress, or better able to manage their responses to it, or whether being at or near the top offers some protection against stress. But looking at these recent results in relation to the earlier studies it might be reasonable to conclude that leaders, *in general*, are less stressed than subordinates, hence healthier and more likely to live longer, in spite of greater responsibilities, the perception of "loneliness at the top" and perhaps in part because of a having a sense of greater control and high rewards for high efforts.

It is important to remember that, just because scientific studies have found that, on the whole, leaders have less stress, it doesn't mean that no leader is stressed, or you can't be a leader if you are. There are always many external factors outside a leader's control which impact on their success and it may be the ratio of within/without control factors that is a key factor in how much stress is experienced.

All three of us authors have worked with great leaders who have suffered from stress, mentally and physically, and have seen a number of positive outcomes when leaders have become more practiced in stress management through coaching, meditation, reframing and other methods. We have also seen examples of exhaustion, illness and burnout. Chapter 9 gives you some techniques to develop resilience and learn how to understand and manage stress in yourself and others. A good social life, with friends and family, is now known to be a key buffer against stress, and has been shown to increase not only our sense of wellbeing and happiness, but also more measurably, longevity and health.

Leaders have more testosterone AND less cortisol

Two very interesting studies, published in 2010, proposed a link between testosterone and cortisol that reinforces the relationship between leadership and low stress. There is considerable evidence linking high testosterone to the achievement and maintenance of high status and dominance in primates and other mammals, especially when under threat. Evidence for the effects of high testosterone on status in humans has been much less clear. This research found that it is not testosterone levels alone that predict dominance in humans, but the interactions between it and cortisol.[4] The combination of high testosterone and low cortisol appears to be a predictor of status and dominance in people, whereas high testosterone alone and low cortisol alone do not correlate with dominant behavior in competitive situations. Two studies are not proof, but offer a persuasive argument, taken into consideration with many observations of behaviors that are associated with leaders.

Lower cortisol is not only linked to decreased stress but also to what social scientists call "social approach", that is, an easy openness to other people, a counter to anxiety and social avoidance. Looking back at the four-step change process in Chapter 2, this might also be a factor in greater openness to the therapeutic relationships that facilitate change in the brain.

Entrepreneurial leaders have higher risk tolerance/ better ability to manage risk

Research conducted by Barbara Sahakian and her team[5] at the University of Cambridge shows that entrepreneurs are more comfortable with risk taking than managers. Not a surprising finding perhaps. Risk tolerance has also been shown to be positively correlated with higher levels of testosterone. It is therefore plausible that leaders are more likely to be tolerant of risk than those lower in the hierarchy. Entrepreneurs also scored more on personality impulsiveness and superior cognitive flexibility, the latter also a frequently mentioned characteristic of leaders. This research has not been extended to look at other kinds of leaders, but some similarity in traits and behaviors between entrepreneurs and innovative leaders looks reasonable (see further Chapter 4).

Leaders are more likely to have a well developed pre-frontal cortex (PFC)

You now know that it is the PFC that is critically involved in most of the higher executive functions of the brain, such as focusing attention, self-control, planning and complex problem solving. This part of the brain (which is relatively larger in humans than in any other mammals) is extremely well connected with all other parts of the brain, and is like the CEO of the brain (to reverse the analogy of Chapter 2, where the CEO of a company is like the PFC). Our working memory, the crucible for our conscious thinking and problem solving, is located there. A part of the PFC (the right ventrolateral PFC, or RVLPFC) has been shown to be particularly active when we exercise both self-control (the ability to manage our impulses and instinctive responses to stimuli – to stop ourselves doing something, whether reaching for another chocolate or responding angrily to a colleague who needs something explained for the third time) and cognitive control. Examples of cognitive control are our ability to change the way we think about something, for example, to reframe an unpleasant situation, or to overcome an instinctive bias against a person who holds a belief that we do not agree with. Self-control enables us to manage, or regulate, our emotions, and this may be one of the key reasons for leaders' lower levels of stress. Self-control has been demonstrated to be a key attribute of people who are thought to be trustworthy.[6]

With a better developed PFC, leaders are not only better able to focus their attention top down, but also have the self-control necessary to switch that attention when needed. This flexibility of mind has been noted in entrepreneurs (see Sahakian et al), and is often mentioned in relation to good leaders. Leaders who are able to respond quickly and adapt effectively to changes in their environment are more likely to help their organizations survive and even thrive in turbulent times.

Leaders are confident

Higher levels of testosterone are also positively correlated with confidence, which is often mentioned in the management literature as being a characteristic of leaders. In Amy J Cuddy's inspiring TED talk, "Your body language shapes who you are",[7] she demonstrates how holding a power pose for two minutes raises your testosterone levels, reduces your cortisol and can increase your confidence. This chimes well with the findings that it is the balance between testosterone and cortisol levels, *not testosterone alone*, which provides an indicator for leadership. As you will see in Chapter 4, higher than average levels of testosterone are not always a good thing. They can be predictors of excessive risk taking, aggression and antisocial behavior, and possibly lower levels of empathy.

Confidence, a sense that one is more likely to perform well, is reinforced by each success, so might arise from the effects of practicing self-control over time. Self-control (as famously measured in the Mischel Marshmallow Test), turned out to be a better predictor of success in exams, at university and in later careers than other tests such as SATs and IQ. This reinforces common sense. You are more likely to be successful if you are focused and hard working, than if you allow distractions, temptations and tantrums to get in the way, however high your IQ (see Box 3.1).

> **BOX 3.1 SELF-CONTROL AND MARSHMALLOWS**
>
> The Mischel Marshmallow Test looked at young children's ability to delay gratification by resisting the desire to eat one marshmallow while the researcher left the room, in order to gain more marshmallows on their return. Further studies confirmed the strong correlation between being able to delay eating the marshmallow and success in later life. Other work challenged some of the assumptions behind the test, claiming that not enough attention was given to the children's circumstances: were they brought up in environments where food, if uneaten, was taken by others?
>
> It would be interesting to see who would be successful in 30 years time if that test were repeated today, when multitasking and multiple media are more the norm.

Confidence might also be influenced by the sense of greater control that you have the higher up you are in decision making. A confident leader is more likely to feel optimistic about outcomes in the future, more likely to feel that they can influence events positively and thus less likely to be anxious. Women, on the whole, appear to find it harder to achieve confidence and that may be linked to their levels of testosterone (see Chapter 11 for a discussion on difference, diversity and gender). If indeed leadership is better correlated with the balance between testosterone and cortisol, and not absolute levels of testosterone, and that balance can be managed through practice, and confidence increased, then the chemistry of gender is not the barrier to leadership for women it might have been once thought to be.

Leaders are good influencers – and great storytellers

In the individualistic Anglo-Saxon cultures, with heavily technology and knowledge dependant economies, and highly educated mobile workforces, the ability to influence is a more powerful tool than the power to order someone to do something. An order will get something done in the short term, and to solve a crisis it is a good leadership tool, but in the longer term, a leader needs people to be motivated to contribute to their organization's success, to exercise their initiative, to develop innovative and creative solutions to customer problems, to engage both rational mind and emotions – in other words, to work effectively at the peak of their capacity and beyond, without detailed direct orders.

Communications skills are naturally crucial to influencing, and we will be examining these in more detail in Chapter 5. No-one disputes that excellent communications skills are essential for leadership, but the importance of storytelling as one of these is sometimes overlooked in a business context. Stories, narratives with a timeline, with characters and a plot or point, go with the grain of the brain. Stories are how we learn to make sense of a lot of things about the world when we are little. Stories follow the way we lay down autobiographical or episodic memories. In other words, "our reality derives from the stories we tell ourselves".[8] They follow the brain's own patterns of thought because they feed the brain's need for meaning, for events and actions to have causes and effects, for reality to have a reason for the way it is, for goal directed actions and social scenarios. Stories are more easily memorable and re-tellable. Some of the most powerful leaders in business are superb storytellers. Steve Jobs' introductions of new products at Apple became legendary. Some include personal elements that increase the emotional content of the story, and make it easier for their listeners, at all levels in the organization, to identify and empathize with their leadership. Good – and true – stories told by a company's leaders can shape the culture and brand of a company. A leader's credibility can be severely damaged if they get carried away by storytelling, so that their stories about the market, the company's future prospects and the way it behaves are not consistent with its values and the lived experiences of staff and stakeholders. However good stories told around the reality of how the organization behaves towards others, how it benefits communities and society as well as customers and shareholders, how it believes in and supports its people, can influence emotions, and help develop strong motivation, commitment and loyalty. In our work we increasingly hear the need for people that can look at a set of numbers and visualize the story of what those numbers will mean for their people, their customers and society at large. So the elements of a good leadership story might include:

- A simple, memorable storyline – with a beginning, middle and end.
- Strong characters.
- Plausible reasons for events.
- Explicit goals for actions.
- Emotional language.
- Consistency with the reality of the people, their organization and their values.
- A clear vision of what the future might hold.

You can find out more about the power of storytelling in Chapter 5.

Leaders set clear goals for themselves and for others

The human brain is geared towards enabling goal driven actions. Again the PFC plays a key role in marshalling the brain's resources and energy towards achieving what we intend. Goals, whether conscious or unconscious, help focus our attention. Because the brain's various networks compete for resources, and our conscious thinking processes are especially energy hungry and ferociously competitive for working memory capacity, putting in the effort to set conscious, explicit, goals is a way to mobilize our brain to achieve success. Some leaders are said to be highly motivated by winning in competitive situations (also linked to testosterone levels). Achieving a defined goal might be a form of winning, which triggers the reward systems in our brains. Non-conscious goals, often short term, might conflict with or distract from our conscious ones. A widely experienced personal example is dieting. My long-term goal is to lose weight to improve my health. In the short term, I experience a craving for chocolate, so when busy, distracted or stressed I find I have opened the biscuit pack in my drawer without realizing I have done so. In a business context that might mean that whereas the long-term goal is growth in new markets, I have a fear of what failure might mean for my reputation, so I keep putting off that investment decision, without being able to acknowledge the reason. Articulating goals clearly helps us to reflect about them because using language helps us to think. Writing them down is a form of practice and can also act as a social contract with ourselves or others, which tends to give us a stronger chance of achieving them. Our brains are also constantly striving to interpret the meaning or intention behind other people's actions and behaviors, to the point that, if it isn't clear or explicit, we make up our own explanations. Thus setting conscious goals, articulating them, communicating them clearly to others and finding ways of motivating others to share in them, is a way for leaders to reinforce the direction of their own and others' minds and actions towards desired outcomes and away from distractions and competing intentions.

Leaders are like experts

In order to be successful, leaders need to be competent, to have sufficient knowledge in order to act in ways which are more likely to benefit than harm the organization they lead, more likely to lead to success than failure. Luck might play its part, but on the whole it comes more easily to the prepared mind. Competence is sometimes taken as a need for domain expertise in the specific area of business, industry or market in which their organization operates. How often are search firms tasked with finding someone whose track record is in a similar company, industry or profession? But the best technology expert in an IT firm does not always make the best leader. The professor who has won a Nobel Prize for advances in pharmacology might not be the best person to run the company that produces the drug, or even to run the lab they work in. There is plenty of anecdotal evidence that leadership is normally contextual, that few leaders survive dramatic changes in circumstances or industries. So in a stable situation it might work well to look to match experience, but in times of growth or turbulence it might be worth looking for a track record of managing change and disruption, even in a different sector.

Expertise takes time, self-discipline and enormous effort – whatever the domain; as mentioned in Chapter 2, it takes about 10,000 hours of practice to become an expert, whether in chess, basketball or artificial intelligence. What expertise means for the brain is efficiency. Experts can see patterns and meaning where others see a blur – and they can see them more quickly.[9] They can, in other words, see both wood and trees. Seeing patterns and meaning leads to more efficient chunking of the mass of relevant information that needs to be processed consciously and unconsciously, so that working memory can do more in less time and better decisions can be made. Experts are better able to assign probabilities and therefore are more likely to be better managers of risk. They are also more robust under pressure.[10] Their instincts are more likely to be reliable, their feel for a situation to be more accurate. These are traits that are often recognizable in leaders.

So what kind of expertise do leaders need? They need sustained, continuous, practice in the underlying skills of leadership:

- Be able to focus their attention.
- Change that focus when required.
- Reflect critically on their thoughts, attitudes and behaviors.
- Manage themselves so that they can mobilize their will power, persist in adversity and calibrate their attitude to risk and uncertainty.
- Regulate their emotions and moods.
- Balance their intuition with their rational thinking.
- Maintain their health and energy.

• Spend time and effort on developing relevant skills and knowledge for their area of activity so as to focus on the right issues, more often than not, and to have a reliable intuitive response to what comes at them, when circumstances are relatively stable.
• Hone their ability to relate well to others.

The capacity to persist through problems and difficulties, the resilience to bounce back after setbacks, coupled with the courage to change focus and direction when necessary are mentioned less often but can make the difference between success and failure (see also the discussion in Chapter 9).

This is the scaffolding for a whole range of leadership skills and behaviors: flexibility to choose from a variety of leadership styles, behaviors and perspectives, self-discipline to learn, to challenge and analyze, capability to take decisions, whether alone or with others, that are more likely to be the right ones, emotional awareness and attunement so as to be open to other people's diverse ideas and perspectives, and ability to focus on others' needs and wants, not just ones' own. Sustained practice of self-reflection and self-management, together with empathy, may also generate some valuable side effects. Understanding and fulfilling the need to maintain a strong social network reinforces not only health and wellbeing, but core values such as fairness and respect for diverse others.

Leadership can be learned

The PFC can be developed and its capacities enhanced through focused attention and practice. This is good news for both organizations and leaders, because it means that leadership qualities and capabilities can be learned and improved though experience together with training and development. As we have already emphasized, this is not to claim that it is an easy process, or one that can be delivered in the classroom, or through traditional methods and programs of learning. Developing an increased ability for self-management and consistently practicing the self-discipline required to interject the "free won't" between impulse and action, or instinctive thought and spoken word, depends on tremendous motivation and will, and years of practice, reflection and feedback (see further discussion in Chapter 7, especially Box 7.4). There is evidence that this may be easier if supported by the right kind of relationship with a coach, facilitator, mentor or trainer who understands how the brain works and can offer useful tools and techniques to reinforce the practice. There is also evidence that mindfulness meditation can improve self-awareness and self-control.

Meaning, values and ethics

You have already learned how the brain automatically assigns meaning to everything we perceive, including signals from our body, through the emotions, on a spectrum from fear to love. At the most basic level, which we share with most mammals, this meaning is intended to help us survive through appropriate actions, fleeing from threats and danger and approaching opportunities to reproduce, sources of food, warmth and social support. Evolution has shaped our brains, and is continuing to shape them, so that the human brain is capable of constructing very sophisticated, complex meanings from everything we receive through our senses. Our brains are at the same time our most advanced feature, our USP, and the reason for a potentially fatal weakness: our complete dependence on care from others for at least two years after birth. Perhaps as a result, and certainly vitally for our survival as a species, our brains have in fact been "critically tuned" to social interactions, to understanding and communicating with other people, to living and working with them. The infant brain is shaped to a significant degree by its interactions with the environment, but most importantly with the primary caregivers. It is then not surprising that our brains fundamentally seek meaning in social interactions, to make sense of the reasons for, and effects of, the human actions they perceive[11] and to make sense of their own place in their relationships. Perhaps it is also not surprising that when we speak of needing to find some meaning in our lives and work we are mainly talking about finding and fulfilling our social purpose, one that gives a value to us in the context of our society, what Maslow called self-actualization.[12] It is part of a leader's role to create or maintain and communicate the core meaning of an organization and the people who work in it and with it. Meaning can be the most powerful motivator, an incentive that transcends money.

When we speak of the values we hold, these are complex cognitive and emotional constructs shaped by our experiences and the societies and cultures which form our environment. Their purpose is to enable us to survive and thrive, in a context of much more sophisticated and subtle threats and rewards than saber-toothed tigers and a cache of honey. Some values worked well when we were all hunter gatherers on the plains of Africa and work well now too. Fairness is one such value that has deep instinctive roots. Others might have been protective then, but destructive now. A respect for equality and diversity might need to be worked hard at: it does not come naturally when our instincts tend towards defining like-us as more likely to be friend, and not-like-us, more likely to be foe.

A leader's values are critical to the impact of their leadership. Like goals they are lodestones for behavior. Leaders who are aware of their most dearly held values are thus better able to articulate them and align them with their organization and the people they lead for the better – or sometimes, worse. In this book so far we have been talking as though our assumption is that leaders and leadership are good, that is, beneficial for their organizations, the people they work with and through and their society. And yet we all know of leaders who have been successful in the short term, but have been the cause of great injustices, unimaginable human suffering and appear evil in thought and deed. Genghis Khan, Stalin and Hitler are obvious, albeit extreme, examples.

We all know people in leadership positions who combine both good and bad leadership behaviors, sometimes in the same meeting. The danger is to underestimate the complexity of the brain, to minimize the effects of the complexity of human organizations and not to believe that leadership is something that needs constant effort.

We have experienced leaders who are successful but dishonest, until they are discovered (remember Madoff), or who are responsible for great increases in the bottom line, but are bullying and destructive of others' self-esteem and creativity. Investors are often accused of short-termism, but some of those who write on leadership might also suffer from that trait. Perhaps the ability to create a sustainably successful organization should be a key part of the definition of a good leader.

Risk tolerance can turn into risk addiction. Dominance and influence can turn into aggression and manipulation. These behaviors are often acquired during a rise to leadership or as a result of trying to hang on to a dominant position sometimes to the point of destroying the organization they lead. Self-reflection, self-management, emotional regulation, a strong sense of personal values, an explicit commitment to ethical codes and a well exercised PFC can protect against, but not wholly exclude, such hubristic behaviors. Perhaps the self-reflection of a leader who has been at the top of their organization and led it from success to success can be helped these days by an app which plays the role of the slave standing behind the triumphant Roman general and whispering "remember, you are only mortal".

A society's ethics are encoded in law, but tested daily in everyday social interactions. There are laws that seem to us good – and others with absurd unintentional consequences. The arts and cultural activities that surround us – books, TV, films, paintings, music and museums – provoke and challenge us to feel and then think about what we value and how we apply those values in contexts which are at one remove from our lived reality and thus might help us find the distance to reframe some of our perspectives. In our early teenage years what is good or bad might look like white and black. As we mature and gain in experience and self-awareness, we see that these issues are sometimes more grey – killing another human is wrong, but might euthanasia for a person dying slowly in great pain, who has chosen it, be a good thing? Is every person equally responsible for their own actions? Is a psychopath ill or evil? Science does not have answers yet, and perhaps never will. We don't understand enough yet, and even understanding would not be sufficient, but there are implications for the field of neurolaw in terms of *mens rea* (Latin for "guilty mind").

We have begun however to have some idea around what might lie behind some bad or even catastrophic judgments. When the brain's energy levels are low, and we are overloaded with conflicting demands, powerful emotions, stressed or fearful, the limitations of our PFC cannot cope and our passionate impulses take over. The constant demands of high public office might underlie the resource deficits that lead to toxic personal decisions, such as affairs or accepting improper gifts. We do not intend to go into the ethics of leadership in depth, but wanted to flag that leaders' values and ethics are a key part of their impact and thus have to be a part of their development and constant practice. They cannot be compartmentalized as a private matter.

What do our brains need from a leader?

We do not like the word follower. It gives the wrong impression, implying that the leader is in front, forging one path, and the rest are behind.[13] Those who are within a leader's sphere of influence need to be capable of forging their own paths, of independent, innovative and creative thinking and actions. It is no longer possible to be the holder of all relevant knowledge or always the generator of the best ideas or decisions. Most of our common endeavors need just that, to be shared with others. Leadership is about relationships, but these are dynamic and a person might be the leader one day, in one context, and a group member of the commons the next. So in this chapter we talk about leaders and their relationships with those they influence or direct, as between leaders and the people they work with and through, always bearing in mind that these will often be shifting roles.

We are beginning to understand what a member of a group needs in order to be comfortable taking their lead from someone else. There are certain requirements imposed by the way our brains work. Above all, as emphasized in Chapter 1, we need to be able trust our leaders.

Trust is a feeling, a mental action or state, involving relying on another (individual, group or organization) to behave in a way consistent with the "truster's" assumptions and values, in a context where there is risk to the "truster". You now understand how trust is influenced by the hormone oxytocin, which also influences our affection and bonding with others. We trust those who are credible and reliable and are more likely to trust someone if we feel that they are concerned about us, not just themselves. There is thus a strong correlation between trustworthiness and self-control, perhaps because perceiving someone to be capable of managing themselves and their emotions implies that they are less likely to behave irrationally, erratically, impulsively and perhaps even dishonestly and selfishly.[14] Indeed self-control has been called the price we pay for admission to a society.

Our brain needs a leader to create environments that *feel* safe and certain, even when the world is far from being either. We also need leaders who communicate well, who make understanding them easy, who create processes that are fair and transparent, so our brains do not waste precious effort in second guessing them or trying to understand what to do next.

We want leaders who help us give meaning to our lives, who demonstrate that they value us. We have seen how good relationships are absolutely critical to our wellbeing, so our brains need leaders who develop supportive relationships in which we can innovate, create and develop ourselves. We need leaders who embody certain attributes, whose attitudes, thoughts and behaviors are aligned and not conflicting, so that they are models of the kind of behaviors that will lead to success for us as well as our organization. We need them to be there physically or virtually, often enough for us to have a meaningful, consistent relationship. We need them to be sufficiently attuned to us and our emotions so that our relationship is mutually supportive, not just one way. We need to believe in our leaders. Leaders need to be successful, and in some cases, success trumps everything else: a notorious example being Steve Jobs whose relationships with staff were, on the whole, corrosive but who led Apple to spectacular growth and success – twice. Leaders who fail more than they succeed, for whatever reason, are less likely to be credible, so leaders also need some luck!

A model for discussion

A well developed and practiced PFC and its executive functions are at the heart of leadership. The most fundamental characteristic of leadership is the ability to manage oneself. This in turn depends on constant self-reflection and practice. Leaders are likely to have a good balance of testosterone and cortisol, so that they are confident, manage stress and risk well, have good focus, enjoy winning in a balanced way and have an easy authority in their group. They will have put many hours of effort into acquiring and practicing expertise that helps them succeed.

These fundamental brain-based characteristics are likely to manifest as an open, agreeable, goal-oriented, self-controlled and reflective personality. The leader with a well developed PFC is likely to have clear, aligned goals, to be self-confident and resilient. Other members of their society will be more likely to trust them, to accept willingly being persuaded and

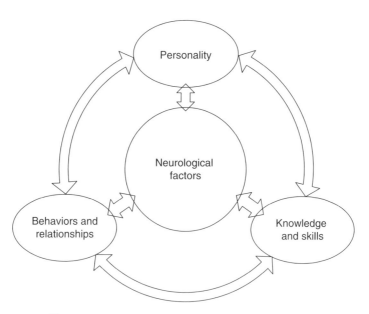

FIGURE 3.1 A new neuroscience-based leadership model

Source: © K Chisholm 2014.

influenced by them and to take them as examples of "good practice". People will feel valued and will be keen to do their best to maintain that value in the eyes of the leader. They will therefore feel more secure, and perhaps also more in control, as trust is mutual

People who are influenced so that they feel more in control of their role, more engaged with their own organization, who feel they are contributing to the wellbeing of others in their community and society are more likely to be self-motivated, loyal, productive, creative and healthy. They are more likely to be open to feedback, to seek learning opportunities and to be on a journey of personal development.

Summary

We need leaders to behave in certain ways, to do certain things, to have a good relationship with us, but also to be – or be striving to become – a certain kind of person. Leadership then is the unique combination of who you are, how you think, what you do and how you relate to other people (Figure 3.1).

Actions and reflections

- Know yourself. Practice mindfulness, examine and test your values, listen profoundly to others' views, especially when they are different.
- Have integrity and clarity of purpose, articulate your values and goals and be ruthless in prioritizing them.
- Work hard. If you don't love what you do and respect the people you work with think about alternatives.
- Practice focusing your attention, develop expertise in your field and in connecting to people and remember to balance cognition and intuition.

Chapter

Testosterone, Risk and Entrepreneurship

"Our doubts are traitors, and make us lose the good we oft might win, by fearing to attempt."

Shakespeare, *Measure for Measure*

The "trouble with testosterone" starts *in utero* (in the womb) when the embryo with the XY gene gets its first flood of testosterone and starts the journey to becoming male. All embryos start out female and it is only after a few weeks that they start to differentiate in terms of gender. Female embryos carry the XX chromosomes and males the XY.

There are of course, fascinating exceptions such as the XXY "super females" who have more than their fair share of testosterone leaving them stronger, faster and hairier, with a better sense of direction and ability to read maps upside down than your run of the mill XX, but that's another story.

If we stick to future leaders, then what we are looking at down the line is a group of mostly men, a few women, less than half of all of them below the age of 30 and most over 35. The age cut-off is interesting because testosterone levels start to decline in men around the age of 30.

Women also have testosterone, but much less than men (men have about eight times as much, but as metabolic consumption is greater in men they actually have to produce about 20 times as much per day).

Testosterone is an anabolic steroid hormone like insulin and growth hormone. It is secreted from the testes in men and the ovaries in women. Catabolic steroid hormones include cortisol and adrenalin (mediators of long- and short-term stress). When the ratio of anabolic: catabolic is high you have high performance, when the ratio is low you have stress and poor resilience.

When the ratio of anabolic: catabolic is high you have high performance, when the ratio is low you have stress and poor resilience.

Mind and body, body and mind

Even though psychology has informed business for decades there still sometimes seems to be an assumption that there is a cut-off between mind and body, with little or no interaction between them. Since the advent of sophisticated scanning techniques, our increasing understanding that neuroscience is drifting below the neck and physiology is drifting above the neck is growing through visibility of the exquisite interaction between nerves and hormones (the neuroendocrine system) in the brain and body as a whole.

The tiniest change in a cell, chemical or electrical signal in the body, gives rise to some compensatory, complementary or inhibitory response in the brain and vice versa. Like when you feel threatened so your adrenal glands pour out a little adrenalin, then you start to breathe faster and your heart rate goes up. Or when you take a few deep breaths to calm your mind.

• What are the characteristics that you admire in the leaders of today? Might they include focus, determination and drive? These are strongly correlated to testosterone levels.

- Would you say that the leaders of yesteryear were too ruthless, too much in "command and control" mode, too aggressively pace-setting? These are correlated to higher testosterone levels.
- Are you seeing future leaders evolving to be more collaborative, trust building and coaching in style? These may not be correlated, or indeed may be inversely correlated, to testosterone levels. More likely they are correlated to oxytocin and serotonin levels.

Also it is important to remember that in such complex behaviors these chemicals and hundreds more are cascading around brain systems having inhibitory and excitatory effects on each other to create the entire outcome. Here we have concentrated on testosterone, but for all the physiological reasons that there are not many women in senior positions in large corporates are we going to witness a shift to leaders, boards and organizations becoming more well-rounded, more balanced, more able to mitigate our physiology and less skeptical of the interplay between physicality and behavior? In the next decade, will neuroscience research reveal the similarities in the physiological signature of professional athletes, elite soldiers and experts in various fields, especially in terms of financial risk taking, innovation and business leadership?

will neuroscience research reveal the similarities in the physiological signature of professional athletes, elite soldiers, especially and experts in various fields, especially in terms of financial risk taking, innovation and business leadership?

These are some of the exciting questions that we address in this book and that will be answered over time by the millions of dollars worth of research being carried out in the US and Switzerland. What we do know is that the brain and the body "rev up" together for a fight, flight and fright situation.

Think of the rugby player in anticipation of kick off who can "hear every voice, see every blade of grass": that is the effect of testosterone on the brain augmented by noradrenalin from the *locus coeruleus*.

It is actually postulated by neuroendocrinologists that our adrenal glands may register risk before out conscious minds do.

Experiments show that men and women can have a similar appetite for risk, but that men are more willing to act on partial information, which has obvious advantages and disadvantages in business.

The "winner effect" experiments (endogenous steroids and financial risk taking on a London trading floor) have been published in the Proceedings of the National Academy of Sciences by Coates et al.[1]

These are based on the knowledge that an animal that has recently won a fight (either male or female) is statistically more likely to win the next fight due to testosterone-induced increases in the oxygen carrying capacity of hemoglobin and increased confidence and appetite for risk. Victory keeps raising testosterone levels in an inverted U-shaped dose-response curve. This means there is a tipping point beyond which the animal starts to pick too many fights and its risky behavior impairs its ability to survive. Looking at profit and loss, on high versus low testosterone days on a trading floor it becomes apparent that traders learn over time to get higher reward to variability ratios.

How do we modify behaviors that are so biological in their basis?

There is increasing evidence from brain scanning that:

- Mindfulness training can regulate the neuroendocrinological (nerves and hormones) system and increase fold density in the brain to induce calmer states, partly through regulation of cortisol and melatonin production.
- Physical training regimes such as the Nordic practice of sauna and snow bathing (or swimming in cold water) can improve emotional stability, providing superior immunity to both despondency and euphoria, through sufficient production of dopamine and noradrenalin to keep us motivated and alert.

• Stress followed by recovery (in the previous bullet point, thermal stress) but also episodic fasting like the five:two diet may also develop resilience to learned helplessness for the future.

Maintaining a degree of balance between risk aversion and greed has been likened to staying within the boundaries of motivation that does not tip over into addiction.

Risk, relationships and decisions

Let us turn more specifically to risk and the nature of relationships, which involves quite a few different hormones. In a book called *The Arabs: Journeys Beyond the Mirage*[2] journalist David Lamb tells the following story from the ultra-conservative kingdom of Saudi Arabia:

"Saudi Arabia", wrote David Lamb, "is more comfortable building a consensus than pioneering a policy. It works, if goaded, behind the scenes, and it does not take risks" (see Box 4.1).

BOX 4.1   RISK AND CULTURE

An American oilman who had lived in Saudi Arabia for years recalled a night, in June 1967, when a Saudi friend stopped by his home to say goodbye.

"I'm going to war", the Saudi said. "I leave in the morning." There were handshakes, embraces and words of farewell.

A week later the American was taken aback to see his friend at a party in Riyadh. He asked what had happened.

"My brother went", the Saudi said. "I had some business to tend to."

As it was, the Six-Day Arab-Israeli War was over anyway by the time the two Saudi brigades reached Jordan.

Imagine a world in which no international discussions could be had without there being a brain-chemistry profile on each of the participants.[3]

- *Who is low in oxytocin, then?* Not much chance of making real progress towards any kind of consensus there, then.
- *Who's creaking on cortisol?* Was it just stress at the time of the blood sample or is the guy always too uptight to listen to reason?
- *Are the Italians as tanked up with testosterone as they portray themselves?* Who is the most attractive woman we can field to keep them happily distracted as she threatens quietly to abandon them if they do not share our point of view?

Such a scenario is not beyond the short-horizon bounds of possibilities. The lengths to which, it is said, secret services would go during the cold war to get samples of world leaders' urine and feces, in order to see what current diseases might have impact on foreign policy, were considerable – not least of all diverting the whole of the waste plumbing system of one hotel at which General de Gaulle was staying. There aren't many things that can't be justified politically if risk is to be minimized through an advantage gained.

But that's at international level. What of more commercial or private matters? "Decision making" is the rubric under which academics put it. "Neuroeconomics" or "behavioral economics" are the trend-setting terms, precipitated perhaps by Ormerod's *The Death of Economics*[4] nearly 20 years ago. The new economists wonder about what is going on in the brains of real individuals, not just economists, when key factors are being weighed (or not) in the making of a decision. Old or classical economics – utility theory – begins to give way to attempting to understand why small shifts in circumstances (in the world or in the individual) can have very large consequences. Chaos and complexity underpin everything, remember?

A key and difficult issue for all studies of individuals however is that all brains are different. Although they start with very similar potential (given normal biological variations coming from normally-distributed genetic differences), what happens in life from embryonic month four onwards shapes any particular brain to be the specialized and individualized organ that it is, as we have already discussed.

In *The Psychology of Military Incompetence*,[5] written well before the neurochemical study of the living brain was possible, Dixon could only use concepts such as "the Anal Character", "Anti-Effeminacy" and "Muscular Christianity" to explain decision-making processes, imbued in part as he was, in the period of writing, with what are now seen as outdated Freudian or cultural descriptive "explanations" for human behavior. Nowadays, if not quite everything has a neuro- prefix, there is nevertheless a search for more specific ways of understanding what goes on in the human mind – or at least in its physical manifestation, the brain.

So catchy titles appear, such as:

Fooled by Randomness (2004).
The Black Swan (2007).
Flirting with Disaster (2008).
Predictably Irrational (2008).
The Triggers to Yes (2008).
On Being Certain (2008).
The Age of Empathy (2009).
The Big Short (2010).

All explore from one angle or another the nature of decision making and, by implication if not explicitly, the nature of risk; and seek to raise in your mind the possibility of some explanatory processes for what happens in the workings of the neural networks.

Zhong and his colleagues,[6] for instance, suggest that dopamine controls what is happening when gains are being made; while serotonin has that function when losses are being made. Serotonin is not only the feel good chemical but it also has inhibitory functions too. And both dopamine and serotonin inevitably have a marked effect upon the individual's perception of any given situation.

Given that no behavior happens without neurochemicals happening first, the increasingly fascinating question arises as to whether our brain *controls* our risk taking or in fact *responds* to our risk taking because we control our brain? If the former, then how will neurochemical science provide the means of selecting good risk takers? It is 20 years since Leeson's activities caused the 1995 collapse of Barings. What if it were possible in the future to guard against such mavericks by knowing more about their brain chemistry?

Why is it, for instance, that in the corporate world one can quickly identify "types"? It is unlikely that an audit accountant type would be found in the creative functions of an advertising agency – and vice versa. If our developmental neurochemistry defines who we are and hence the kinds of jobs we seek, is that a matter of choice? Or is it only the rationalization of a process that drives us in one direction rather than another? And can that same process get embedded in the culture of a country, as has just been suggested?

Risk taking is theoretically described as having four main attitude patterns – being risk averse towards moderate prospects and long-shot hazards; and risk tolerant towards moderate hazards and long-shot prospects.

Various regions of the brain have been identified as being involved in risk-based decision making; but the science of how the various regions of the brain are interconnected (connectomics) is itself proceeding along such new directions that much of what the last five years has produced is likely to have to be re-evaluated. Genes are also getting much involved. Twin studies from both China and Sweden suggest there is a considerable hereditary element in risk taking. So research is moving more and more towards creating a model of risk decision making that links the decision maker's attitude with genetic make-up.

And then there is our old friend, the right ventrolateral pre-frontal cortex (RVLPFC), to be taken into account. Situated in the inner surface of the right half of the front part of the brain, it is involved in complex creative decision making. As the brain is an energy hungry system (using about 25 watts of the available 95 watts that the whole body runs off) any reduction in the available energy to a key decision-making part of the brain will have an impact on the quality of those decisions. This is why interpersonal relationships are so key to good decision making inside organizations. Not only do high levels of trust make people feel good, they also free people to use their abilities to best corporate advantage.

The neurochemistry of trust raises the possibility of moral markets and the nature of relationships and economic prosperity – as Zak proposed in 2012.[7] But trust and risk taking are not just two sides of the same coin. In a recent thoughtful paper on the biology of human trust[8] it is recorded that while oxytocin increases trust in a risk-taking simulated game, testosterone has an antidote effect on oxytocin and *de*creases trust in social situations but *in*creases the appetite for financial risks.

Maybe measuring testosterone on the way into the trading floor would predict the outcomes for the day – and cortisol levels say who should be kept off the floor.

So the neurochemistry of risk taking is being actively explored, as is trust between people too. The way a person trusts him- or herself in the act of making decisions is also an area that is on the edge of research interest. "Trusting yourself" still tends to be more to do with self-help advice than laboratory experimentation. But it is the foundation of real-life risk taking – even for those who seem always to make bad decisions, for they are the only ones that that person could have made.

What is certain is that the continued exploration of risk taking is well on the agenda of experimental neuroscience. So one day we may be able to trust what its findings mean.

Neural Tethering Model©: a new approach

What might the interplay of testosterone and oxytocin – of risk and trust – mean for leaders today? We introduce here a model of Neural Tethering© – mobilizing your neurons (literally using your brain) through self-awareness, focused attention, repetitive practice preferably

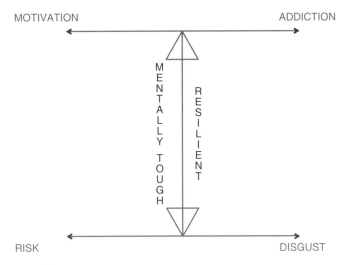

FIGURE 4.1 / Neural Tethering Model©

Source: © Swart 2013.

with the additional help of a therapeutic relationship to keep yourself on the right side of the spectrums of risk, disgust, motivation and addiction.

Use this model to identify and keep track of triggers and behaviors that may not be serving your ultimate goals. The model is partly based on some research by Andrew Lo in the financial engineering department at MIT, which shows that:[9]

- Financial gain activates the same reward circuitry as cocaine. Risk-taking activities resulting in a series of lucky gains may induce a potentially destructive feedback loop.
- Financial loss appears to activate the same fight or flight circuitry as a physical attack, sidestepping brain functions ("rationality") in favor of emotional processing and elevating heart rate, blood pressure and alertness. Once triggered, this circuit overrides most other decision-making components and is very difficult to interrupt.

- Despite its adverse reputation, moderate emotional processing appears essential to making sound risk–reward tradeoffs. Both too much and too little emotion can trigger irrational behavior.
- Risk seeking (risk averse) investors process potential monetary gain (loss) along the same circuitry involved in the use of cocaine (contemplation of disgusting things).
- Economic preferences often involve complicated interactions among multiple brain components and therefore may not be stable over time.
- There are inherent limits to how much you can process "what others are thinking" into your own financial arbitrage strategies.

With our backgrounds in psychiatry, psychology and education we authors have all witnessed that motivation and addiction are on a spectrum. This seems obvious when it comes to drugs and alcohol: you are motivated to seek something that makes you feel good, but at some point it is no longer good for you but you still keep doing it.

you are motivated to seek something that makes you feel good, but at some point it is no longer good for you but you still keep doing it.

People are beginning to see things like carbohydrates or processed sugars as things that they can also become addicted to. However we see a more silent enemy creeping in to our society. People and organizations are loath to admit that their jobs and even things like sport are addictions parading as something benign or even to be aspired to (see Box 4.2).

BOX 4.2 CARTER: A CASE STUDY

Carter loves his job so he works harder and longer, his children are being raised by someone else, the pressure to maintain the lifestyle and the private education for those kids is ever present and mounting. He pounds himself at the gym to cope with all the demands and his repressed resentment, but he's releasing more adrenalin than serotonin and often has difficulty sleeping.

He has too much to do but doesn't want to look like he cannot cope with it so Carter satisfies all those cravings for caffeine and sweet treats, but still feels irritable and snappy when he gets home (after the kids' bedtimes). His reassuringly expensive family holiday assuages some of the guilt (guilt is an emotion closely related to disgust). The pills for high blood pressure, heartburn and insomnia deal with the rest.

Sound familiar? If so, you are not alone – far from it. It is a silent epidemic akin to the Prozac nation of nineties America. But what can you do about it especially if it all leaves you feeling a little helpless and with an impending sense of doom? Back up to the Neural Tethering Model©, where you first have to be able to recognize where you are on the scale of motivation to addiction. You have to be prepared to be deeply honest with yourself and/or your coach/therapist asking:

• Have you bitten off more than you can chew?
• Are you so driven that it borders on dangerous?
• Do you obsess over details and find it difficult to say no when you are tipping over onto the wrong side of the scale?

Start to look out for the behaviors that manifest when you are taking on too much. Perhaps you become overly (self) critical?

If you can recognize these signs pretty quickly and bring yourself back to the motivation end of the spectrum you can consider yourself resilient.

If you can pre-empt tipping over into (self) destructive behaviors you would be considered mentally tough.

Ideally you want to be able to move the vertical bar that connects the two spectrums towards the left hand side so that more time is spent in the healthy zone and your threshold for risky or "addictive" behaviors is higher (Figure 4.2). That is the tethering aspect – grounding yourself at a place from which you can manage how you respond to situations around you thoughtfully whilst retaining the ability to pick yourself up and move forward if you have a bad patch, as opposed to beating yourself up and giving up.

Used consistently, this model not only builds proactive behavior, it also guards against procrastination.

In Chapter 2 we mentioned Daniel Kahneman's System 1 and System 2 and Steve Peters' human and chimp characters, and this Neural Tethering Model© asks that you begin to recognize activity from these two parts of your brain as different voices. This is akin to metacognition or literally "thinking about thinking", so when you instinctively reach for that fourth coffee of the day you can ask yourself if you really need it or if it is just a bad habit that will actually slow you down and leave you lying in bed later with a whirlwind of thoughts in your mind?

If you need evidence that this is the wrong thing to do please see this excellent video on taking breaks, naps and the effects of caffeine on memory and motor (movement) tasks – take a nap, save your life:

https://www.youtube.com/watch?v=nG2sJjwO2QQ.

Basically we are asking you to listen out for and recognize the voice of temptation versus the voice of reason and decide whom to identify yourself with. Repetitive practice will embed delayed gratification as a natural behavior. In fact mindfulness meditation is the best way of learning to press that pause button between the chimp and the human as it causes increased gyrification in the brain.

Meditation causes short-term state changes in the brain like gamma wave states and longer-term trait changes in the anterior insula, between the left PFC and amygdala and by increased gyrification,[10] which together mean one can be calmer and happier.[11]

You start by using this information and the model to work on your relationship with yourself so that you become self-authoring and less vulnerable to external events that trigger stress responses or bad habits in you.

Later you can use this model to manage your relationships with others – your family or your team – both to assess where you are risking a relationship through certain behaviors and also to help the less self-aware see when they are crossing that line from being motivated to live up to their high standards towards activities that are actually jeopardizing their career.

Entrepreneurs

"For I must tell you friendly in your ear, sell when you can: you are not for all markets."

Shakespeare, As You Like It

This ability to be resilient, mentally tough or filled with confidence and self-belief garners a lot of interest in terms of the differences between entrepreneurs and traditional CEOs. There is some work being done with brain scanning of these two groups at the University of Reading in the UK, which will be worth keeping an eye on.

In Spain, Peter Bryant and Elena Ortiz Teran have looked into whether entrepreneurs' brains are wired differently and their research suggests that they are. In their *Harvard Business Rreview* article of December 2013[12] they postulate that founder entrepreneurs must be:

- Alert.
- Tolerant of ambiguity.
- Able to respond quickly when opportunity knocks.

Combining studies in the lab with interviews in real life situations their evidence supports the view that:

- Founders think differently in decision making especially about problems and opportunities.
- Founders embrace ambiguous problems more quickly, using simple rules to move forward, then dedicate more effort to resolve ambiguity and uncertainty during later stages of decision making.

They do discuss that these factors will probably be multifactorial in their explanation, involving genetic factors, early development and learning as well as adult experience of problem solving and decision making. And this approach begins to arise as a theme of applying neuroscience to leadership – work with what you have and create the conditions for success in your environment:

- Physically
- Mentally
- Emotionally
- Spiritually or values-driven.

Summary

We believe that applied neuroscience is the zeitgeist for leadership. When that happens, common parlance adapts remarkably:

- Think of people wondering whether it would "throw a spanner into the works" when discussing risk post industrialism.
- People talking about "docking and re-synching" as a way of checking in on trans global relationships post merger.
- How will our brains incorporate the language of neuroscience into business over the coming months and years? Will millennials want to work for serotonin start-ups?

As we have discussed as a theme in this book, the brain is not hardwired in adulthood so we should not be surprised that entrepreneurs' brains are at one end of a spectrum; and we should not take this to mean that we cannot think differently should we have the inclination. What can leaders do with all the information in this chapter?

- Recognize the biology and regulate it – at individual, company and policy level.
- Focus attention on the pros and cons of testosterone-fuelled behavior.

- Choose a physical training regimen to improve mental resilience.
- Train and incentivize your people in a way that discourages short-termism and encourages meaningful benefits to themselves, their team, the company, the customer and society.

Actions and reflections

People are starting to use neurochemical language to describe themselves and interactions that can be both fun and enlightening. Play around with:

- "Lots of oxytocin flowing between those two".
- Look out for high testosterone behaviors such as strutting around with a puffed up chest.
- Spot cortisol when someone has started to develop a bit of a pot belly and sits slumped at their desk.
- Notice your own serotonin levels and triggers for change by tracking your mood with an app or diary. You may never experience a full blown mental illness like depression – although more than one out of 20 Americans 12 years of age and older reported current depression in 2005–6[13] – but anyone can feel low, endure some kind of personal crisis or simply have too much to do and not enough serotonin to keep doing it with a smile on their face.

Use the Neural Tethering Model© on your own or as a leader with your team to start a conversation about risk profiles and encourage diversity of thought around how to keep the team healthy, aware, focused and continually developing even in the face of ambiguity and change.

5

Why is the Soft Stuff so Hard?

"No man is an island entire of itself; every man is a piece of the continent, a part of the main."

John Donne

In the past decade or so it has often been said that for leaders, it is the soft stuff that is the real hard stuff – a quote that has even been attributed to Jack Welch. While it is generally agreed that the hard stuff is what can be measured, definitions of the soft stuff are legion, from brand design through emotional intelligence, to talent development, engagement, innovation and "people issues". Sometimes the distinction is made as if between IQ (Intelligence Quotient) and EQ (a measure of Emotional Intelligence[1]). Most people agree however that the soft stuff, whatever it is, isn't measurable and that for sustainable business success, leaders need both.

Ask most CEOs what they find hardest and the answer is usually people related. Douglas R Conant, formerly CEO of Campbell Soups, writing in *Strategy and Business*[2] defined the soft stuff as: problems of intention, understanding, communication and interpersonal effectiveness. So this chapter deals mainly with the soft stuff of the human relationships that leaders need to deal with.

We know that the brain is exquisitely tuned to social
relationships, shaped by and shaping our relationships
with others from birth onwards. So why should
relationship issues be so hard and what can the
neurosciences tell us that might help?

Our perception of the world is a fantasy that

Our perception of the world is a fantasy that
happens to coincide with reality.[3]

Perhaps the most fundamental reason is the extent to which each individual's brain creates their own version of reality, of the world around
them. Beginning with our time in the womb, genes, their expression and
experience interact, so that even in identical twins, brain connections are
forged differently. This accelerates after birth, as our experience of the
world through our senses increases in volume and complexity.

Our brain is programmed so as to assign meaning to our perceptions,
through the emotions (see Chapter 1). I may not be able to have conscious
access to some of the experiences that have shaped my meanings, and
therefore might not be able to explain why, to me, a desk means conformity as well as a piece of furniture on which I do my work (see Box 5.1).

**BOX 5.1   YOUR BRAIN CREATES
THE WORLD**

The brain creates complex layers of meaning from the combined sensory inputs and relevant existing cognitive patterns,
which will be different to anyone else's, although with more
or less overlap. I might try and fully explain how I see even an
object like a desk, but your frames of relevance will be different
and therefore you may assign different layers of meaning to the
words I use.

Abstract concepts, such as justice, and values, such as good or bad, can
be even more difficult to convey. I may think I know what you mean by
integrity, by exceptional customer service, by loyalty, but I will have given

these my own, unique combination of meanings. And once you combine concepts with complex environments, different cultures, different business processes as well as relationships it is not surprising that what is obviously "a perfect plan to solve the slide in sales" to me is a sad mess to you, or what you agreed with your customer was different to what your customer thought he had agreed with you.

In the absence of full sensory inputs our brain will attempt to fill in what is missing, using past experience to anticipate what might be happening. In the absence of the ability to fully understand what you intend, my brain will make the equivalent of guesses. The analogy is with our eyes' ability to interpret a rapid series of still photographs as a movie, or to see pixels as a whole picture. We stitch reality together from the bits we perceive and process.

This attempt to create a whole story when we have only parts is a natural, innate tendency of our brain without which it might be difficult to survive in an uncertain and rapidly changing environment. However in a complex corporate environment, it can lead, for example, to a multiplicity of interpretations of the same strategic planning document. In some exceptional circumstances our brain's intuitive interpolations might turn out to have catastrophic results. And all of this, even assuming a common language from birth, a common cultural environment and common system of education.

Do you understand what I mean?

On the one hand our brain creates its own version of reality, making perfect communication impossible. On the other the brain evolved to meet needs that arise from living in large groups and complex societies. Although other animals communicate with sounds, movements and vocalizations, human languages are uniquely powerful tools, not just for communication but for self-reflection too. Putting a feeling into words (naming it too) enables a human to examine it and even, in some cases to regulate it, to manage its intensity. Language also enables humans to transmit complex concepts and skills from one generation to the next, underpinning the development of cultures.

When our brain is attempting to fill in the meaning of another person's intent, from their words and/or actions, we are using an ability to interpret another person's mind, known as "theory of mind" or ToM (also known as the ability to mentalize – see Box 5.2).[4] This is a highly complex function without which operating effectively in a complex society would not be possible.

BOX 5.2 THEORY OF MIND

Having a Theory of Mind (ToM) means that we can distinguish between our self and others, understand that other people's behaviors are driven by their goals and beliefs, not ours, and that our knowledge and perspective is different to everyone else's. According to Chris and Uta Frith, children will develop the full capacity for ToM by about the age of five, but begin to be able to distinguish between what they know and what another person knows earlier. For a clear and accessible explanation see further their 2005 article "Theory of mind", *Current Biology*, 15(17): 644–5.

Neuroscientists have begun to look at how this amazingly useful ability works. Some maintain that our ability to interpret another person's intent involves a specific part of the brain containing "mirror neurons". These fire in similar patterns as if to create the same movements, expressions and reactions that we are observing in another person. One theory has it that mirror neurons evolved "as a prelanguage way" of learning and sharing innovations.[5] Others claim that types of brain cell known as spindle cells or VEN (von Economo neurons) are key to interpreting others' intent from their behavior. Helen Gallagher and Chris Frith[6] have mapped a number of brain areas that are especially active when we are interpreting other people's intent. Some of these areas are also very active when people engage in cooperative activities, involving choices about shared benefits,[7] and are also engaged when someone is listening to stories or watching cartoons involving people. We can mentalize about scenarios, real or imagined, in the present, past or future.[8] Our mentalizing capabilities appear closely connected to our ability to monitor social situations, and our own position in them, involving areas (such as the amygdala) which are engaged in processing emotions (ours and others). Not surprising if we consider that intent is shaped by emotion – think of likely actions shaped by fear and disgust, or desire, for example. ToM is most likely to involve a significant number of (the most evolved) parts of our brains, in complex interactions which have not yet been fully mapped or understood.

ToM and empathy

Empathy is not just the ability to understand that others have emotions and feelings and to feel some concern or distress about them as a result, but the ability to feel as they do, (or nearly as they do) to "take a step in their shoes". Empathy is one precursor to behavior that is beneficial to others – known as prosocial behavior.

As a senior manager, with many years' experience of leading teams in a number of different organizations and good listening skills, I can imagine how you might react if I talk to you about a proposed redundancy, even if I have limited knowledge about you and have never spoken to you on this subject before. My experience and everyday practice in using ToM mean that I am quite likely to be right. If I am empathetic and can feel your pain at your loss, I may express myself in ways which show respect, maintain your dignity and make what I say easier for you to hear and deal with. I may think of more options of help the organization can offer. But my brain's tendency to make guesses and take energy saving short cuts, together with the sheer variety and individuality of people mean that I might also be very wrong – and I need to remember that.

Communication: the fundamental tool of leadership

The importance given to communication for leadership can be summarized in a recent quote from a *Forbes* online contributor, Mike Myatt: "It is simply impossible to become a great leader without being a great communicator".

Humans communicate with their whole body, with intentional as well as non-intentional movements, with stance and stillness, with both what is and is not actioned. For example, if your boss makes eye contact with a pleasant expression when you see her in the corridor you are quite likely to interpret that as meaning that she is, if not friendly, at least not inimical. The absence of a smile, or eye contact, can be interpreted as a potential cause for apprehension. And those reactions can happen without our brain being consciously aware of what is happening and why we are feeling as we are. At levels below our conscious awareness our brain is using its automatic ability to assign intent to a whole range of signals from other people to which our conscious brain, with its limited processing capacity, does not always pay attention.[9] For Matthew Liebermann, the widespread brain networks that underpin theory of mind have considerable overlap with what he calls "the default network", which underpins brain activity when we are not consciously focusing on something. In other words our brain spends significant time and resources on socially meaningful activity. As Gallese[10] says, "most of the time, our understanding of social situations is immediate, automatic and almost reflex-like."

So without a conscious attempt to interpret, I assume your purpose in your movements, without you saying a word. As you walk down the corridor, without looking at me, I immediately assume you are showing that you do not value me. This assumption can have a range of impacts, depending on my own state, my previous assumptions about this relationship, how confident I feel: I may challenge my feeling by reflecting on how much more likely it is that my boss is very busy and too absorbed in her own concerns to notice me. On the other hand, my sense of self-efficacy might be undermined and my motivation plummets.

Why does all this ToM and empathy and communication stuff matter?

Integrity

First of all, if we communicate through our whole bodies, then having integrity and being true to what we believe as a leader is more than just an ethical desideratum. Our actions and our behaviors need to be consistent with what we say, otherwise we might not be trusted or believed. If what we say and do conflicts with our emotions, values and beliefs, then that conflict could be communicated through physical movements, such as fleeting expressions, or tensions, such as hunched shoulders, undermining our credibility as leaders. On the other hand a passionately held conviction, expressed with the force of our own belief, will ring true.

Embodied communication

Secondly, how we behave or move, the way we say things, our expressions, can be more influential than our words. An experiment with giving feedback using contradictory facial expressions, so that positive feedback and praise was given "with frowns and narrowed eyes" and critical feedback was given with smiles and nods, shows that those who received the former felt worse than the latter.[11] Faking a warm smile tends not to work,[12] but leaders can use self-reflection and practice to choose words that better match both what they believe and what they want to achieve and thus have an approach that is more aligned with their own emotional reactions and lead to a more productive conversation (see also Chapter 2).

Emotional impact

Thirdly, emotions are contagious,[13] and our behaviors are shaped by the people with whom we interact. Again this is likely to occur without our being consciously aware of what is influencing us and why. Some have called this "resonance". Leaders are carefully observed and their emotional impact is likely to be greater,[14] as they will be influential both through conscious and non conscious processes. This is one of the reasons why leaders need to be self-aware and to hone their skills in managing their emotions.

Empathy

Fourthly communication is a two way process. If I as a leader cannot easily "read" or empathize with others, and attune my own style to suit their current circumstances and emotions, I am likely to create undesirable consequences. For example, if I am full of the success of a new multi-million, multi-year deal with a major client, but the organization is in the process of a restructuring as a result and people are losing their jobs or likeable colleagues, how I outline my vision of a future after success will be critical to maintaining motivation for the next deal and the one after that. As Boyatzis says, leaders who have been promoted for their expertise, drive and focus on results often fail to make the top jobs because they lack emotional or social intelligence, the ability to understand, empathize and attune to what their clients, staff and stakeholders really feel and think.

The speed of intuition

Finally, think about presenting a new strategic plan to a large organizational community. It might take some people several minutes to understand even the basic thrust of the words of the plan. However their brain "gets" the fundamental message in what the whole person communicates in fractions of seconds – for example, "I am confident and excited about the future" or "this is a risk I am worried about".

Influencing attitudes

The combination of language and embodied communication is a very complex and rich source of information, most of which is processed below our levels of consciousness. This enables large numbers of brain regions to work together rapidly to give meaning to these inputs. The advantages of this kind of processing are speed and the number of parameters that the brain can deal with. What can you do as a leader to use this insight to achieve your goals?

Recognize that in order to influence attitudes you need to engage the emotions and feelings of your listeners and that means engaging your own too. Engaging strong emotions also increases the chances of your message being remembered. Again being able to use appropriate and relevant language, imagery and embodied communication are key factors. What might work when you are trying to inspire your whole workforce might not work with your accountant or a financial analyst. However even conveying quarterly results to analysts or financial journalists requires more than just conveying numbers and facts. It is critical to be trusted and believed. This is where the importance of relevance, integrity, congruence and your own emotional states become very important. In order to influence attitudes, be prepared to reveal your own emotions and to use emotional language.

The power of relationship

Leadership communication, in order to be effective, needs to build a relationship between people. I am more likely to be influenced by someone with whom I have a relationship of trust, and with whom I share some beliefs. A trusted leader who communicates with integrity can develop relationships of trust with people all over their organization, even with those whom she has never met. Those relationships can, in turn, become the basis for changing beliefs, attitudes and behaviors.

Storytelling: why stories work

We've gone some way towards explaining why being able to tell a good story is so important for leaders. Good stories are influential. Great ones inspire cultures and beliefs. Inspirational leaders are often called great storytellers – remember the elements of a good leadership story in Chapter 3.

Stories are easily memorable, as they follow the pattern used by the brain to lay down episodic memories, with a timeline – beginning, middle and end – and agents with whom we can identify. If a (false) story is consistent with what our brain expects, coherent and plausible, it can be more persuasive than the truth. Our brains are constantly using past patterns to predict the future. When the future doesn't fit with what we expect (one step fewer than we expected in a staircase, for example), we experience dissonance or discomfort. A story that "fits" with our expected patterns keeps us in our comfort zone. Equally, our brains are always searching for meaning, for a cause to an observed effect, for a purpose for an action. A story that gives us plausible reasons and causes tends to be believed (think of conspiracy theories versus coincidence, for example).

A story is a whole, and one part might trigger others, thus making it more memorable and easily re-tellable. Some call the capacity to be easily retold part of "conversational capital". Some stories appear to be fundamental or archetypal, like myths, and in the telling and multiple retelling help shape the values and cultures of a community or organization, for example, the great start-up story, where the founders of the organization were young, experienced great hardship and were misunderstood, but worked all hours, were creative geniuses, stayed true to themselves and the great benefits their product – simpler, better designed, more usable – brought to the world, and made the company into a global success.

There is evidence that in reading or listening to stories, our brains mirror some of the activities of the agents in the story, for example, smell words cause our olfactory system to fire, actions our mirror neurons, emotions our emotional networks (see note 16).

A story that makes sense of a chaotic, complex environment enables staff to perform better because it lessens the brain's fear of uncertainty and the discomfort caused by ambiguity. It creates a good feeling, due to the ease with which the brain accepts what the story is saying.

A good story can be the stimulus for motivation, wanting to belong to the group about which the story is being told. Daniel Kahneman says that "caring for people often takes the form of concern for the quality of their stories, not for their feelings".[15]

There is also some evidence that reading a lot of fiction improves our ability to empathize with others, and improves our social awareness,[16] implying that the mirroring leads to empathizing with the actors in stories, as we do with the real people in our lives. If a leader tells a great, plausible, story about themselves, with emotion, which reveals values that are common to the majority of listeners, they can resonate with the "hero" and it creates a kind of relationship.

The brain is selective and takes many short cuts

The reality our brain creates for us is not only the result of each one of us filling in the gaps in perception differently. The gaps in perception are not just a function of the physical limitations of our senses or the processing of their signals, but also of the way that what we perceive is driven by our attention. Our brains are highly selective in what they choose to notice and pay attention to. The assignment of meaning happens initially subconsciously, and if my brain decides that an input is not significant enough – to me – it will not process it to the point where I might become conscious of it. So I literally might not see, or hear, a message you are trying to convey, unless it is placed in a context which has significance for me (sometimes known as selective inattention – but this is not a conscious process).[17] Or the brain may be fleetingly aware of it, but not store it in long-term memory. Unless the stories created by leaders have relevance for their people, they will not be remembered or even heard.

The brain has a range of strategies (heuristics or biases – see Chapter 6) below the level of consciousness, to work more efficiently and minimize energy use. These are used because they worked well in the past. Some of them are individual, learned through experience. Others are biases that appear to be hard wired. Scientists have identified over 150. These can affect the way we understand others, communications and relationships.

Our brains are biased towards processing inputs that reinforce existing beliefs and ignoring those that don't. This is known as *confirmation bias*, and it crops up in all sorts of contexts. A story that confirms people's existing beliefs – "we are the best at understanding our customers' needs" – is more believable than one that challenges this. Equally, stories that chime with other biases, such as recency or proximity, are more likely to influence decisions. For example, on my way into work I read an article in a trade magazine about rising customer confidence, so I am more bullish about my quarterly result projections, rather than basing them on an investigation of the data, which would tell me that this was a statistical exception.

The availability heuristic, the tendency of the brain to go to what is immediately, easily, available, either because of its recency or because it is a personal meaningful experience, may skew the results of a whole team. If we are in secure, predictable and trusting environments, as well as with enough time, then we can more easily engage that part of our brain that has the capacity to reflect, focus on and critically analyze a situation. In a project team meeting we can question and accept the challenges of others. We can take time to seek relevant data outside the team and apply not only our own knowledge but that which we obtain from others. Under time pressure, in uncertain, changing, distrustful environments we might rely too heavily on our brain's ability to fill in the gaps, which may have worked well in circumstances where we have both extensive experience and expertise, but might be letting us down in tasks which involve new and complex issues. We might hesitate to show uncertainty, or even that we do not have all the answers. Challenges become threats to be rebuffed, not an excuse to innovate and improve. We stop looking outside our own, team-created, reality for what might help us create a better product, or calibrate it against what customers might find easier to use, or get it to market more quickly and efficiently.

Leaders need people who can work well together: cooperation, collaboration and altruism

In a powerful article, "Rebuilding companies as communities",[18] Henry Mintzberg makes the point that humans are social beings that cannot easily function without a social system that is larger than "us". We now know social relationships and feeling part of society to be important to both mental and physical health. Isolation in old age is correlated with stress and a compromised immune system. There is evidence that taking an active part in a network of friends and neighbors, or in groups with a common interest or activity is protective against Alzheimer's. Exclusion from a group or community can be literally life threatening.

Behaving in ways that promote benefits for the group, not just the individual, are essential for inclusion. People who cheat, who take much but give little find themselves punished and/or excluded.[19] Again the evolutionary benefits of behavior that promotes belonging are easy to understand. A leader who demonstrates fairness, who creates and maintains processes that discriminate fairly between good and bad performance, between those who work cooperatively and those who work only to promote themselves, who has processes to enable individuals to articulate their own goals as subsets of the corporate ones, creates a platform for people to work together towards the good of the whole.

Being employed in a small start-up, or in a rapidly growing small company, can feel like being part of a family, with everyone related and engaged in ensuring the success of the group. In large organizations that sense of relatedness and common purpose is harder to achieve. We have spoken before about trust and fairness and how important both are for successful leadership. A leader who creates an environment of trust and clarity of purpose, who emphasizes the extent to which people are similar rather than different, for example through the creation of a strong brand with which staff can identify, makes it easier for large numbers of people to work together towards a common goal. One who delegates appropriately, who reinforces the status of those whose efforts are for the good of the company or group will create an environment which does not feel threatening and in which cooperation, creativity and innovation can flourish.

Cooperation and collaboration benefit groups, communities and societies of which one is a part, with the implication that one will have some share of the benefit. Altruism is benefitting another person or group without expecting something in return, and indeed sometimes to the detriment of one's own situation. There is a lot of controversy around this concept and some doubt whether it truly exists (*The Selfish Gene* shaped much modern thinking about altruism serving the need to preserve one's genetic inheritance). Yet altruism is beneficial: like social connectedness, doing good for others has been shown to be good for both mental and physical health. Even just thinking positively of others, as in compassionate meditation, can lift mood and reduce stress. Altruism gives meaning to our lives and enables us to think well of ourselves. It is a "feel-good" activity, with the brain's reward networks signaling pleasure.

Motivation

One of the biggest soft stuff questions we have all been asked at different points in our careers is "How do you motivate people?" Leading those who are motivated to pursue the same goals as you is easy. The unmotivated but bright and able employee, who does the least they can get away with, the one who is the equivalent of the sulky, passive-aggressive 14-year-old at the back of the class who doesn't really want to be at school, is one of the challenges faced by leaders and HR teams. Perhaps the greater challenge is leading the highly intelligent, highly qualified, highly motivated individual who profoundly disagrees with the direction you are taking and has enough authority to take others with them. This situation is very familiar in academic, public and charitable organizations.

Although there are many theories about motivation, it is not yet fully mapped. We know we keep referring to the role of emotions. They are so fundamental, as the response states which enable the brain to assign meaning, (based on experience or instinct) to sensory inputs: whether something is to be approached or avoided. This occurs almost entirely outside our conscious awareness, and very quickly – within 80 milliseconds. Emotions thus are motivational directors, they serve to mobilize the body's (which includes the brain) resources, their energy, in one direction or another.[20]

We know that avoidance emotions are both more numerous and most often stronger than approach ones. We also know that of the avoidance emotions, fear serves to focus the brain sharply and effectively on the threat causing the fear, restricting its ability to deal with anything else. Another factor is the strength of the "loss aversion" bias. Our brain feels a loss much more than a gain. That is why a work environment built on fear, on threats of losing your ranking, reputation, even your job, can be so counterproductive: it is one in which creativity, innovation and cooperative problem solving are restricted. Leaders who can engage the attachment emotions have a better chance of motivating people, not only towards improving individual performance and creativity but towards contributing to the community (see also Chapters 1 and 2).

There is evidence that people are strongly influenced by their values, for example, wanting to make a contribution to society is a strong motivational factor.[21] Explicitly identifying the goals you set with the widest benefits to customers, clients and society helps give meaning to the work you are asking people to do. Certain values, such as fairness and altruism seem to have evolutionary benefits to the extent that some would call them hard-wired. Working towards the greater good, towards helping others, can be not only motivational, but also capable of reducing stress and increasing our resilience and sense of wellbeing. Being explicit about values, yours and those of your organization, enables you to create processes that reward desired behaviors.

There is some evidence to indicate that people who set goals for themselves, whose focus is forward or future looking rather than on what has been achieved so far, are more successful. Helping people set their own objectives within overall organizational goals can increase motivation by increasing the possibility of success. Showing respect, genuinely listening, taking account of others' views and publicly acknowledging their contribution can also motivate engagement and cooperation. Rewarding those who collaborate well by increasing status and/or autonomy can be more motivational than financial rewards. Finally, where idealistic differences are causing problems, finding some higher level common ground – we are all in this to help society – that is hard to disagree with might create enough motivation for a compromise route to achieve organizational goals.

From the work of Mihaly Csikszentmihalyi on *Flow*,[22] and the earlier writing of Albert Bandura on self-efficacy, we know that work done well, that stretches us enough, but not too much, from which we get immediate feedback, which takes us beyond ourselves, can give the brain pleasure. It can also help us develop a sense of confidence and our own social worth.

As a leader, to encourage and maintain motivation means putting people in the right place, so that the level of work they are asked to do is socially relevant, meaningful, challenging but not impossible, in an atmosphere of positive encouragement, with clearly articulated goals. It means timely and appropriate feedback, good delegation of autonomy and responsibility, and fair and transparent reward structures.

Summary

Understanding the ways in which we communicate and how we impact on and interpret other people, can help leaders work towards behaviors that support better relationships, at work and at home. Motivation ultimately depends on the emotions. As leaders, being aware of our impact on the emotions of those we work with is essential. Focusing our behaviors, communications, structures and processes on eliciting emotions on the attachment end of the spectrum is the key to our success.

Actions and reflections

- Keys to effective communication for a leader are conveying meaning which is retained and influencing sustainable action. Remembering that every listener will have their own context for what you say and remembering the limited capacity of working memory, what can you do to make your content easier to understand?
- Take the time to try to understand what knowledge, assumptions and biases your audience is most likely to share. Imagine yourself in the audience. What are you expecting to see and hear? What do you want from that?
- Live your values and demonstrate your integrity clearly. Show that you value others by understanding their different contexts, meanings and motivations.
- Remember the emotional power of story and drama, of building antici-pation, expectation, of the unexpected, creating surprise – an emotion that enables changing states. Think of Steve Jobs introducing the iPad.
- Give people the benefit of the doubt. Do not assume that, because you have explained something as clearly as you possibly can, they misunder-stand willfully – their brain has just interpreted what you said or wrote, or both, in terms of its own, unimaginably rich, context of meanings.
- Follow through. Powerful and effective communication is not enough without the underlying systems and processes that support fairness, trust and finding meaning in work.

6 chapter
The Challenge of Decisions

"We stand at the crossroads, each minute, each hour, each day, making choices."

Benjamin Franklin

How much of your day is taken up by making decisions? If you include seeking and selecting the information you need, negotiating with others to ensure implementation, and all the decisions you make to monitor outcomes, you might say that is how most of your time is spent. And that is not even taking into account deciding *not* to have a snack between meetings, deciding *not* to take that call from a very well-networked ex-colleague, or not to stop off for a drink on the way home – again.

According to Goldberg's book, *The New Executive Brain*,[1] there are two kinds of decisions, veridical, based on fact, finding a/the truth (what sockets should we use in China) and adaptive, what is right for this purpose at this time (you are also choosing the questions to which the decision is the answer). Goldberg maintains that:

- Most leadership decisions are priority or preference based, made in ambiguous environments, and thus adaptive in nature.
- Mental processes for veridical and adaptive decisions are different.
- In adaptive decision experiments, men tend to be more context dependent and women more context independent.
- These strategies work best in different scenarios.

Decision fatigue and will power

You may have noticed that the last section contained decisions about resisting impulses or desires. In an experiment quoted by Baumeister and Tierney, in their book on *Willpower*, people spent at least a fifth of their waking hours resisting the desire to eat, to sleep, to take breaks. Decisions and will power are linked in that they both use the same sources of energy. Making decisions, using will power to resist something or to persist in something difficult have been demonstrated to be energy intensive for the brain, itself the most energy intensive part of the body.[2]

The decision itself, not the preliminaries of deciding, appears to be the most tiring part of the process and the importance of the outcome to affect the amount of energy expended. Making a few choices from an online retailer might be a pleasure for a fashionista, but having to make very many choices is still significantly more tiring than just browsing. Some salespeople know this, and will exhaust you with minor option choices on a car, before asking you to make the more expensive decisions, by which time you are less able to exercise considered judgment. Prioritizing what is important is therefore crucial.

Decision and will power fatigue explains why it is so easy to:

- Go "off message".
- Make mistakes.
- Succumb to temptation.
- Avoid difficult issues after a hard day as a leader (see Box 6.1).

BOX 6.1 DECISIONS ARE HARD WORK

- Deciding, like will power, depletes the brain's resources.
- People have less stamina in difficult tasks after taking a lot of decisions.
- The brain needs glucose to create the neurotransmitters that convey messages between neurons.
- A cup of tea with sugar or a biscuit can help, but low GI carbohydrates, like oats, might be better for your health.

Observations of the work of judges showed that they tended towards default options (e.g. refusing parole) after long hours on the bench, but were more willing to take a more difficult, positive, decision (allowing parole) earlier in the day, or after a mid morning snack and immediately after lunch.[3]

Emotions, intuition and rationality

Making decisions is a complex set of processes which uses a large number of parts of our brain, and depends as much on our emotional systems,[4] as on the workings of our pre-frontal cortex (PFC, that part of the brain significantly involved in strategic thinking and planning). These processes are not yet fully understood, but through a combination of imaging technologies such as EEG, psychological experiments and observations where illness or brain damage causes distinctive behavior, we are beginning to understand just how challenging decision making can be for human beings.[5]

As you know by this stage in this book, emotions are the brain's way of assigning meaning to inputs and directing energy flow. Fundamentally they signal whether:

- We need to pay attention.
- Something is good or bad for us.

- Something is to be approached.
- Something is to be avoided.

Antonio Damasio showed, in *Descartes' Error* (1994), that without access to emotions, people could not take "rational" decisions about personal, work and social issues, especially anything involving risk or conflict, even though they could solve logical problems perfectly well. Without emotions, people would take decisions that were against their own interests, would not be able to run their business, would not even be able to choose what clothes to wear in the morning. Equally, extremely strong emotions, such as fear or desire, may affect decision making adversely, by narrowing the brain's focus to the point where options are unrealistically restricted.

It is therefore important for leaders to be self-aware, sensitive to their own and others' emotional states and able to manage themselves within tolerances that avoid extremes.

Follow your gut?

Emotions may emerge in our conscious mind as an intuition, or a preference or repugnance we cannot immediately explain. Our non-conscious processes do an enormous amount of work, before a thought or feeling breaks into the spotlight of consciousness. We have frequently heard that we must follow our instincts, intuitions or "gut feelings" (see Chapter 2 for the differences between them). In many cases our intuitions and feelings will be better guides than trying to work out what we need to do step by rational step, with plenty of numerical analysis. This is especially the case where there are very large numbers of parameters, and where we have a lot of experience, practice and hence expertise. Our conscious thinking processes, which use working memory as a holding tank, can only manipulate seven items of information (plus or minus two) at one time. Although this number can be significantly expanded by "chunking" information (the brain's ability to use grouping together to enable working memory to hold more elements, for example, chunking numbers by grouping them in threes and fours as we often do to remember telephone numbers), it is still minute compared to the amount of information that we process below the level of consciousness: just think of how we navigate our car through a well-known route, for example.

Of course the quality of our decision making, itself based on varying amounts of experience that has been tested and assimilated, will be crucial to the effectiveness of those decisions.

Learning how to access some of what is happening in our non-conscious minds can be useful. For my colleague Marc, many years ago, it took a walk in the woods. He let his mind dwell on the beauty of his surroundings, instead of focusing on his career, and the answer to what he wanted to do, a creative new idea, popped into his head. He had, of course, done a lot of conscious thinking and planning work up till that walk.

Expertise increases our chances of getting it right through intuition, when there is some measure of continuity and predictability or a rule base in the environment in which we are operating. There are however a depressing number of areas which are too uncertain to allow for the acquisition of skills and expertise. I can trust my intuition if I am choosing a sofa for my living room, or even a house I want to live in, or discerning a pattern in a chess game, recognizing a friendly look or an abstracted one, or a signal in a radar trace that might be an enemy plane, but my predictions of which shares will go up or down are as accurate as luck might make them, and my ability to predict political scenarios is close to random. There are always exceptions, but analysis of the predictions of expert investors and political pundits have shown that their predictions are accurate less than 50 per cent of the time.

Checks and balances

Harnessing our conscious thinking processes to challenge and revise our intuitive judgments can help us make better decisions. For example, I have a strong feeling that one interviewee out of the five we've seen is the best. I believe that, whenever I have made hiring mistakes in the past, they have been because I was persuaded to ignore my intuitions. My decision is likely to be better however if I have had the discipline of filling in a form against pre-set objective criteria, so I am not only using my intuition, but my rational judgments are fresh in my mind as well. I challenge my belief and feelings by asking whether I prefer this candidate because she reminds me of an old colleague, or because she looks like "one of us". I might ask a colleague from another department, who is less involved in the detail, to sit in the interviews. Equally an assessment form might include the question: "How do you feel about the possibility of working closely with this person?"

Learning from past mistakes

Examining past decisions objectively is almost impossible. Hindsight cannot be eliminated. Your brain cannot fully "unknow" what it now knows, (short of damage, hypnosis, amnesia or forgetfulness due to conditions such as dementia) including the results of your past decisions, so any evaluation of the past will be tainted with knowledge you did not have at the time. What you can do, as a leader, is not waste time unpicking bad decisions retrospectively, but firstly, elicit the knowledge gained from that experience in a way that can be used by others, and then examine the processes you used at the time to come to decisions and see whether they can be improved in any way. Questions to ask of yourself or the team might be:

- What more could we have done to improve the conditions for our decision?
- Could we have uncovered and considered more or better data/ information?
- What would have enabled us to do so?

In one example, a team found that one of their occasional members had some crucial information, which was not shared until there was already a lot of commitment generated for the chosen path. That person, not having attended all the meetings, hadn't felt comfortable about sharing uncomfortable facts.

Decisions about stopping a project which has acquired momentum and has significant sunk investment are notoriously hard – and are often criticized subsequently. Emotional investment and commitment[6] can be such that inner warning signals, external comparators and advice are ignored.

Rather than ask: "Why did we decide to go on for that extra year?"

You can ask: "How did we decide, what processes can we put in place at our project reviews to give us a better chance of better decisions next time and who else should we involve?"

Not deciding is bad for you

Memory discriminates between finished and unfinished tasks, and unfinished tasks and unmet goals keep being brought back to our attention, thus taking up very valuable conscious brain energy. This is known in psychology as the Zeigarnik effect (Box 6.2). So over-long to-do lists and deferred decisions keep repeating like badly digested garlic.

BOX 6.2 THE ZEIGARNIK EFFECT

The Zeigarnik effect is the tendency to remember unfinished tasks more than finished ones. Named after the psychologist who first thought about it, when once in a restaurant he noticed that his waiter remembered the orders and seating positions of a large table, up until the time when he had finished serving. Sometimes thoughts about unfinished tasks can be repetitive and/or experienced as intrusive and unwelcome.

There are many reasons for delaying a task or decision, it might be:

• Emotionally laden (involving guilt or someone whom we fear).
• Require input from many other people.

- Ill-defined.
- Challenging to a core belief (if I fail this I am a bad manager).
- Simply because deciding what to do about it requires information we do not yet have.

A series of experiments suggested that the non-conscious mind was not nagging the conscious mind to "get on with it and finish the tasks" but, more subtly, to take a firm decision as to what to do about each of them. Some could be finished quickly, some delegated. Others needed a plan. And if the plan was specific enough, the non-conscious mind seemed quietened.[7]

Understanding decision making better helps leaders manage workloads by working with the grain of the brain:

- Prioritizing.
- Making timely decisions and specific plans.
- Focusing on clear, doable actions.
- Focusing on the future not the past.
- Balancing feelings and logic.
- Using techniques like timetabling, bring-forward files and delegation wisely.

Heuristics, biases and fallacies

So far in this book, focused attention has been a "hero". It is fundamental to changing the wiring of our brain, and amongst many other benefits, enables us to practice will power, to learn, and through its regular exercise, to strengthen our prefrontal cortex. We have mentioned a downside: focused attention is extremely energy intensive.

It is however in decision making that leaders can most easily find some of its more unfavorable side effects. Attention can be a double edged sword.

The brain has many ways of sparing resources. Rather than expend energy on conscious, focused attention – based thinking, it often uses a number of short cuts, familiar paths and networks which operate below the level of consciousness, intuitively and very quickly. These are known as heuristics and can lead to biases and fallacies.

Even when you, as a leader, are aware of this and consciously use your focused attention to solve a problem, a side effect of attention is that, because it is so energy intensive, it takes resources away from actions other than those involved in the focused activity, that the brain might have taken. Although this is a distinct benefit when we are trying, for example, to get rid of a habit such as smoking, it sometimes leads to ignoring information, data, people, – inputs into the decision making process that would have been useful in solving the problem in hand. This too can result in some biases and fallacies.

Heuristics

Heuristics are experience-based processes for solving problems, often relying on trial and error. The term has been used in psychology for unconscious, instinctive or learned processes which are quick and tend to work in most cases, but can lead to mistakes. Systematic errors are known as biases. Fallacies are mistakes in reasoning or belief, which may, in some cases, also be due to biases or heuristics. Being subject to cognitive bias doesn't imply a lack of intelligence. It simply reflects the way the brain works – we all have biases. We have selected some examples, which we believe will be both familiar and useful to you.[8]

Affect heuristic

Affect heuristic is a term psychologists use to describe how emotions shape our most fundamental view of the world and our attitudes. Our immediate emotional response to a stimulus, for example seeing a face, colors our perception of the person, without being examined or challenged. It is not surprising, as the role of emotions in our brain is to tell us what to approach and what to avoid. This served us well when our societies and choices were relatively simple, clustered around the basic needs of survival, reproduction and physical wellbeing. What is surprising is the extent to which humans still follow emotional direction without subjecting it to rational analysis and examination.[9] If someone reminds me of a favorite, wise, uncle, I am more likely to see them as a good candidate for a job, than if they remind me of a treacherous friend – but I will not be aware that this is why I feel warm towards one candidate and quite hostile to another. I will be able to rationalize my decision effectively, after I have in reality taken it, but without knowing its real basis. The affect heuristic most likely underlies other cognitive biases, such as the halo effect.

Halo effect

Experiments show that attractive individuals are perceived to have attributes, such as intelligence, capability, kindness, trustworthiness, that actually have nothing at all to do with looks. It is not just physical attractiveness that has a halo effect: for example, liking a colleague may make it easier for you to accept one of their ideas. Equally, having positive associations with just one aspect of an individual, for example, liking the name Ivan – or liking tennis in this case – may mean you might see more good in a job candidate named Ivan than in others.

Conversely having perceived an individual as careless because they were late for their first meeting, it becomes difficult to see them as committed and effective (sometimes this is known as the "horn effect"). First impressions tend to have a lasting influence. The halo effect is defined as being influenced by a single factor (looks, name, lateness) so that it colors many others. It is not only individuals that can attract a halo effect: products, companies, projects, places, can all be subject to it. The reasons behind the halo effect are not known, but it could be because the brain finds it easier to extend an emotion than to change it. We know that emotions are persistent. For example, they outlast episodic and semantic memories in some patients with Alzheimer's. An elderly Alzheimer's patient might not remember the person in front of them as her daughter Sandra, but she still feels a connection to this person and shows signs of pleasure when Sandra visits.

Being aware of the halo effect can matter hugely to a new leader who comes into an organization from outside. They need to be ready with a coherent, authentic, powerful image and story that work together to create the right first impressions – which are, at the same time, genuine and sustainable. We know leaders who think hard about this, from the perspective of the people they will be working with, and create a lasting legend. We also know others who are perhaps more anxious and focused on their own thoughts and forget something crucial like smiling at the receptionist, when they greet their first employee.

Availability heuristic

We have already described, in Chapter 5, some ways in which ease of avail-ability colors our judgment. This heuristic can cause all kinds of distortions in the way we assess probability: for example, a recent high profile bank-ruptcy will increase our estimation of the probability of business failure. A recent presentation by a team leader who was not on form, might increase our estimation of the chances of failure of a project his team is responsible for delivering. Instead of working out the probability of a project's success based on a number of factors, we substitute the easily available personal feeling of disappointment at one bad presentation.

Where events or actual instances are not available, for example in install-ing a new system based on new technology, the ease with which we can imagine what might go wrong, or right, will color our estimations of the time the project will take and any contingencies we might build into the budget. Very large and complex IT projects based on untried systems are notoriously difficult to plan for.

Availability of information can also color our evaluation of our own contributions on a team or in a partnership compared to that of others. "I always end up doing all the report writing", "You never do the washing up", are familiar types of criticisms based on the most available data, our own actions. Leaders who are unaware of this tendency might both over-estimate their own contribution but also pay too much attention to team members who constantly claim that others are not playing as significant a part as they are.

Ease of availability might also underlie what Kahneman called "WYSIATI – what you see is all there is". Our brain constantly creates and re-creates our subjective reality, in the form of a running narrative. Our brain fills with guesses gaps in the story due to ambiguity, uncertainty or lack of data. Just as we construct a whole image from the pixels on a computer screen, or see realistic movement in a Disney cartoon, our brain stitches together the inputs of all our senses. These guesses are themselves constructed from our experiences. However the story, constructed from what is available to our brain, cannot use information that is inaccessible at the time it is being constructed.

Jumping to conclusions on the basis of what is in front of us, however limited the information in amount and quality, can be advantageous, in giving significant meaning to external signals quickly in a complex and dangerous world. A leader who waits too long for all the information to be available would be severely hampered in today's fast changing economic environment. People therefore make confident decisions easily on inadequate, or one-sided, information, if what is there is consistent and coherent, and fits their beliefs.

Yet in order to make good decisions, we often also need a conscious effort to bring to mind other instances, go and find more relevant information, or simply to find ways of challenging that quick intuitive judgment. A classic example of this is first impressions. Another example is a decision made on the basis of successful past experience, when the context has changed. Ignoring the wider context can be one of the side effects of intensely focusing attention on the decision in hand. A leader who can create the habit of challenging themselves through self reflection – perhaps stopping to think about the wider context more generally – and/or makes time to consult others who are perhaps not so intensely involved may find their decisions improving.

Anchoring

Anchors are numbers which exert an undue influence on our calculations or estimates. They are numbers presented to us vividly and recently as part of the framing of a problem or decision. For example, anchors can be an initial value from which we start a calculation, and from which we make insufficient adjustments. Experiments have shown however that anchors can be numbers introduced in the setting up of a conversation, negotiation, charitable donation or experiment, that affect participants' estimates of amounts or value. Examples are the use of reserves in auctions, or advertised house prices. When two separate groups were given different estimates for the value of a property, their own calculations, whether they were prospective customers or expert house agents, were influenced by the initial numbers they were given. If I am asked, as the seventh question, to guess the number of Green voters in the last German elections, my answer may be unduly influenced to include a seven. Might anchors account, in part, for the unreliability of some market research, where potential customers, given a list of price options, are asked how much they'd be willing to pay for a product or service? Negotiators and salespeople are normally well aware, through experience if not theory, of the power of anchors.

Priming effect

Priming operates by making it easier and quicker for the brain to pay attention to something. If the word fish is introduced in the conversation, or a picture of a trawler, then your brain will recognize words and images relating to fish and fishing more easily and quickly.

Priming is said to work at two levels: a thought is primed, which although unavailable to conscious processing, can affect behavior. Priming might also work in both directions: actions influence thoughts as well as the other way round. For example, people asked to put a pencil in their mouths in such a way that their lips are stretched into a smile, tend to report feeling more amused when looking at cartoons. People asked to nod while they listen to a message tend to agree with it more than those asked to shake their heads from side to side (depending on culture).[10]

Framing

Different ways of presenting information have an effect on how it is perceived and used to make choices. Positive framing, "there is a 50 per cent chance of succeeding with this proposal", rather than negative, "there is a 50 percent chance of failure", may influence the decision to proceed. You are more likely to buy 90 per cent fat-free yoghurt if you are on a diet, than a yogurt which contains 10 per cent fat, even if the two are identical. Framing is sometimes used in surveys to elicit a more desirable response, in the knowledge that people tend to choose the middle of three options. Apparently there is also a distinct preference in shoppers for goods that are in the middle of shelves. This is also sometimes known as the context effect. Framing plans and proposals can be very important to their success and a leader's ability to understand and take into account their audience's own likely frames – that is, those against which they will be looking at the proposals, is more likely to be influential.

Confirmation bias

People have a tendency to seek and retain information that reinforces the beliefs, ideas and hypotheses they already have. Although the brain mechanisms for alerting us to danger, to the unusual, the unexpected, to change are efficient and rapid, given a choice we tend to select confirmatory data, rather than looking for what might upset the status quo of our beliefs. Even scientists, who are trained to be critical thinkers, are often subject to this bias without being aware of it. Confirmation bias may be in part due to the availability heuristic. Our focus is more likely to be on what we believe we know, and thus make confirmatory information by association, more easily available to our memory, for example. It may also be due in part to the brain's preferring a less resource intensive process, in that it is easier to reinforce existing connections than to forge new ones, that is, to change our minds. Awareness of confirmation bias might help us adjust the processes we use to evaluate ideas and projects so that we consciously use ways of looking at data and arguments that challenge what we want to achieve. Using a "Devil's Advocate" approach can help.

Narrative fallacy

We have seen the power of storytelling. One of its weaknesses is that stories, even when they are false, can be very persuasive. Stories enable us to make sense of our experience, and simplicity, specificity, clarity, coherence and consistency make them plausible. The brain creates our reality by weaving its interpretation of the meaning of sensory inputs into a coherent narrative and covering the gaps with best guesses. Storytelling therefore fits the way the brain works and is a most effective way of communicating. Too effective sometimes, as we are prone to believing a good story, because it is good and we can understand it easily.

Stories often collapse time, one sentence covering years. Missing the time element – duration neglect – can cause problems, because time does matter. The heroic success story, where two young men work in a garage and create a multi-billion dollar IT company underplays the years of hard work, the proportion of failed start-ups, persistence in the face of mistakes and failures, the late nights ending in despair or arguments, and the personal cost of a start-up that grows exponentially. The end of a story, especially one that ends dramatically with a happy ending, can unduly color our perception of what happened before. Looking at stories of the past so as to learn lessons for the future can have pitfalls, which leaders need to be aware of.

An example is when a story is told about a major project success or failure in the past. The less information the narrator has, the easier it is for them to create a compelling story, even if it misses out key facts, and is constructed from hindsight. Understanding the past and being able to explain how and why things happened is very difficult, but the language we use to tell our stories or even to recall the past tends to give us the feeling that our understanding is better than it is. "I knew that the project was doomed from the start" is an overconfident statement likely to be influenced by hindsight. Using stories of the past to base a decision about a future project should be balanced with other information.

Leaders must be persuasive storytellers, with the discipline to examine the stories they tell so as to avoid distortions that they themselves end up believing.

Leaders who make mistakes

No human being can make the right decision all the time. All the biases and fallacies that we have chosen are common ones. We have been guilty of all of them at some point in our careers. We hope that we have not been guilty of too many of them in one go! Leaders should be able to acknowledge their mistakes, take responsibility for them and their outcomes, learn from them and help others avoid them. Leaders who can admit mistakes might be better trusted than those who try to bend reality to avoid that. Adversarial political systems, such as those in the UK, make it especially difficult to admit error, leading to extreme risk aversion in the civil service (doing nothing is better than being the cause of your minister apologizing to parliament for something you caused to happen).

If as a leader you have great ambitions and a desire not only to enable your organization to succeed but to make some contribution to your society, then taking some risk is inevitable and enabling wider learning from your mistakes essential.

Summary

What then does your brain need in order to take a good decision?

It needs you to be at your peak capacity to deal with the most difficult decisions you face: not unduly stressed, hydrated and with enough energy resources. It needs a good balance between intuition and rationality, the ability to regulate emotional states and a good deal of focus and attention. Rigorous prioritization, planning and responsible delegation will help you to avoid constant worry about unfinished business. What can we do about heuristics, biases and fallacies? Very little without enormous effort over a very long period of time. A useful approach is to be aware of them, to understand when you and others might be most liable to them, and to use self-reflection and especially diverse and external inputs to increase the chances of mitigating them.

Actions and reflections

- Consider whether you are avoiding a decision because you are feeling fearful or embarrassed at the thought of possible consequences; and find a way of managing that, with help from a colleague, manager or coach, or getting help with the decision from someone who isn't as emotionally involved.
- Use reflection to engage your conscious thought processes. Use chunking techniques, for example, including many items under one simple heading, to enable your working memory to cope with complex issues.
- Exchanging views and ideas with others, especially people with significantly different experiences, helps overcome a tendency to consider only information readily available, or that which reinforces what we already believe. Being able to name emotions, feelings and intuitions helps us manage them in our thinking.
- Practice exercising your will power, so that you pursue decisions even when they are difficult, and avoid substitution of easier problems for more difficult ones. This is not only useful for your own decision making, but sets a good example.

- Deliberately seek to expand the range of options under consideration. Get external help for this: diversity matters. Use priming to expand your repertoire of ideas; deliberately list words which are opposite to the ones you might use for your options.
- Practice reflection on your instinctive reactions. Try to see your own patterns, so that you can begin to recognize situations which might trigger them.
- Practice reframing issues, broadening the frame by stepping back and expanding both the number of options and the context in which you are considering them. Look at your options from different perspectives. Frame them both positively and negatively. Consider not just the evidence you do have, but what is missing from it.
- Focus on one important issue at a time. If you feel pressurized by too much on your desk, delegate less important decisions, don't just delay them. Make very specific plans.
- Manage your own expectations, set goals that are a stretch, but doable, do not set impossible targets for a decision, which will demotivate you when you cannot meet them.
- Make the decision-making processes work for you and your team. Consider a pre-mortem, where you go through all the questions you would ask if a project failed, before you take the decision to start.
- If you feel tired, or demotivated, replenish your resources, have a drink of water and a piece of fruit or a biscuit, go for a short walk in the fresh air, take a power nap, meditate for five minutes, speak to someone you value, or whatever works for you.

chapter 7

Changing Yourself –
Changing Others

"Hardly any faculty is more important for the intellectual progress of man than ATTENTION. Animals clearly manifest this power, as when a cat watches by a hole and prepares to spring on its prey."

Charles Darwin, 1871, The Descent of Man

A great deal of the work of a leader involves change – in their own and others' performance, behaviors, skills and attitudes. As we have described already in Chapter 2 our brain is changing all the time: every new stimulus or thought creates some new connections, familiar stimuli and thinking reinforce existing connections and every mental and physical action is the result of activating new or existing networks of connections between neurons (Box 7.1).

BOX 7.1   NEURONAL CONNECTIONS

What we mean by connections are the physical exchanges of chemicals (neurotransmitters) and electrical charges between synapses at the ends of axons and dendrites. These are the cable and branch-like protrusions from the main body of the neurons that carry signals between them and are covered by a myelin sheath, which provides protection and insulation and has an effect on the speed and reach of the signal transmission. Frequent transmission of signal between neurons makes subsequent transmission easier.

However, in order for someone to change their physical or mental behaviors sustainably, that is, to create new habitual or default behaviors, their brain needs to create new AND robust connections between neurons. We also know that the adult brain remains plastic (i.e. changeable) throughout life and that its connections can be changed by learning and practice. Remember the example of London black cab drivers, who have a much larger mid posterior hippocampus than that of ordinary drivers.

Habitual behaviors

As adults, most of what we do on a daily basis, how we react to familiar stimuli and effect regular goals, is habitual and automatic.[1] Experience shapes patterns of behavior through which we normally achieve our daily goals, walking downstairs, eating breakfast, walking to the bus stop, answering the phone, typing on our computer: if it works reasonably efficiently, we will use it. We do not need to consciously plan how to walk. Unlike a toddler who has to work out how to get from the chair to their father's knee, walking is so automatic it just seems to happen when we need it to.[2]

Such habitual behavior is the result of many years of learning and practice. It is the result of neural networks being reinforced through repeated use to the point where their activation is the easiest option for achieving certain goals in certain contexts. A useful analogy is like the deepest of several connected channels running down a hill: water will find its way there by itself. Goals do not have to be conscious in order to trigger habitual behaviors: a friend who worked long hours for years found that, when she retired, just walking into her kitchen triggered a desire to eat, because for years, she had had a meal on coming into her kitchen straight from work – at whatever time.

New behaviors take time and conscious effort to learn. Learning can be described as the forging of new connections. Once forged and successfully repeated over a significant period of time, these connections become the deepest channel, the default path for signals in the brain, and it is now believed the neuronal pattern may physically be recreated in the brain, from primarily in the right hemisphere to primarily in the left. Changing such habitual behaviors can be very hard.

Think about your own deeply engrained habits (see the case study in Box 7.2). Not just those like smoking, eating or drinking, which are constantly in the news, but some of the small things you do every day or week. For example, how do you normally react to an interruption – with a smile or a frown? Think about how that affects someone who is trying to bring you important information. How do you usually start your management team meetings? Do you go straight to the points you want to make or do you encourage a range of inputs? Might you be unconsciously limiting your knowledge of the organization's performance? It can take months or years to create habitual mental and physical behaviors. Changing these involves the creation of new pathways, which with use over time become the easier, default routes for neuronal signals to travel, the deeper channels. The old connections if not used, are gradually pruned.

BOX 7.2 MARINA: A CASE STUDY

Marina, a very bright and able colleague, who managed the IT system at the heart of providing customer information and support for a large services organization, was known as difficult because she had the habit of starting most responses with the word no. This had served her well in the past, when she was the junior receiving orders and requests from everywhere, as it gave her time to think and plan, but as the leader of some 200 sales, clerical and IT staff it was a significant disadvantage. A mentor helped her see the need for change and she worked hard at becoming more approachable.

What do you need in order to change your brain?

In Chapter 2 we introduced you to the factors that need to be in place for a brain to change so that it enables new patterns of mental or physical behaviors. The first was **focused attention**. Although adult brains continue to be plastic, and we have some 86 billion neurons capable of roughly one million billion connections, we do not have infinite capacity. Our brain is a competitive environment in which different parts compete for resources. These resources can be chemical, such as the oxygen and glucose that are required for energy, and hormones which trigger particular effects, and physical, such as the limited capacity of our working memory which can hold only some five to nine items at one time, and the speed at which a signal can pass across a number of neural connections.

Some people might say that the brain is inherently lazy. That is memorable shorthand for saying that the brain is so resource intensive that, wherever possible, it will choose the most energy efficient path.[3] All of what we know as the higher order executive brain functions, anything complex involving working memory and the pre-frontal cortex (PFC), such as conscious processing of inputs, conscious decision making, complex problem solving, memorizing complex concepts, planning, strategizing, self reflection, regulating our emotions and channeling energy from them, exercising self-control and will power, are very energy intensive.

Attention appears to be the mechanism by which these limited resources are focused on a particular stimulus, physical activity or mental task (and by extension, taken away from other areas), and hence allow for new neuronal connections to be forged and progressively strengthened and old unused ones to be gradually pruned (see Box 7.3).

BOX 7.3 PRUNING CONNECTIONS

The pruning of neuronal connections happens throughout life, but there are two periods when it is most intensive and causes massive changes: around the age of two (the terrible twos) and adolescence. It is the reason teenagers need so much sleep and fuel, and underlies changes in their personalities and moods.

It would appear that the presence of top down, focused attention is necessary for significant changes in the brain.[4] But for leaders, focusing attention is not enough. Attention needs to be focused on what is most important and relevant, and that means the capacity to rapidly switch the focus of attention when necessary – to be flexible as well as focused.

These new connections are sustained and embedded through the second factor, deliberate **practice or repetition**. Forming a new network or pathway of multiple connections (or mental map as many people call it), is not enough, as a new connection is fragile. For it to remain usable it needs to be used again and again until it is well established. "Use it or lose it" is indeed a critical principle.[5] Re-using a set of connections, such as those created as a result of learning a new skill like driving a car, not only improves that skill but gradually changes the location of that map in the brain so that it needs less conscious attention and hence fewer resources and effort to accomplish. The difference between being an experienced driver on a well known route and a novice on a new one is one we all recognize. Studies have shown that London black cab drivers' mid posterior hippocampus starts reducing in size in retirement after a relatively short time. Use it or lose it indeed.

Underlying focused attention and practice is the need for the **motivation, will power or self-control** to change. Without this, focusing attention and practicing will not be sustained enough to deliver the long-term robustness of the new connections that are required for long-term change.

Finally, the **environment** has to be conducive to focusing attention. In situations of danger and uncertainty the brain's resources are driven by the overwhelming need for survival. This need focuses attention on the sources of danger and on trying to predict where the next threat will appear, on escape or full frontal battle rather than on an innovative or creative solution, on avoiding risk rather than managing it towards a new suite of products, market or way of doing business. And of course, the most important part of our environment is other people and our relationships with them.

The factors explained

Focused attention

Focused attention is driven both "bottom up" and "top down", that is, by external stimuli that we do not control, or by our goals and will. Our attention is focused involuntarily on "bottom up" stimuli that are most relevant to us, either through instinct "learned biological importance", social significance or unexpected, surprising change to a pattern. For example, when we perceive an immediate threat, such as a car that is veering towards us at speed, or perceive a personally meaningful signal, such as a craning of necks when we walk into a room, or a sudden drop in a share price on our screen. Attention is voluntarily focused, "top down" in service to our conscious goals, for example, when we want to do something that is of interest, like hitting a tennis ball, solving a problem or understanding what a customer really wants. Top down attention can also be focused through non-conscious goals. The human brain appears geared towards enabling goal driven actions and both these kinds of attention are goal directed, ultimately leading to action of some kind.[6]

The discovery that it is the presence of focused attention that determines whether a significant change in brain structure occurs, not just repeated actions, was made initially by Michael Merzenich and his team in the US in the 1970s and 1980s. Although receiving and processing a stimulus will create changes, in adults, unless accompanied by intense emotions, these are less lasting than those created by deliberate attention.[7] Another way of looking at this is that it is the process of focusing attention which enables the brain to "work on something" by directing energy and resources towards the neural networks involved.[8]

It is also possible that "focal, conscious, directed attention" is necessary for the capture of explicit memory (semantic and episodic)[9] and thus is most significant for the creation of a coherent and consistent "story of the self".

Remember the high cost of attention: it is very energy intensive. Voluntarily focusing attention while distracted by competing stimuli, for example, working against a deadline on a major client project while worrying about a promotion, tends to deplete resources also necessary for other acts requiring self-control or exercising will.

A well known example of how goal driven, focused attention shapes what our brain "works on" and suppresses reactions to stimuli which are not, at that point, relevant to our goals, is the "gorilla suit" video. This is an experiment involving a film in which a woman in a gorilla suit walks several times between a number of people throwing a ball between them. The viewer is asked to count the number of times the ball is thrown in a particular way, or something similar. When asked after viewing, only about 50 per cent of people noticed the gorilla,[10] even though it is a truly exceptional, surprising stimulus.

The ability to focus attention and keep it focused can be improved through practice. There is now considerable evidence that mindfulness meditation is one way of practicing that does just that. Practicing focusing attention, as in mindfulness, also appears to facilitate the rapid switching of the focus when necessary.[11]

Repetition and practice

As mentioned in Chapter 2, the effects of practice can be explained at neuronal level by the "Hebbian" principle of "cells that fire together wire together".[12] Repeated firing of neurons at the same time strengthens their connections and increases the speed and efficiency of the linked network or networks. Linked firing is also thought to be involved in the creation of memories. The corollary is that neurons that fire together only once, or only a few times, have fragile links to each other, unless the experience is highly emotionally charged.[13]

Repetition and practice works not just for the motor cortex, but for sensory and cognitive activity. Practice needs to be sustained over a significant amount of time. Depending on the activity,[14] various amounts of time have been mentioned in experiments. Klingberg describes an experiment in which it took five weeks of cognitive training to change patterns of activity in the frontal and parietal lobes (op cit p. 122–3). Depending on the complexity of the activity, other experiments cite variously four and a half months, 144 days or even three months (for learning to juggle)[15] for a new brain map, equal in complexity to an old one, to be created in the motor cortex. Other experiments have shown changes after only an hour's practice of a simple task, for example, typing of a memorized sequence of letters.[16] An experiment in 1995, by Alvar Pascual Leone, with some participants practicing on keyboards and a control group just thinking about the same movements, demonstrated that both groups changed the relevant motor cortex area. Mental, as well as physical, practice changed the structure of the brain.[17]

As we've already seen, in the brain, neurons and connections that are not being used are regularly "pruned", throughout life, so repeated practice or use of neural networks or pathways is essential – absolutely necessary to sustain change.[18] This repetition has very significant and desirable side effects: firstly, like attention (and indeed perhaps because of it), in a competitive environment it takes resources away from other networks; secondly, it has the effect of reducing the resources required to follow or use this network, thereby, over time, making it the preferred or easier neural pathway. One possible reason for this, other than the increased speed and efficiency already mentioned, is that routinization reduces the amount of attention required. New networks tend to be developed in the right hemisphere, and routinized ones seem to be "relocated" or re-allocated to the left, where they can work with less conscious attention.[19]

This has the most profound significance for leaders who are grappling with significant organizational change. It really cannot happen overnight if it involves changing beliefs, attitudes, ideas and behaviors. Changing people needs time and changing deeply held beliefs takes a lot of time. The director of diversity for a very large, market dominating multinational technology company, which was losing 80 per cent of its women within ten years, was shocked to hear that the executive board expected a week-long training program to solve their approach to gender. Changing the attitudes of staff in a public sector organization that was changed into an agency and then a private company took years. Looking back this might explain the decline of business process reengineering: you can reengineer processes and financial flows within days, IT systems might take longer, but people will take longer still.

Motivation, will power and self-control

Motivation, will power and self-control are closely interconnected and not enough is yet known about their underlying neural correlates to enable us to differentiate them or understand exactly how they link and or overlap. We will be defining the sense in which we are using them, but with the health warning that the science is far from fully explored. We believe that all three need to be harnessed to achieve significant, sustainable behavior and attitude change towards a consciously set goal. Humans are motivated, moved to act, in responses directed by our emotions' evaluations of external and internal stimuli – in the spectrum from escape/avoidance to attachment/attraction.[20] This can be both conscious and non-conscious. Emotional reactions can vary not just in the *value* they attribute to the stimulus, but in the *level* of arousal or activation, both influencing motivation to act. Like attention, emotions are capable of focusing resources. Extreme avoidance and attachment emotions, both evolutionarily essential for survival, tend to focus attention and energy very quickly and sharply on the stimulus, and thus diminish capacity for perception of other stimuli and engaging in other more complex cognitive activities,[21] such as decision making. The downside being that for humans in sophisticated social situations, this kind of laser-like focus and motivation for immediate or long-term actions might not always be the best adaptive responses. If I am motivated by fear to avoid my boss then my focus and energies will be on achieving that, rather than on doing a great job that will delight my client. Even if I rationalize that doing a great job will help me avoid my boss's anger, I will still have less capacity for achieving it, as my focus will be my boss, not my client.

B O X 7 . 4 F R E E W I L L O R F R E E W O N ' T

Whether or not humans have free will is still hotly debated. In 1999 Benjamin Libet established that some 100–200 milliseconds before a conscious decision to move a finger, for example, a readiness potential was measurable in that part of the brain that controls that finger movement. Libet concluded that our non-conscious mind had made the decision before our conscious mind was aware of it – hence no free will. But he maintained that our conscious mind had about 150 milliseconds to choose between allowing and countermanding that decision – hence free won't. These findings are still controversial. The meaning of the readiness potential has been disputed. They may however explain why exercising will and making decisions are such hard work.

Motivating others to change, to engage all their resources to achieve the goals that you have set for the organization is one of the greatest challenges leaders face. We know that motivation arises from the emotions. One in particular, "surprise or startle" appears to play a very special role in changing attitudes and behavior. It creates the possibility of an "aha!" moment, or discovery. Coaches startle or surprise their clients in subtle ways when they are finding change difficult to achieve, when they seem stuck. This emotion seems to allow the brain to pause, and in that moment, to allow for the possibility of change. Leaders also use surprising acts, words or speeches to create the same effect. The leader who comes in on Wednesday and announces a restructuring that will start with immediate effect is creating an extreme example, a disconnect between the familiar past and the future, which disrupts habitual behaviors and ways of thoughts and creates the opportunity for challenge, innovation and change.

That human will or will power (defined here as the determination to pursue a chosen action or goal) exists has been demonstrated by experiments, pioneered by Roy Baumeister (see further Box 7.4).[22] It has also been shown that, like focusing attention and decision making, exercising will power is energy hungry, and there are measurable effects of energy depletion and fatigue after a test of will power. A key manifestation of will power is self-control or self-management, the ability to resist instinctive or impulsive desires, to temper or reframe intuitive reactions, regulate emotions and feelings, remain focused on an activity, thought or goal, however long term, and balance both emotional and rational/logical (so called hot and cold systems) processes in decision making.[23]

A lot more work is needed to understand will in terms of neuronal structure and activity (or indeed whether it is possible to differentiate from self-control) although exercising self-control appears to correlate with increased activity in the right ventrolateral pre-frontal cortex (RVLPFC),[24] regardless of the context – for example, suppressing an unwanted thought, resisting an immediate temptation or dampening an inappropriate emotion.[25] According to Baumeister, will power, like a muscle, can be trained through repeated practice – but with appropriate rest periods to avoid fatigue.

In order to change behavior to achieve a goal, exercising will or self-control to keep attention focused on the goal and on the changes needed would seem a key part of the top down process. Will is also essential to persistence in practicing until the change is successfully embedded and routinized, and potentially also to the capacity to monitor progress (also necessary for achieving a goal according to Baumeister[26]).

There is some evidence that motivation can be manipulated by incentives.[27] Incentives engage an emotional response. In experiments with students, adding a financial incentive to a set task meant that motivation was increased and students pushed through fatigue to work longer on a task than those without the incentive.[28, 29] There is also evidence from experiments involving real-life issues of self-control, such as giving up smoking and dieting, that the right kind of incentives can increase motivation. Because the value of incentives is linked to the strength of the emotional response, it is not always the obvious rewards that stimulate the largest motivational benefits. A financial reward that is less than expected can create very strong feelings of disappointment, even anger (due to loss aversion), or one that is below the team average may elicit shame at the loss of status. Incentives need to be appropriate to the individual and their circumstances and non financial rewards – such as a new title – can also create very strong motivation. Increasing motivation increases self-control, and enables people to work harder and longer to achieve a goal.[30]

Motivation and will can thus be seen as parts of the brain's mechanism for bottom up and top down focusing of attention on what is most important and relevant and enabling self-control towards the achievement of goals.

Environment

In Chapter 3, we saw that part of a leader's role is the creation of environments which make it easier for people to achieve organizational goals. These leaders are sometimes known for "making their own weather", both within the organization and, more rarely, outside it, amongst key stakeholders. These are indeed the leaders who recognize that it is easier to work with the grain of the brain than against it. Having recognized the paramount importance of focused attention to enable change, of emotions for motivation and the need for practice over significant periods of time, they are more likely to create environments in which individuals and teams can change themselves and each other. Such environments will have reduced distractions, they will have many opportunities for the corporate goals to be clearly articulated and repeated, and the goals will be few and coherent, not conflicting.

Having explicit goals appears to increase motivation. There is some evidence that writing them down not only helps clarify them but also increases the chances that we will achieve them – perhaps by making them more real, or treating them as part of a contract with ourselves or others. Ensuring that there are not only long-term goals but medium and short-term ones as well, that they are public and that progress towards them is monitored and is seen to be monitored at the individual, team and group level also helps in achieving them. Setting clear goals which do not conflict with each other is a way of ensuring that we direct our and others' minds and actions towards desired outcomes and away from distractions.

Such leaders are likely to have a focus on, and appropriate incentives for, longer-term advantage rather than short-term gain, but with again clear operational plans for the steps that need to be taken to make that advantage a reality. Leaders will rely on relationships of trust at all levels and will not use fear as a tool. They will engage and involve stakeholders and acknowledge and respect their emotional as well as rational reactions and goals. They will encourage monitoring of both individual and team progress, and will have the ability to use a coaching style to support change and self-management throughout the organization. They may even explicitly encourage mindfulness and have spaces where individuals can be quiet and meditate.

Summary

Understanding what the brain needs in order to change (focused attention, practice, motivation, conducive environments and relationships) enables leaders not only to change themselves but to make it easier for others to change in desired directions. The process starts with self-awareness and self-management. Leaders can change themselves in ways which facilitate improved communications and relationships of trust. That enables them to create environments and embed a range of motivational factors in processes (such as reward systems) and structures (such as allowing for appropriate autonomy) which support others in succeeding to change themselves. Goals will be clear, coherent and well articulated.

Actions and reflections

- Use the power of goals, whether conscious or non-conscious, to act as triggers or primers for focusing attention.
- Consider how you can create many opportunities for others to practice desired behaviors. Anything that supports practice is useful, such as getting self-help groups to do role plays to help with, for example, changing the way you might deal with a crisis, setback or refusal, having easily memorized protocols which are reinforced in rehearsals or drills, or embedding regular coaching as part of a change program.
- Engaging in mindfulness meditation, even for a few minutes a day before important calls or meetings, is a great way of developing better control over the focus of attention and the ability to switch it when needed. There are now apps that can help with regular meditation practice.
- Setting an example of how to avoid unnecessary distractions and offering training in how to avoid them (e.g. in time management), and discouraging multitasking when there are important projects to complete or problems to be solved can both help focus and improve efficiency.
- Providing a varied and appropriate mix of incentives, which, with feedback, are closely linked to the desired actions and the outcomes of which can help people be more motivated and overcome fatigue. Incentives can be extrinsic, a bonus or time off, a better title or bigger office, praise and acknowledgment, or intrinsic. Intrinsic incentives can be the satisfaction of achievement, the triumph of winning, a sense of usefulness or worthiness, of belonging, being in a state of flow and the joy of an "aha!" moment of discovery after struggling with a problem. These kinds of incentives can be facilitated by enabling individuals to work at levels which suit their abilities – so that they are stretched but not overwhelmed, by giving them a sense of control over their work and environment, by offering tasks which are meaningful, useful and engaging, through timely feedback which reinforces a sense of being effective, through work that is conducive to flow. They also arise more easily in environments which facilitate creative thinking and flexible

team working, where people are valued for their strengths and supported in overcoming their weaknesses.

- Finally, where appropriate, allow people to have sufficient time to develop expertise. Frequent changes in department or area of work is fine when the skills you want to develop are transferrable, such as communications or relationship skills, but can get in the way of performance when in-depth domain knowledge is needed.

8

chapter

Elite Performance, Brain Agility and Engagement

"Always bear in mind that your resolution to succeed is more important than any one thing."

Abraham Lincoln

Businesses are more focused than ever on excellent performance and acquiring a competitive edge through interventions such as executive coaching and leadership development. What can we learn from the London 2012 Olympics and Paralympics? As South African athlete Oscar Pistorius famously said, "every race is won or lost in the head." Pistorius, a double amputee, ran in both the Paralympics and Olympics but fell from grace when he was put on trial after a tragic shooting of his then girlfriend, for which he was later found guilty of culpable homicide. Remember from Chapter 1 that surprise is the potentiator emotion that can flip you from survival to attachment or vice-versa.

It was interesting to witness how our brains moved along the basic emotions spectrum during his trial in 2014, the shocking nature of the incident

Remember from Chapter 1 that surprise is the potentiator emotion that can flip you from survival to attachment or vice-versa.

moving us from the joy and excitement of the Olympics to anger, disgust and sadness.

In the corporate world, the caliber of self-awareness, physical and mental preparedness and self-belief we saw underlying excellence in the Olympians and Paralympians is highly valued, so what makes us perform really well and how can we maintain or improve our brain fitness (see Box 8.1)?

BOX 8.1   BRAIN AND BODY CHALLENGES

In the business world we are increasingly aware of the importance of integrating logic and emotion via the left and right hemispheres of the brain (although this is a gross oversimplification), but the brain–body connection should not be underestimated, plus all the things you have to deal with across your everyday activities like working with people:

- In different time zones.
- From different global cultures.
- Where one or both of you is speaking in a language that is not your mother tongue.
- When you or they or both of you are living in a country that is not the one you grew up in.

Not to mention mergers and acquisitions of different business cultures along with the differences in genders, hierarchies and generations X, Y and the baby boomers.

Hone your senses. The five senses are how your brain knows what is going on in your world, through your nose, tongue, skin, eyes and ears:

- Smell – through your olfactory nerve.
- Taste – through your facial and glossopharyngeal nerves.
- Touch – via your somatosensory system.

- Vision – via your optic and oculomotor nerves.
- Hearing – from your vestibulocochlear nerve.

Smell

This is the most emotive sense because the olfactory nerve travels directly from the nose to a part of the brain that is close to some of the emotional centers, the limbic system. All the other senses involve nerves that travel around the skull before carrying information back to the brain. The hippocampus is the part of the brain where emotions are linked to memories and some peoples' most vivid memories are strongly associated with smells. The smell of the sea, freshly cut grass or the damp smell of earth after it rains can invoke strong childhood memories.

Which smell most strongly evokes a childhood memory for you?

Lavender is the most potent naturally occurring neuromodulator. It can balance the emotions, calming people when they are agitated and invigorating people when they are melancholic (see Box 8.2).

BOX 8.2   ART: A LAVENDER CASE STUDY

Art, a CTO who tended to become quite "assertive" during board meetings, used it and it became a bit of an in-joke so that other members of the executive committee would say "get the lavender out!" when he started to get worked up. We all know that a bit of humor helps to relax the brain so either way it seemed to work. Years later, people are still smiling about that little bottle of lavender he used to carry around. Even his wife knew what it meant if the bottle was out on their nightstand.

Taste

In terms of brain optimization, it revolves around really savoring a cup of tea or a piece of chocolate to give your brain a minute between meetings and bring yourself back to the present. This is a form of mindfulness. When we are not mindful, challenges can deplete our resilience more markedly.

When an interaction with someone leaves a bad taste in your mouth, what does it mean?

And are you able to see this for what it is rather than get bogged down with historical emotions that no longer serve you? In the next chapter you will discover many ideas and techniques for minimizing these sorts of unhelpful pathways in your brain.

Touch

In terms of brain–body connection touch is about considering the information your largest organ – the skin – is providing you with. There is a map of the body in the sensory cortex of the brain called the homunculus. It appears somewhat distorted as the parts of the body with the most sensory neurons are most highly represented. So the lips and fingertips appear much larger than the arms and legs.

When you feel the little hairs on the back of your neck stand up or goose bumps, what is your ancient neural architecture telling you?

Finnish scientists have even produced "Bodily maps of emotions" which shows where different emotions are manifested in the body across global cultures. The results have been reported in the *Proceedings of the National Academy of Sciences* and really need to be seen in full technicolor:[1]

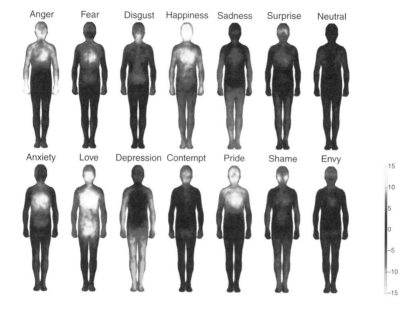

FIGURE 8.1 Bodily maps of emotions

Source: Reproduced with permission from *Proceedings of the National Academy of Sciences*.

Vision

This is probably the sense we use the most. Novelty is good for the brain so look out for something new every day. The social neurosciences tell us that the most eye contact occurs between two women, least between two men and moderate between a man and a woman. Eye contact is also one of the ways we build healthy neural architecture in our children. Think of the Romanian orphans who were fed, washed and clothed adequately but not given any cuddles or face to face contact. The proportion of them that grew up with attachment disorders and mental health problems is legendary.

Notice what happens if you really look someone in the eye when you shake his or her hand.

Bill Clinton was particularly good at this and utilized it to build trust and rapport and perhaps more …

Hearing

If you have a list of goals you are trying to achieve or behavioral habits you hope to embed, then try reading them out loud. When you read things out loud you use three parts of the brain so it reinforces the message to your brain much more strongly than reading alone:

- Wernicke's area which understands written and spoken language.
- Broca's area which has functions linked to speech production.
- The temporal lobe which holds the auditory centers of the brain.

We use this when coaching to save us repeating the same message three times. It is also the reason that parents and teachers ask children to repeat things back to them, not only to make sure they have understood it but also to embed it in their brain. Knowing something like that and that a rhythmical speaking style has a positive effect on what people remember should allow you to create certain hooks that make things stick in the minds of people you need to rely on. Ponder why we remember nursery rhymes or catchy slogans so well sometimes to the point that we cannot get them out of our minds (see Box 8.3).

BOX 8.3   AARON: A CASE STUDY

A senior Law firm Partner, Aaron, once arrived at a session, highly agitated and talking at 100kph. I thought "I can't coach someone in this state" so I handed him my iPhone and earphones and asked him to listen to a piece from Swan Lake for 3 minutes. At the end he sighed and looked at me. I asked him to acknowledge how much his mental state/mood could change in just 3 minutes and to use music in this way himself going forward.

Brain Olympics

- Bronze – Resilience
- Silver – Energy
- Gold – Higher purpose.

With the basics in place, what can you do to attain bronze, silver or gold in the Brain Olympics?

Bronze

At the bronze level you should be regularly ensuring enough good quality sleep. Six to eight hours is recommended although this will vary from person to person. As long as you are waking up refreshed and dreaming enough, you are probably allowing sufficient time for the brain to rest and build up resources for resilience. The main reasons that this does not occur are listed here – try to avoid these things as much as you can:

- Misuse of caffeine (caffeine should be avoided after 2pm due to its long half-life which means that is can remain in the body for eight to ten hours after consumption). Some people are especially sensitive to the effects of caffeine, others find no effect from it whatsoever and some people can drink a mug of it just before they go to bed. Try to work out which category you fall into.
- Use of substances such as nicotine and alcohol. These should be minimized generally and avoided altogether for two hours prior to bed time as they stimulate the brain.
- Use of digital media should be ceased one hour before going to bed due to effects of unnatural light from the screen on the pineal gland and also the cognitive stimulation from dealing with the information on the screens and you certainly should not be sleeping with your smart phone or device next to you due to the effects of wifi and 3G or 4G signals on your brain waves.

One of the most incredible findings from brain science research in 2012 was about how the brain cleans itself of toxic waste byproducts whilst we sleep. The "glymphatic" system relies on cerebrospinal fluid to flush out neurotoxins overnight, including one called beta amyloid which is found in clumps in the brains of people with Alzheimer's disease. This was followed up in 2013 by research that identified "hidden caves" that open in the brain while we sleep, allowing cerebrospinal fluid to flush out neurotoxins through the spinal column. The implications of this research cannot be overstated: failing to get enough sleep may prevent the brain from being able to remove neurotoxins that can eventually lead to neurological disorders like Alzheimer's and Parkinson's.[2]

Too many leaders think they are fine with working on much less sleep than an average person because the sleep-induced IQ loss (say 5–8 points) does not matter much if you're riding on a 130–50 background. Whereas for someone on the population average of 100, a (reversible) loss of 8 points is very consequential. Estimates show a whole night's sleep forgone costs you about a standard deviation in IQ (*personal communication* Prof Shane O'Mara, Institute of Neuroscience, Trinity College, Dublin).

No matter who you are, when your brain is rested and resilient, you can:

• Perform better under pressure.
• Regulate your emotions.
• Multitask.
• Think flexibly and creatively.
• Solve complex problems.
• Be responsive to behavioral demands.
• Make the best decisions or choices in the short and long term.

Silver

This is about doing all the above, as well as meeting healthy nutrition, hydration and basic exercise requirements.

Oxygenating your brain with exercise or at least deep breathing as opposed to the shallow breathing or breath holding that dominates when one is chronically stressed. Recommendations would involve doing

30 minutes of cardiovascular exercise on most days of the week. The serotonin boosting effect of this can be equivalent to the effect of a low dose of an anti-depressant and has been reported to boost productivity at work on the days exercise takes place in the morning by as much as 15 per cent. Combined with the beneficial effects of fresh air and being exposed to sunlight, this has serious brain boosting power, as oxygen and glucose are vital fuels for the brain. The pineal gland needs sunlight to regulate our sleep–wake cycle and there are cascade effects on mood and stress levels.

Glucose from a healthy, balanced diet, rich in antioxidants and supplemented with vitamins and omega oils is important. The brain, although only 2 per cent of body weight, consumes 20 per cent of its glucose intake in a critical "just in time" delivery system and cannot store glucose for later use. This should encourage the practice of regular eating to avoid defaulting to unconscious biases and low trust levels. The brain is constantly scanning out for threats and if there is not enough fuel available it will not be used to generate trust, but saved to ensure survival. And this does not only mean you may misjudge or devalue others. You may underestimate yourself or have lower levels of self-belief when not well fed and watered.

Hydration is critical – a 1–3 per cent decrease in your hydration levels negatively affects your memory, concentration and decision-making power. You need to drink at least 500ml of water for every 30lbs of your body weight, per day, and more if you are drinking lots of caffeine or sweating profusely.

Gold

With resilience and energy in place, work on the integration of the various brain areas involved in personal and professional development, there is time to move towards fine-tuning intuition, not only focusing attention but shifting that focus flexibly when required, unleashing innovative capability and thinking about leaving a legacy. To achieve this, like any Olympian, the talented and ambitious leader's efforts would be boosted with a coach on board – in this case concentrating on brain based techniques for sustainable behavior change including mindfulness, which can free up cognitive resources for creative thinking by connecting people to their underlying wisdom rather than allowing distractions from negative thoughts and anxieties (more on this in the following chapters). As Alvin Toffler says, "the illiterate of the 21st century will not be those who can't read or write but those who cannot learn, unlearn and re-learn."

"the illiterate of the 21st century will not be those who can't read or write but those who cannot learn, unlearn and re-learn."

Most people drink caffeine every day, whether it's that morning mug of coffee, cups of tea throughout the day or (diet) colas; some people (statistics show more students but a growing number of executives) even take the drugs like Ritalin that are for ADHD (Attention deficit hyperactivity disorder) or narcolepsy (the illness where people suddenly fall asleep) to keep themselves awake, then need a sleeping tablet to help them switch off. Smart drugs such as these and ones like Modafanil – normally used for dementia – are currently illegal in the UK as cognitive enhancers for otherwise healthy people because they can have side effects, but they are more available in the US and of course widely available on the internet without regulation. We suggest you stick to the natural stuff until side effect free nootropics – cognitive enhancers – are designed. It's only a matter of time due to the combination of demand and the massive amounts of funding going into brain research and development. If you would like to be less forgetful, sleep better, not get as stressed and make better decisions, you could supplement your healthy balanced diet with antioxidants, B complex vitamins, vitamin D, magnesium, coenzyme Q10 and omega oils that keep your brain and nervous system healthy. There is also evidence that green tea extract induces neurogenesis – growth of new neurons – in mouse brains. Although green tea does contain caffeine it also contains high levels of EGCG or catechins, which are antioxidants with anti-inflammatory properties thought to be protective against diseases like Alzheimer's. Green teas also contain l-theanine, which can induce alpha waves in the brain associated with better mood, cognition and lower stress.

An understanding of neuroplasticity and the practical application of neuroscience to business have revolutionized leadership development producing more gold medal-winning executives all around the world. We all know that the adventurous, curious childhood spirit can get squelched by corporate life and to avoid this you need to shift individual mindsets and business cultures. The systems dynamics literature from MIT Sloan School of Management clearly shows that every interaction exists within a system and that there are knock on effects everywhere as well as difficulties in making changes if the system does not accommodate this.

So what can you do as a leader?

Current theory includes ideas to promote innovation such as:

- Rapid prototyping (failing fast and often).
- Resource cutting (necessity is the mother of invention).
- Design thinking (discussed further in this chapter).
- Disruptive innovation (discussed further in this chapter) – and see also the section on innovation in Chapter 10.

In Box 8.1 in this chapter we mentioned integrating logic and emotion but indicated it is more complicated than that. We touched upon other considerations in using your brain such as culture, generations and physicality. The Leadership Brain Agility© tool (Figure 8.2) is based on utilizing thinking from six different parts or systems of your brain (referred to as bubbles) to improve the flexibility of your decision making, risk taking and leadership ability. There is no right or wrong way of using this tool – rather it is about honing your strengths whilst remaining very aware of your development areas and realizing that your key stakeholders, clients, direct reports or family members may have various differing approaches to yourself. It is diversity of thought, after all, that leads to step changes.

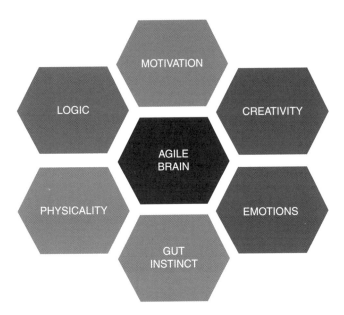

FIGURE 8.2 / Brain agility model

Source: © Swart 2010.

Whilst it remains a gross over-simplification that the left correlates to logical, rational, analytical thinking, and the right to more creative, intuitive thinking, it is probably true that most people think predominantly in one of those ways, then has to more purposefully refer to the other way of thinking. Most right-handed people (80–90 per cent) have a dominant left hemisphere, and left-handed people are about 50/50.

Which mode of thinking do you think is primary for you, regardless of handedness?

Logic

Most people reading this book would answer that question by saying logic – so, apart from confirming that this is about the scope and scale of your technical, analytical skills and competencies, we are not going to dwell on this bubble.

Creativity

The kind of versatility, adaptability and thinking outside of the box that leads to innovation, this bubble is key to some of the ideas expanded on later in this chapter.

Physicality

The most under-rated bubble seems to be the brain–body dimension.

The brainstem becomes the spinal cord which gives rise to all the nerves that go out into the body and bring back information from the outside world. Above the brainstem is the deep, older neural circuitry of the limbic system (seat of our emotions), and wrapped around all of this is the modern, logical cortex which we humans have developed much more than other animals (including monkeys) as it is involved in future planning and articulated speech. Because speech is such a great short cut to being understood, we take much less notice of things like nervous laughter, blushing, flinching or butterflies in our stomach. If you play sport or do yoga you are more likely to be in touch with signals from your body (interoception as described in Chapter 2), but this is a particularly important one for men, because even though male and female brains are more similar than they are different, men tend to have a smaller vocabulary for emotional language, and information crosses between the left and right more slowly – but this can be improved with time, education and social expectation. Wearable technology such as the Fitbit, Nike Fuel Band or Jawbone UP band have really helped people become more mindful about what they are doing with their body. We discuss stress, resilience and energy later in this chapter.

Gut instinct

Due to the inordinately large nerve supply from our guts to the limbic system and basal ganglia, a gut feeling is based on data that may be more based on experiences we pick up in life than data we use every day and keep front of mind. Increasingly we are hearing leaders saying they regret it when they look back and realize they ignored their intuition or sixth sense, in favor of logical thinking.

Can you think of any examples of how this has affected judgment and decisiveness in your life?

Emotions

As well as physical feelings we need to be able to monitor our own and others' emotional feelings. Being self-aware is the first step and being able to understand and respond to other people's emotional state (empathy) is the next step to emotional intelligence (see also Chapter 5).

Motivation

Finally, having an understanding of your own agenda, for example, for a meeting, as well as the motivators and drivers of your team, leads to diversity of thought, avoids "group think" and opens the door to innovative organizations. As a leader this is about your values, integrity and the legacy you would like to leave.

Leadership Brain Agility©

Imagine your 100 per cent brain resource at the center of this model (Figure 8.3). Take a minute to think about how much you use the various brain areas, as a leader – this may vary depending on what is demanded

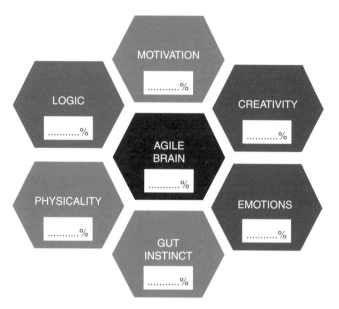

FIGURE 8.3 / Brain agility model© percentages

Source: © Swart 2010.

of you, but pick from how you are on most days. You can then repeat the exercise for other situations. Allocate a percentage to each of the brain areas before you continue reading.

This tool is about being able to move between these different brain areas when required of you. So if you are well practiced at using the different parts, it will come easily when required, as you will have an established pathway in your brain. The good news is that neuroplasticity means that we can develop in areas we are not used to using well into adulthood.

Learning a new language or a musical instrument – which are known as "attention intensive" exercises as opposed to things like crosswords and Sudoku – probably increases the process of neuroplasticity in the adult brain. Neuroplasticity occurs through three main mechanisms as described in Chapter 2.

Most people find that they use one or two of the brain areas most of the time, another one or two some of the time, and one or two hardly at all. Or at least they are not aware of using it. So pick wisely which area to concentrate on and that will benefit you the most. If there is something you do not feel you can or want to work on, then find a right hand person that complements your skills or fit yourself into an organization that value your current strengths.

Here are some simple tips and techniques for practicing using these different areas of your brain – remember practice makes perfect in the brain because neurons that fire together, wire together – it is a "use it or lose it" type of organ.

However the brain will struggle to take on more than two new habits at any one time, so we suggest the following process of "spiral learning":

- Pick one brain area and two habits relating to it or two brain areas to work on in the first instance.
- Once you have practiced that skill and it feels more natural because it has become a habit move on to one or two new brain areas or skills.
- Continue around the model in this way until you are comfortable that you could respond appropriately to different situations and people.
- Investing time in your agile brain is an essential key to sustainable leadership. Leaders who can surf ambiguity and learn adaptively will do better in future in the face of inevitably accelerating change.

Use logical analytical thinking, which equates to competencies, scope and scale of your technical skill and your thoughts:

- Talk through issues with a peer, mentor or coach.
- Write notes or a to-do list by yourself and read it out loud. Then you are using the part of brain that produces the written word, the part that articulates speech, as well as the part that hears your voice through your ear and into your temporal lobe (as described earlier in relation to "hearing" giving a tiny insight into how your senses and these six brain

bubbles interplay to produce the amazing capabilities of your brain and body).

Creativity relates to versatility, adaptability and your business vision:

- Use drawing instead of writing, or a mind map instead of a to-do list.
- Use colored pens – preferably at least four not including blue or black, and no stick men, letters or numbers.

Movement relies on a system called the basal ganglia at the base of the brain, around the brainstem.

Physical feelings include your energy, resilience, and ability to really listen. Are you tired? Are you jet lagged? Did you have breakfast today? These can all affect your quality of thought:

- Pay attention to things like nervous laughter, sweating, blushing, flinching or butterflies in your stomach.
- Try listening to people to really understand their point of view, rather than interrupting with your ideas.
- Maintain good eye contact whilst you are listening.

Gut instinct is about intuition, judgment and decisiveness. Look out for signs or stories in life that guide your sixth sense. And also look inward for that "gut wrenching" doubt and indecision versus the "I just knew it in my gut" kind of confidence. These can often manifest as actual visceral feelings as the viscera or internal organs are actually supplied by nerves communicating with the brain. One can only guess that is where the metaphor comes from. This is really something that develops with wisdom, and there are no short cuts to gaining that apart from fully embracing life and all it throws at you, to sculpt your brain as much by your response as by the event itself. Only meditation can accelerate this as far as we know currently.

Emotional intelligence is about empathy and trust. Our basic emotions such as fear and trust are deeply seated in the limbic system – specifically the amygdalae:

- Keep a journal of your feelings or check in on your emotional state at least four times a day to raise your awareness.
- Try to listen out for whether people around you say "I feel" or "I think" more and respond accordingly.

Our basic drives are for sleep/wake, hunger/thirst and sex. These originate in the Reticular formation, and involve the basal ganglia.
Motivation is about your values, integrity, capacity for action and legacy:

- Try to put yourself in the shoes of others – what is their raison d'etre?
- Which factors motivate and de-motivate yourself and others?
- How can knowing about this help you work better with your team?
- How can knowing yourself better help you achieve purpose and meaning at work, as a leader and in life?

The d.School at Stanford University uses design thinking as a methodology for practical, creative resolution of issues that looks for an improved future result. As a style of thinking, it is the ability to combine empathy for the context of a problem, creativity in the generation of insights and solutions, and rationality to analyze and fit solutions to the context.

Roger Martin, Dean of the University of Toronto's Rotman School of Management and author of *The Opposable Mind: How Successful Leaders win through Integrative Thinking*, argues that integrative thinking is a feature found in successful leaders and defines it as "the ability to face constructively the tension of opposing ideas and, instead of choosing one at the expense of the other, generate a creative resolution of the tension in the form of a new idea that contains elements of the opposing ideas but is superior to each." This would reflect superior frontal cortex functioning.

"I think one's feelings waste themselves in words, they ought all to be distilled into actions and into actions that bring results."

Florence Nightingale

Are you interesting?

Why would you wish to integrate the functions of the brain – what would be the advantage as a leader? We propose that "the integrated leader" is able to engage people on a level that really gets the most out of them and sees success start to happen through others not only as a result of their own direct actions (Box 8.4). This is true leadership and is more likely to engender step changes in innovation, or even disruptive innovation – an innovation that helps create a new market and value network, and eventually goes on to disrupt an existing market and value network (over time), displacing an earlier technology.

BOX 8.4   ENGAGEMENT

Ask yourself the following questions and try to answer them from the point of view of one of your peers or direct reports. Think of someone specifically when you answer these questions:

- Are you engaging?
- Do your people want to engage with you?
- What is going on when there is an interaction between two (or more?) of you, and your peer or direct report is feeling engaged and interested?
- Where is your attention when you feel engaged?

We should begin by postulating that these are probably mutually occurring events – that is, to be engaging you are *engaged*. This is similar to the concept from the social neurosciences that to encourage trust in a relationship – and by relationship we mean any interaction between people, at work, at home or socially – you must be open to trusting rather than being in a stress or fear state which others could become aware of on a primal level.

This can be explained to some extent by the existence of mirror neurons in the brain, which we introduced in Chapter 5. Imaging studies have shown that brain regions that are thought to contain mirror neurons are active not only when the person carries out an action but also when they observe another person carrying out the action. Mirror neurons may also be similarly involved in empathy, in that they ensure that the moment someone sees an emotion expressed on your face they will sense that same feeling within themselves. At an unconscious level we are in constant dialogue and attunement with anyone we interact with therefore gaining an understanding of how they feel.

This loop backs to the hypothesis of reciprocity in terms of being engaged. On a deep, primitive level of instinct within the emotional centers of the brain we can sense if another person is interested in us, and this is more likely to make us engage with them. More recently a study[3] has disputed that these mirror neurons carry out as sophisticated a function as was previously thought so an additional explanation could be the contagion of neurotransmitters and hormones that is discussed further in Chapter 10.

A more obvious version of these is the idea that if someone begins to mirror your body language, an atmosphere of rapport and engagement is developing. Unfortunately this has been misused by the likes of the stereotypical "used car salesman" using techniques like NLP (neuro-linguistic programming) to try and induce a state of rapport by purposely imitating the body language and spoken language preferences of the "customer". So looking out for and playing back language such as "I feel" versus "I think" or using visuals and metaphors depending on what you pick up from the person you are interacting with can be perceived as anything from emotionally intelligent to highly manipulative. Practice, focus attention and be aware. This is something that really needs to be authentically "who you are" because first impressions are not only powerful but we now know they are more objective than we could have imagined without the power of evidence from brain scanning. In 2011, Rule et al published the following findings in *NeuroImage*[4] (see Box 8.5).

BOX 8.5   THE AMYGDALA RESPONSE

The human amygdala responds to first impressions of people as judged from their faces, such as normative judgments about the trustworthiness of strangers. It is unknown, however, whether amygdala responses to first impressions can be validated by objective criteria. They examined amygdala responses to faces of CEOs where real world outcomes could be measured objectively by the amounts of profits made by each CEO's company. During fMRI scanning, participants made incidental judgments about the symmetry of each CEO's face. After scanning, participants rated each CEO's face on leadership ability. Parametric analyses showed that greater left amygdala response to the CEOs' faces was associated with higher post-scan ratings of the CEOs' leadership ability. In addition, greater left amygdala response was also associated with greater profits made by the CEOs' companies and this relationship was statistically mediated by external raters' perceptions of arousal. Thus, amygdala response reflected both subjective judgments and objective measures of leadership ability based on first impressions. The finding that the left amygdala responds both to subjective perceptions and objective indices of others' success suggests a neural mechanism for consensus and accuracy in our first impressions of others.

As the modern, logical cortex of our brain has developed we have tended to lose sight of the information we get from our gut instinct and motivation centers, but they are there and deep down we know if someone is authentic or not. Whether we choose to acknowledge this is another story, but the superficial attempts at being interested or engaging do not usually last long and are not compelling.

To come across as genuinely interested, a socially appropriate level of eye contact and a style and level of listening that is about attempting to understand the other person rather than interjecting with a clever question or even an anecdote of your own on the topic are the key foundations. When two people do this an emotional resonance loop develops between their brains on several levels:

- Dopamine is released in the reward areas of the brain – this neurochemical is associated with getting something you *want*.
- Opioids are released when you get something you *like*.
- Serotonin release is associated with being in a good mood.
- Oxytocin is in the air when trust is growing or when you are falling in love. It is a hormone that induces a calm, warm mood that increases tender feelings and attachment and may lead us to lower our guard. This is perhaps the hormone most fundamental to being interesting.
- Noradrenalin intensifies the effects of all of the above and is involved in attention and concentration.
- Cortisol (stress) levels should be low in this scenario.

Evidence from research into interpersonal neurobiology would suggest that being engaged is to feel curiosity, a desire to know more, and is a manifestation of the surprise/startle emotion combined with excitement and trust.

Music communicates to us emotionally through some element of the unexpected and can also help to induce a state of relaxed alertness in ourselves, or others.

The brain is all about inter-connectedness – our genetic make-up combined with all our life experiences from the womb to parenting styles, learning preferences, talent choices, social milieu, gender, culture, relationships and many more factors create a unique blue-print of who we are, what we find interesting and who we engage which continue to shape us into the future. In a phrase, engaging people, would be to be aware of and able to regulate the impact of our brain on that of another. It is about providing enough, but not too much novelty, challenge and choice to inspire and motivate.

Summary

Neuroplasticity means that we can develop these skills even if they are not already a strong part of our toolkit. We can learn explicitly through training and reading, as well as implicitly through the lessons we pick up in life. Brain based coaching engages executives through both explicit and implicit brain learning areas, as well as through logic and emotion centers, to change and sustain leadership behaviors that motivate and inspire others into high performance.

But how might this have a direct contribution to the bottom line of your business?

In their 2008 paper "Man's search for meaning" in the *Journal of Economic Behavior*, Dan Ariely and colleagues show in a laboratory setting that subjects in less meaningful conditions exhibit reservation wages that are consistently much higher than the subjects in more meaningful conditions. Occupations that are traditionally regarded as meaningful (medicine, art, science, education) are invariably associated with large and "noble" goals. Individuals presumably derive satisfaction from a feeling that their work promotes these goals, which in turn leads to lower reservation wages. If you are managing or leading in professions other than these and particularly in some that have been vilified in recent years, this is really worth knowing as part of your toolkit for motivating individuals and boosting organizational productivity. Meaning can be found in the smallest thing and as a leader it may be your job to help people identify and deliver it.

Actions and reflections

There are plenty of ideas and exercises for reflection interspersed throughout this chapter. Because of what we know about how the brain works we did not want every chapter to have the same lay out and you need to remember not to take on too much at once or the brain will become de-motivated by too many open tasks. Here is a checklist relevant to this chapter: pick two or three topics at a time to do one thing toward improving whenever you have time to move forward another step in your brain:

- The five senses questions.
- Bronze, silver and gold activities.
- Leadership Brain Agility© exercises.

9

chapter

Stress, Resilience and Confidence

"Worry affects the circulation, the heart, the glands, the whole nervous system. I have never known a man who died from overwork, but many who died from doubt."

Charles Horace Mayo

It is a familiar story. You have taken over as CEO of an international telecoms company that had dominated the market, but is now struggling to compete with innovative products and services from competitors who barely existed a few years ago. Chosen because of your track record in turning around technology-based businesses and your credibility with market analysts, you find that the change required is much more widespread than you expected.

Major customers are showing signs of restlessness, your products pipeline is not healthy and your biggest market is taking a long time to recover from the recession. The previous CEO, who had led the company for a long time, had been charismatic, dynamic and over-optimistic. His style of command and control left a big vacuum and you have inherited some critical people-related problems. Your wonderful marketing director has had a heart attack; your HR director resigned; your remaining senior managers seem cynical, wondering whether you have been brought in to break up the company; your technologists are stressed and directionless; and the board's expectations are unrealistic.

You are spending more and more time at work, travelling to see customers and trying to get round all departments and businesses around the world. You have begun to wonder whether this was a disastrous career choice and it is affecting your sleep, your digestion, your confidence and equanimity. How can you begin to make change happen in the right direction?

Stress

Stress happens when people feel under threat:

- When you are frightened by change, uncertainty or anything new.
- When your self-esteem is attacked.
- When you feel that the demands on you – internal or external – are beyond your control or capability to meet.

In a business environment, in the politically stable developed world, stress is usually psychological, that is, in response to how people *perceive* themselves and their world. Understanding the causes and effects of stress is crucial for a leader in a volatile environment so let's look at various statistics and perspectives to see if they really are giving us the same message.

We are currently in an era where the pace of change and financial uncertainty has created an unprecedented rise in stress. We are beginning to understand the breadth and depth of its consequences and crucially, its impact on productivity. Stress can affect your:

- Thoughts – do you find it difficult to concentrate and be creative without getting distracted? Are you worrying about your position to the point that your self-esteem is lower than you remember it being in your adult life?
- Emotions – do you feel irritable and angry more often but do not know how to express or release these feelings?

- Behavior – if we asked your children, would they say you are short-tempered and grumpy a lot of the time? Does your staff complain that you are locked away in your office and never available or not visible to people down the food chain?
- Physical symptoms – do you clench your jaw, grind your teeth, take tablets to deal with symptoms of acid reflux, get headaches or back pain, take more than an hour to fall asleep or lie awake way before your alarm goes off in the morning?

Have you been ignoring these signs or doing things that deal with them superficially but do not get to the root cause? Any of these things could lead to absenteeism in the workforce but up at leadership level where it's not ok to show any weakness and you cannot afford any time off, what happens? How do you keep going, how do you manage short-term and what is the cost? These are some of the things we have heard people at CE level share in coaching sessions:

- "I'm paranoid that people would like to see me fail as the leader of this business."
- "I don't think I can keep going at this pace, without dying early, from stress."
- "I have no idea how to connect with my kids."
- "I'm (self) destructive and I don't know why."
- "I often feel like I will be found out for being a fraud."
- "I'm terrified of ending up like my father who died alone."
- "I've been using drugs and alcohol to deal with my stress, and I feel bad, but can't stop."

When we talk about these in any kind of public forum the usual response is one of relief that one is not the only angst ridden, self-doubter in the world! So you are not alone, you are not just a statistic; but the statistics are scary and you are exactly the kind of person that can take this knowledge and do something about it at an organizational or policy level. Health and safety statistics in the UK show:[1]

- The total number of cases of stress in 2011/12 was 428,000 (40 per cent) out of a total of 1,073,000 for all work-related illnesses.
- The main work activities attributed by respondents as causing their work-related stress, or making it worse, were work pressure, lack of managerial support and work-related violence and bullying.

And The Huffington Post reported in 2013:[2]

- The astounding cost of work related stress to the economy has reached a massive £6.5 billion, demonstrating how prevalent an issue stress in the workplace has become in the UK.
- There were 10.4 million days lost to stress, with the cost of "sick" days being £618 per day, meaning workplace stress totaled £6,427,200,000. With presenteeism also on the rise, meaning employees coming to work disengaged, tired, unmotivated and too stressed to work, businesses could see these costs rise if they don't take action.

The rise of chronic diseases, obesity and stress in the modern world are well known but there is also evidence of a rise in the incidence of more acute events due to stress, such as heart attacks. There is now clear knowledge that stress, even in the absence of chronic risk factors such as high blood pressure, cholesterol or smoking, leads to more heart disease and strokes. And yet it is deemed acceptable to call in sick because you have back pain or food poisoning but not because you are stressed, fatigued, depressed or anxious. Perhaps you do not think it is unacceptable or at least you do not agree that it should be – but would you do it?

If you regularly read the *Financial Times* then you know the names of all the (very few) senior people in financial services who have had the strength to do this in the last five years. So no-one would judge you harshly if you would rather tell a white lie because the chances are they would do the same, just as not so many years ago most people would not be open about their sexuality at work if they were not "straight".

There are several mechanisms by which how you feel affects your health – chemical or hormonal (arising from the endocrine system), nervous (arising from the brain, spinal cord or peripheral nervous system) or psychological (coming from your thoughts and perceptions).

Stress triggers the production of some of the most powerful chemicals that affect how your brain and body work.

Adrenalin from your adrenal glands (sitting just above your kidneys) is often correlated with increased "sympathetic" activity in the autonomic nervous system commonly recognized as the "fight, fright, flight" or short-term stress response.

Cortisol (from another part your adrenal glands but stimulated by the hypothalamic-pituitary axis in the brain – see Box 9.1) is associated with longer term or chronic stress responses.

BOX 9.1 CORTISOL

The steroid hormone cortisol is a key part of our stress response: it mobilizes energy, affects the immune system and essentially enables the brain to cope better with the stimuli that have created the stress. We know that a level of challenge can be beneficial, heightening our ability to respond to stressors such as falling in love, or such as threats to our status or survival. Chronic, sustained, unavoidable stress, which stimulates an excess of cortisol is very harmful, and can lead to cell death in the brain, and even, in extreme situations, to death. Indeed chronic stress has symptoms very similar to aging in the brain, and excessive cortisol causes significant damage to the hippocampus, crucial to the retention of memory.

Although there is much evidence that stress creates changes in the immune system, it is far from proven that these changes are anything other than adapting its responses to deal more effectively with threats to health and damage to the body, with possibly occasionally damaging side effects. There is however considerable evidence that chronic, long lasting, stress causes damaging changes in the immune system. This is greater in older people, or those whose immune systems are already weakened, but it is still a significant effect.

These chemicals affect the brain directly, but they can also affect the immune system, and the vagus nerve, which connects the digestive systems and the brain. Experience of stress, sustained over long periods of time can have a powerful and widespread negative impact on your thinking, feeling, health and hence productivity.

Highly intelligent and successful people easily grasp that what you eat, do or do not drink, how well you sleep and whether you exercise affect your *physical* health but it is more of a stretch to realize how directly these basics affect your mental wellbeing and performance at leadership level, where you are essentially being paid to use your brain.

The resultant cost of the aforementioned illnesses, let alone that of more minor ailments contributed to by stress such as colds, flu or muscular and skeletal pain, is significant and needs to be taken seriously. People from all kinds of organizations, from global corporations and the public sector to small local businesses and charities might suffer from:

- Anxiety symptoms.
- Panic attacks.
- Insomnia.
- Acid reflux.
- Even heart attacks and cancer due to work-related stress.

Some of these people are highly driven, motivated and committed individuals who take little or no time off work but have forgotten that "your job is not worth your life". This is something we find ourselves saying much more often than we would like, but the feeling of being indispensable is one that can override so many messages your body is giving you that things are not ok.

This is an issue that is critical for the health of the organization, concerning not only its leaders but coaches, consultants, human resource departments, occupational health departments and employees and is becoming an increasingly huge time commitment for the employment lawyers that collaborate with them.

Lack of productivity costs businesses even more than absenteeism. Now that businesses are recognizing the link between personal wellbeing and business success this should mean that despite on-going issues with business confidence and the need to curb costs, shareholders and other stakeholders accept that leaders invest more than ever in themselves and their people, but it is usually a case of too little too late.

Dealing with stress

Remedies are sought after the event, for example consultants – especially ones with clinical backgrounds – seem to be brought in as an urgent and reactive "fix" rather than to promote health and wellbeing proactively. Between us we have coached people who have only accepted coaching after a mild heart attack, when they are obese and nothing else has worked or they have been given official or unofficial warnings for aggressive behavior, creating a negative atmosphere for their staff and even serious alcohol related issues.

What then, can you do as a leader, to avoid the build-up of stress? First of all, having understood stress and its effects, avoid being the cause of it yourself, and create cultures, structures and environments that make it easier for others to deal with stress. Recognize that stress is inevitable in highly competitive and developed global economies, so develop your own and others' resilience through role-modeling "healthy" behaviors. This book has many examples of helpful strategies and tools you can use such as:

- Physical exercise to release adrenalin and cortisol from your sweat and redress the balance with the endorphins such as serotonin released by aerobic activity.
- Journaling to release the negative effects of survival emotions from your mind.

• Discussion with a close confidante, mentor, friend or coach.
• Ensure you are getting enough good quality sleep.
• Manage your commute to make it a time that you can recharge rather than an extra stress in your day.
• Try not to succumb to fuelling your stress with caffeine, alcohol or high sugar products – recognize cravings for these as a need to do more of some of these other activities.
• Supplement your diet with magnesium and omega oils that keep your brain healthy.
• Any form of meditation (an umbrella term like "sport" which includes football and tennis just as meditation includes mindfulness or tran-scendental), of which there are some specific examples in the section on resilience, but especially yoga nidra guided visualization if you are having trouble sleeping (readily available on YouTube).

Secondly, be aware of your own mindset, behavior and feelings. We saw in Chapter 3 that those in the most senior positions have less stress than those with less autonomy, perhaps because they are better at managing their responses. A leader who is severely stressed over a period of time is a warning bell for the health of the organization. A leader's stress is also highly contagious. They need to recognize that unrealistic optimism can be just as damaging as pessimism, and that a crucial part of their role is developing stories and strategies that reframe the future so as to reduce uncertainty for others. But this has to come authentically from within not just paid lip service (see Box 9.2).

BOX 9.2 CORTISOL CONTAGION

Much in the same way that women who live or work closely together synchronize their menstrual periods within 2 months because of the effect of sex steroid hormones that leak out into the ether from our sweat, men or women who are suppressing high levels of cortisol (you know the type that looks perfectly calm on the outside until the day they snap damaging either themselves or someone else or both) can affect the cortisol levels of people around them because their excessive cortisol will eventually pass into the skin of others and adapt their internal physiology. Whenever we talk about this people nod knowingly and want to move away from proximity to certain people that they know make them feel more stressed. The "estrogen effect" is less powerful now that many women's menstrual cycles are artificially controlled by the oral contraceptive but the reality of "cortisol leakage" is bigger and uglier than ever.

Thirdly, be sensitive to the signs of stress in others. As a leader you need to be adept at tuning into others' emotions as well as in managing your own. In times of great change and turbulence, knowing when to suggest a supportive intervention such as coaching might make all the difference to a key person.

If it is you or a line manager that adopts the coaching style to support a direct report, that process may not be governed by reason or logic but by intuition and empathy.

It does involve some reliance on gut instinct – literally what you feel in your body; that is, butterflies in your stomach, palpitations, the feedback you get from a direct report, blushing or sweating and the shared nervous laughter when discussing an awkward situation in the workplace. These physical sensations can all be used to enhance your impact as a leader, how well you are perceived and your ability to deliver improved performance. It is a "felt" process, but ultimately, the results will show on the bottom line.

Finally, choose any interventions carefully. There is evidence that cognitive behavioral stress management (CBSM) can reduce stress responses[3] so it makes sense that psychology is often the top choice to see leaders and their organizations through tough times (see Box 9.3). The mind does not reside only in the brain; it resides in the body too. The mind–brain–body relationship is fluid and mutually inclusive.

The mind–brain–body relationship is fluid and mutually inclusive.

> ### BOX 9.3   COGNITIVE BEHAVIORAL STRESS MANAGEMENT (CBSM)
>
> CBSM is a short-term therapeutic approach that focuses on how people's thoughts affect their emotions and behaviors. It attempts to influence a client's irrational thoughts while focusing directly on identifying and changing behaviors and thought patterns. CBSM provides opportunities for psychologists to provide information, build a client's emotional and interpersonal skills, and support them through the process. During CBSM a client learns recovery skills that are useful throughout their lifetime. Techniques and skills that are acquired during CBSM help facilitate sustained behavior change and have been shown to decrease the sense of isolation and depressive symptoms while improving immunity.

Once you really start to buy into two seemingly new but interconnected ideas as being totally fundamental to sustainable behavior change, the penny drops.

Pete Hamill's book *Embodied Leadership*[4] quotes neuroscientists from Antonio Damasio (*Descartes' Error*) to Candace Pert (*Molecules of Emotion*) and Raymond Tallis (*Aping Mankind*) who all conclude that the mind is embodied, not just embrained, that there is no strong distinction between the brain and the body, and that the brain is situated in a body it cannot be separated from.

And what if you could therefore get even more benefit from any kind of psychological intervention by ensuring the quality and quantity of refueling and recharging for the brain that has to enable all this psychological work? In Chapter 8 you read that the brain needs rest, nutrition, hydration and oxygenation. Remember the brain is an energy hungry organ with no storage space, which easily defaults to unconscious biases when low on any of these resources. You wouldn't go to the Olympics with a losing mindset so why go to work with an inadequately resourced body?

You wouldn't go to the Olympics with a losing mindset so why go to work with an inadequately resourced body?

With the wealth of psychological experience amongst the coaching profession and the growing interest in neuroscience, it becomes clear how much time and money might be saved by assisting those at risk of burnout and stress-related illness, whatever the issue may be but even at the best of times there is little point bringing in sophisticated coaches and consultants or conjuring up bullet proof strategies and visions if the basic needs of the brain and body are not adequately met especially in the face of:

- Major market disruptions.
- Transitions in role or location.
- Outplacement.
- Personal crisis.
- Organizational change.

In dealing with these, integration of qualities associated with certain brain areas is vital (remember the Leadership Brain Agility© tool in Chapter 8 and especially the physicality bubble), so with the right sort of development tool, executives can progress to adaptability and resilience rather than decline to burnout.[5]

It is very important to have a clear definition of burnout (see Box 9.4). In the psychiatric profession, there is concern that burnout is one of those terms, like "nervous breakdown", where people do not actually know exactly what it means so it can be used in ways which are dangerous or at best misleading.

BOX 9.4   NATE: A CASE STUDY

Nate was a CEO under a lot of pressure from his chairman and their shareholders to reach their year end targets, which it did not look like he was going to do. It felt like the sword of Damocles was hanging over him. The stakeholder relationships got so strained and he began to look so ashen that I challenged him on whether this job was actually sustainable for him. Nate said "I do think I want to see it through. I think it will be worth it." I reminded him of another damaging relationship he had pledged to stay in until it became untenable and said "if that is what you want to do I will support you 100 per cent but you have to ask yourself if it is really what you want or if you are stuck in old neural patterns of fear and survival (high cortisol) in the face of change you are not in control of (low serotonin, low dopamine and tipping point testosterone)". He looked at himself, the behaviors of the last few weeks flashed before him and he just muttered "I never would have realized ... I just could not see it any more ... but it is so clear ..."

The key outcomes of applying neuroscience to business here are:

- Being agile across brain functions is key to maximizing executive performance, leadership impact and resilience because the ability to keep up with change is the main thing that can leverage these advantages for you.
- Integrated leaders and high-performing organizations flourish through the effect of trust (oxytocin) on brain reward systems because people come to work because they love what they do and are excited by future possibilities rather than in fear of changes they cannot control.
- New knowledge about neuroplasticity means that interventions such as brain-based coaching, which combine psychological and physiological insights, make a profound difference to the bottom line of a business through the ability of leaders to flex and adapt to evolving business demands.

Resilience

"There is nothing either good or bad, but thinking makes it so."

Shakespeare, Hamlet

Why does resilience[6] matter? Reflect on your own experiences. Maintaining your stellar track record was easy when the market was on the rise, customers had plenty of cash and desire for your product, the team was fresh and full of enthusiasm, and with plenty of room for growth and promotion. You are now challenged by a situation dominated by:

- The lag in confidence after a global recession.
- A mature market with emerging innovative, cost effective, competitors.
- A mature team competing internally more than externally, having lost sight of what customers might want.

Alternatively, you have just stalled due to:

- A personal setback.
- Illness or injury.
- A death in the family or divorce.
- Threats to your status.

A major customer defection might be deflecting attention and energy from your key leadership goals and tasks. As professors Steven Southwick and Dennis Charney said in their article on resilience, "success can hinge on resilience. Setbacks are part of any endeavor, and those who react to them productively will make the most progress".[7]

Being in charge of any organization in times of change and turbulence can be a challenging and sometimes stressful and lonely position. Being able to manage the stress and not pass it on to others, while maintaining high standards of performance, requires high levels of resilience.

Remember the interesting inverse correlation between stress and leadership in Chapter 3: two studies published in 2012[8] found that people in higher positions of authority have lower levels of cortisol and lower (reported) anxiety. Leadership is thus associated with lower levels of stress (see Box 9.5). This counters the conventional wisdom that the higher up you are in a hierarchy, the more stressed you are. The researchers make it clear that the lower stress levels of leaders may either be a contributory factor to their high position, and/or a result of it.[9] They proposed that a key factor in the lower stress levels is the greater sense of control, a psychological resource known to have a stress buffering effect.

> **BOX 9.5   CONTESTED AND UNCONTESTED LEADERSHIP AND STRESS**
>
> Earlier studies by Sapolsky on non-human primates also showed that, in situations where the leadership was uncontested, higher social ranking individuals were less stressed than lower ones. Conversely, leaders whose position is threatened may not have similarly lower levels of stress than subordinates.

So the ability to manage stress, in particular, to have the resources to avoid or modulate long lasting stress, seems a most beneficial trait for leadership.

Building resilience

Although there is evidence that the baseline to which we manage stress is largely set in early childhood,[10] it is increasingly accepted that we can develop resilience, improving our responses to stress and thus our ability to manage it.

A number of studies have shown that certain personal characteristics are all conducive to managing responses to stress, such as:

- Openness to new tasks and new people.
- A greater tendency towards attachment emotions.
- Feeling in control.
- Not having high levels of anxiety.
- Being secure in one's status.
- Realistic optimism.
- The ability to adapt by reframing stressful events and situations.
- Close, supportive personal relationships.

These characteristics appear to correlate well with three or four of the so-called big five personality traits:

- Openness
- Conscientiousness
- Extroversion
- Agreeableness
- (Lack of) neuroticism.

Other, environmental factors also seem to help such as:

- A stable, safe society
- Good quality schools
- Sufficient resources.

The latter factor has recently gained popular interest especially amongst traders and portfolio managers since publication of the popular book *Scarcity – Why Having too Little Means so Much*[11] (see also Box 9.6).

BOX 9.6   SCARCITY EFFECT

Recent research has shown that scarcity of resources, such as lack of enough time for both work and family commitments, funds for both mortgage and holidays, or even the self-imposed scarcity of a January diet can focus attention on the desired resources and away from the task in hand. See Mullainathan, S and Shafir, E, 2014, "Freeing up intelligence" *Scientific American Mind*, 25: 58–63.

So what can you do to build and strengthen resilience? Studies have shown that how an individual appraises a situation and the extent to which they are subject to intrusive thoughts about it make a difference. Being able to reframe an extreme and long lasting stressful situation like losing a limb in combat or being born with a disability or degenerative disease is a telling example of resilience.

As Southwick and Charney say, "virtually anyone can become more resilient through disciplined, consistent practice". (Our old friends, focused attention and practice are necessary for rewiring the brain to increase our resilience.) More specifically these authors recommend a number of different approaches. In addition to reframing, (which essentially means actively seeking to find more positive ways of interpreting stressful events and situations), not unexpectedly, managing emotions plays a key part.

Being able to regulate emotions is a useful tool for leaders. In addition to reframing and the bullet points listed earlier about reducing stress, other techniques you could try are very connected to the aforementioned desirable personal characteristics and big five personality traits:

- Mindfulness meditation – focusing on the present or a single focus (commonly your breath) which brings about an incredible and pervasive sense of wellbeing with regular practice.
- Compassionate meditation – opening up the heart and mind towards goodwill, appreciation and equanimity to others (and yourself).
- Transcendental meditation – using a sound or mantra which you repeat for 15–20 minutes per day as a method for relaxation, stress reduction and self-development.
- Cognitive bias modification (CBM) training can help develop a more realistically optimistic outlook (see Box 9.7).

BOX 9.7 COGNITIVE BIAS MODIFICATION (CBM)

CBM is a form of cognitive behavior therapy as described in Box 9.6 on CBSM but without the need to visit a therapist. It can be done over the phone with a therapist or even by yourself on the internet using suitable technology. CBM combines evidence and theory from the cognitive model of anxiety, cognitive neuroscience and attentional models, for example, for kids with ADHD. CBM has been described as a "cognitive vaccine".

Most of these are things you can easily do yourself at home and/or at work using a guided meditation from YouTube, a smart device app, a gym membership or wearable technology such as a wristband pedometer (Jawbone UP, Nike Fuel band, Fitbit).

In Chapter 2 we talked about thermal stress or episodic fasting as ways to practice building emotional resilience away from the day job. Another recommendation is to gradually increase the stress challenges you face so that your sense of efficacy and confidence grow as you learn to deal with stress in a controlled way. Sometimes called stress inoculation, this technique is widely used in training in the military and other front line services, where, for example, virtual reality can create realistic simulations of increasingly dangerous and stressful situations, such as accidents or fires.

For many leaders this gradual practice in managing stress is the natural order of their progress into leadership. A leader's sense of confidence and efficacy grows with experience as their roles grow in responsibility and challenge. Leaders learn from mistakes as well as successes, they learn that what worked before might not solve tomorrow's problem and they learn to deal with difficult people-related issues. It used to be said that to be a good leader of a large organization, you needed to have managed a team before the age of 30, giving a lot of time for practice, for learning from mistakes and building confidence as teams get larger and management demands more complex. What we now know about neuroplasticity means you can teach an "older" dog new tricks so fear not if you are closer to 50 or 60 or even 70. Again successful change depends on sustained practice, worth remembering as yet another good reason for delegation, especially when you are trying to develop resilience in others.

Alan Rusbridger, editor of the UK's *The Guardian* newspaper, demonstrates this beautifully in his book *Play it Again*[12] and on his website alanrusbridger.com, which features interviews with three neuroscientists and brain scans before and after learning to play Chopin's *Ballade No. 1* – arguably the most complex one-movement piece ever composed, on the piano in less than one year, when he was in his mid 50s.

Building stronger supportive and trusting relationships also helps, as we know that warm relationships help release oxytocin, which suppresses the release of cortisol. One way of looking at your relationships is through the creation of a network map, with the thickness of the lines representing the strength of the relationship:

- Have you got the right kind of support around you?
- Do you have a sponsor or mentor outside the organization you can turn to?
- If you are the MD is your chairman supportive, and if not can you work together to improve that?
- Are you a key node in your subordinates' network, helping them to become more resilient?
- Do you have a handful of good, close friends, family or confidantes you can discuss your worst-case scenarios with?

Another known way of improving one's emotional states or moods is to be altruistic, to think of others and be active in contributing to a community or to "count one's blessings", regularly, perhaps once a day, remember the good things and people in your life that you are grateful for. These habits can be encouraged at work, role-modeled by leaders, mentors and sponsors, by making thanking people for their contribution an explicit part of meetings, feedback and appraisals, by encouraging company-wide volunteering for a common, relevant cause and reporting these activities in internal newsletters, blogs or websites.

Finally, remember the extent to which your mind and body are part of the same system, indeed are one system. Standing tall, "playing the role", walking the walk of a confident leader is known to boost testosterone levels and reduce cortisol. Amy J Cuddy's TED talk on the subject, "Your body language shapes who you are", emphasizes that two minutes of standing in the power pose boosts confidence (and testosterone). Conversely making oneself small, hunching, taking the pose or position of a suppliant or subordinate, reduces testosterone and increases cortisol levels.

Confident leadership

As a leader you are more likely to be followed when you manage your own responses to stress and are not only resilient yourself but supportive in developing resilience in others, appear confident and can create confidence, rather than anxiety, in others (see Chapter 11 for more on confidence in relation to gender).

The business journalist and author Jonathan Gifford created an engaging book about leadership in 2010: *History Lessons: What Business and Management Can Learn from the Great Leaders of History*.[13] He took as his chapter headings everyday straightforward experiential concepts of leadership, like "Leading from the front", "Bringing people with you" and "Creating opportunities". Each of the eight chapters give three examples of leaders whose qualities exemplify the chapter in question.

Apart from a broad and observational perspective – the first chapter, "Changing the mood", is what makes the book stand out from the general run of leadership writings. Not many management writers would use the concept of "mood". It sounds soft: more appropriate to restaurant design than leadership, perhaps. But Gifford places it first in his list of what history might teach modern management.

For the first example of changing the mood he uses Montgomery of Alamein and his speech in the desert as he took control of a demoralized Eighth Army in Egypt. For the second he takes Queen Elizabeth I, also addressing troops as the Armada threatened England. And for the third he takes Nelson Mandela's approach to reconciliation as modern South Africa started to grapple with the iniquities of the apartheid era.

"Mood" or state of confidence supposes something about the emotional state of others. The military have always known how crucial something called "morale" is. It is mood made apparent in all sorts of signs that generate resilience, especially in the face of the enemy. Underlying "moods" are the "emotions".

And modern neuroscience is beginning to get a bit of a grip on what emotions are about and why it is becoming increasingly relevant that modern leaders understand their importance and how they can manage them – in themselves as well as in others.

The US military – the Marines no less – have come at mindfulness through the idea of "resilience" – a concept that does get executive interest. In mid January 2014 *The New York Times* reported the work of psychologist Amishi Jha[14] who trains Marines in mindfulness and has found that 12 minutes of practice a day creates resilience – maintaining focus under battle conditions – that soldiers with less than 12 minutes practice a day, or none at all, do not have. That is useful to know. But first let's get some terminology straight. Science likes things to be precise and it is beginning to be possible to be more precise about things like "feelings" that have previously been rather imprecise. What, then, distinguishes "emotions", "feelings" and "mood" and where does confidence fall in? If they are going to be better understood and more deliberately managed, what exactly are they?

Emotions are the direction-giving sources of energy within the brain. They are what give meaning to events. Our five senses – touch, hearing, taste, smell and sight – and our thoughts need to have values attached to them if we are going to make sense of them. The emotions are fundamentally responsible for giving those values.

What happens is this. An event impinges on the senses or a thought (the consequence of earlier events) arises internally and sets off electrochemical signals within the brain (including gut and heart). The system needs to know two things immediately about the incoming data. Are they hostile and/or have they been noticed before?

If hostile then body systems will be mobilized within 80 milliseconds. If known, then it will be assigned to pre-existing pathways – *whatever they are* – arising from the unique experience of the individual and brain receiving the incoming data. In this way our own history shapes us all.

Although there is no final agreement about how many emotions there really are, eight seems to be as good an answer as there is at the moment. As a reminder of what was described in Chapter 1:

- One emotion deals with surprise, startle or its mild variant "wonder".
- Five deal with escape/avoidance/survival. They are fear, anger, disgust, shame and sadness. Energy from these goes inwards to looking after the person.
- Just two emotions create the enormously powerful yet oddly fragile processes of attachment – excitement/joy and trust/love, which are the great emotions of all creativity.

Feelings are the manifestations of emotions – in the widest variety of combinations – that become conscious. Feelings are signals that can be named or not, examined or unexamined, explicable or not, but crucially, we are aware of having them.

"Mood" – like "confidence" or any other widely generalized state – seems to be rather like weather. Mood is not attached specifically to objects or other stimuli. That is the province of feelings, which are specific in origin. Mood is hugely inclusive, very much attached to place, occasion or event. Similarly confidence is something that can ripple through a crowd, swell into a crescendo of voices in chorus at a great football match, or define a nation. It is a surging experience, generally, even when quietly surging, defining everything at the moment at which it happens. And it can be very persistent as well as transient and even be built into material objects. Contrast Botticelli's "Venus arising from the waves" with Vermeer's "Woman reading a letter". Mood is magically resident in the painted surface and transmits itself through time.

All these processes are largely managed in the central part of the brain called the limbic system. They are what distinguish mammals from reptiles. What distinguishes human beings from all other mammals is the capacity to attach words to the experience of emotions, feelings and mood and to both convey and trigger experience through the use of words. If you asked a colleague who the "cold fish" or the "snake" is in life or at work, most people would immediately know exactly who you mean. As a leader you really don't want to be the one people think of when asked this question.

This is what leaders need especially to know. Whether you like it or not, everything that you do as a leader by way of communication in every verbal and non-verbal means possible (body language and cortisol molecules) is transmitted from your feeling system into the feeling systems of those on the receiving end – whether it is one person or thousands.

So it becomes incumbent on leaders to understand your own emotional system, how to manage it, how you transmit meaning and how that meaning is picked up and used by those receiving it. For that is where organizational energy comes from and defines the direction it will take.

Which takes us back to Gifford's leaders. Changing the mood is only the start of a process. But all three knew instinctively that, without shifting the mood, behavior would not change. Once the mood has shifted, the possibility of a change in behavior arises, but only if the energy activated by the mood is effectively mobilized purposefully.

This is also why the future of leadership is to understand emotions, feeling and mood and to realize that performance comes from the way an individual mobilizes their energies in the service of the goals of the organization.

Summary

In this chapter we have drawn from the fields of neuroscience, psychology, medicine, history and coaching to highlight some of the issues surrounding leaders and their people in challenging times. We have looked at stress and its consequences and how as a leader you can develop your own resilience and confidence, and those of others. We have looked at some examples of leaders who were successful in the most challenging circumstances. Most of all we have looked at how being attuned and responsive to your own emotions and those of others is such an essential skill for leaders.

Understanding the links between stress, health and performance is not enough; we need to show how the links between personal benefit and organizational benefit can be proactively influenced to deliver sustainable change, to create healthy environments and enable people to learn to develop resilience, flexibility and adaptability, so that fewer remedial interventions are needed.

To have an ultimately scientific approach to leadership and management, organizations need to take into account the importance of health, well-being and physicality as well as motivation, engagement, innovation and skills to their bottom line.

Actions and reflections

- "Turn to" list – make a list of all the people in your life that you can turn to for help, comfort or reassurance should you need it. Include people you have been able to turn to in the past as well as people you could reach out to now (it may be that your parents have always been there for you but that at this age it feels like the roles are becoming reversed). Knowing that they have a safe harbor for times of need makes people feel more securely attached in the world and therefore more likely to be empathic to others and less likely to fall foul of unconscious biases. The implications of this for leadership are huge. Keep this list somewhere private you can re-visit it whenever you are feeling a little lost or "out at sea".
- Gratitude list – list ten things you are grateful for. Try to do this every day or most days of the week. It takes only a few minutes but reaps great dividends. Over time you will naturally move from material things to recognizing your internal resources such as your imagination, determination and ability to see a patch of blue sky when all seems grey. When tested by life you can re-read some of these lists or you may find that having raised awareness of these things you find it that little bit easier to draw on the necessary resources without feeling totally drained.

chapter **10**

Creating the Spark, Lighting the Fire

"(we regard) the human mind[1] rather as a fire which has to be set alight … This also we take as our ambition."

Taken from Lord Geoffrey Crowther, 1969, speech at the inauguration of the Open University

We believe that the individual human brain has immense and as yet not fully discovered potential. "Perfectly ordinary" people have achieved remarkable, extraordinary, things in their everyday life, through improving their focused attention, exercising their self control, and strengthening their will through self awareness, reflection and repeated practice. A beautiful description of this in the sports arena is Alison Mowbray's book on how she became an Olympic silver medalist rower, from a schoolgirl whose best sport was the three legged race.[2] In our view, there is nothing ordinary about people or their potential or what so many people around the world achieve. The truly extraordinary capacity of the brain to change and adapt so as to take in and create new ideas, its relationship with the body and ability to affect its physical manifestations, such as blood pressure or hormone levels, (and indeed the body's ability to change the brain, for example, enhancing mood through exercise or confidence though posture), are only just being experimentally explored.

In our work with individuals and groups in business, government, academia and charities we have come across numerous examples of people whose achievements exceeded their own and others' expectations to the benefit of their organizations and wider society. We have found that high achievers have chosen different paths to success and each of their stories is unique. Again and again we have found that it is not necessarily the brightest people with the highest IQ that have created most value for their organizations and their societies, but those with persistence, resilience, tolerance of failure and risk and above all self-management and will power – all characteristics of the new models of leadership we have described in this book. We have worked with people whose background contains trauma and tragedy, yet who have turned those into a drive to overcome daily challenges and succeed.

We have mentioned before the remarkable extent to which the early interactions with other people in the first few months and years of life shape the brain. That shaping continues, with perhaps less intensity but still with great effect, throughout life.[3] Interactions with the environment, especially relationships with other people, directly shape the development of the brain's structure and function. As Dan Siegel says in his seminal book *The Developing Mind*, "Patterns of relationships and emotional communication directly affect the development of the brain".[4] Some individuals can find inspiration for themselves, through observing remote role models or by setting challenging goals, for example. For others, inspiration comes from parents, teachers and leaders who directly influence them.

The greatest leaders seem to be capable of influencing people across cultures and geographical and time boundaries. In the West we still resonate to Lincoln's Gettysburg Address. Around the world Nelson Mandela, the (current) Dalai Lama and Mahatma Ghandi are often cited as the greatest modern leaders. The names of Henri Dunant and Gustave Moynier are much less well known, yet the organization they founded in the mid nineteenth century, the Red Cross, is still active and evolving today. Isaac Newton and Albert Einstein changed not only our understanding of our world, but *how to think* about our understanding of it. And that might also be said of some philosophers and religious leaders too.

One assessment of greatness appears to be due to the ability to *inspire*, to elicit powerful emotions around disruptive concepts and paradigm shifts, well beyond leaders' own lifetimes. Another might be creating powerful concepts or value-based institutions that continue to exist through *stimulating innovation* by others.

This chapter is concerned with those two aspects of leadership: firstly how to inspire, to use relationships to create the conditions in which people can fulfill their potential for their own and others' benefit, and secondly how to stimulate and nurture innovation. We have touched on some aspects of this in other chapters, but here we look more closely at some of the processes that might be involved.

Inspiration

Fourteen years ago Daniel Goleman published an article in the *Harvard Business Review* that raised the bar in the field of Leadership Studies. In "Leadership that gets results"[5] he identified six distinctive styles of leadership and examined their impact on the climate of the organization and on the people who were being led. Goleman's research indicated that the authoritative style was the most effective. Authoritative leaders, he said, were:

- Visionary.
- Motivational.
- Very clear on purpose and standards.
- Those who, having set the vision, allowed staff the freedom to get there in their own way, to innovate.[6]

Inspirational leaders are generally held to share several of the characteristics of Goleman's authoritative style, notably the ability to create and communicate a motivational vision with great clarity, and the creation of environments which empower individuals to do their own thinking and planning.

In many articles from the study of management, transformational and inspirational leadership belong to the same construct and charisma is often mentioned as part of the same mix. Management research has found that inspirational leadership is positively correlated with improved individual, group and organizational performance and that the ability to articulate a vision is crucial to inspiration.[7] There is however almost no scientific evidence as to whether and how these characteristics might be represented at the level of the brain, and indeed whether they are stable or not. We can *feel* whether someone is inspirational and charismatic, we can measure an organization's increased profits under a transformational leader, but we cannot always say why or how they achieve the results that they do.

How does it work?

We do however have some insights from neuroscience that begin to give us some ideas as to how such leaders might achieve their effects on others. Inspiration can happen at a distance, both temporal and physical, through captured or reported words and actions and through other people's reactions. It can also happen through direct contact. Neuroscience has helped us to understand the power of direct interactive relationships – what happens between brains – to shape and reinforce neuronal connections. We also understand more about the influence of our wider environment, the positive rewards of attachment emotions when we feel we belong, and the negative effects of fear, disgust and shame when we are rejected or we fear rejection. Other people's reactions to inspirational leaders, through affiliation with their causes, through repetition of their words and key phrases may make us want to belong to, or reject, a particular group of adherents.

This ability to engage with others at the level of emotions, that "thing" that happens between brains that is called "affective interaction" is the critical component of inspiration (see Box 10.1 for an example). The expression of emotion through emotional language, physical involuntary effects (such as blushing, pupil widening and mirroring) and voluntary behaviors, images and stories provoke strong emotions in others which in turn elicit motivational energy, a powerful desire to take action (mental or physical) of some kind.[8] A leader's emotional state or mood if strongly felt, whether consciously or below the level of consciousness, is likely to be contagious (see Chapter 9 for why that is so). If inspiration is indeed (as the online Oxford Dictionaries say) "The process of being mentally stimulated to do or feel something, especially to do something creative" then the emotions are crucially implicated. Attachment emotions are also likely to act as reciprocal stimuli (possibly through mirror neurons)[9] and may explain some of the effect of charismatic leaders. Perhaps charismatic leaders both feel and elicit powerful attachment emotions for their cause, their people, their wider community. This creates an emotional resonance around the objects of their attachments. Charisma can go sour when the object of the attention and attachment becomes the leader themselves, rather than something of benefit to the wider group or community. It is also worth remembering, that charisma, (perhaps like other forms of attachment) doesn't always "work" with everyone! Politicians are obvious examples of this.[10]

BOX 10.1   ANDY: A CASE STUDY

Andy, a CEO of a middle sized company, was neither tall nor good looking and he had a squeaky voice, but his eloquence was famous (he used to write and rewrite and practice his speeches a lot) and his vision was lofty. Andy's ability to focus absolutely on whatever person was in front of him at the time and to show his genuine interest in them and that he cared about their contribution made him a magnet for customers and staff alike. Andy had charisma in spades. He was highly thought of by stakeholders and was highly sought after for non-exec roles. He became well known in his field and his next job was head of a large multinational.

There is also some evidence that the ability to convey a
compelling vision, that has meaning and relevance for
a social group, is correlated with multiple strong
interconnections (coherence) in the right frontal
cortex[11]. That could be an indicator both of a
greater ability to empathize but also of the
ability to conceptualize and convey the
"bigger picture", a vision at a greater level of
abstraction. Perhaps it is easier to inspire, to get
more people to resonate with, a vision of less detail
than one with more?

Perhaps it is easier to inspire, to get more people to resonate with, a vision of less detail than one with more?

Good communication skills, verbal and physical, are essential to achieving
results through others (we explored that in Chapter 5). It is not just the
level of arousal created by the emotion – the intensity with which it is
felt and conveyed by the leader – that gives its object importance, but
crucially the extent to which the inspirational leader is capable of relating their own emotion to what matters to others. That requires not just
empathy, but an intellectual understanding of others' circumstances and
a very wide repertoire of the "listening" parts of communications skills. In
addition to conveying – and receiving – emotion, the inspirational leader's
communication skills may include a flexible range:

- Both precise and metaphorical language.
- Appreciation of visual imagery.
- The use of sensory words that enable listeners' and readers' brains to
  mirror the experience.
- An understanding of the language of numbers.
- A sensitivity to how others communicate in different ways.[12]

There is a considerable body of evidence from educationalists that people
learn different things in very different ways; some more easily through
the written word, others through listening, still others through numbers
or images and others again through doing, whether by imitation or not. It
is likely that an inspirational leader needs to find many ways of conveying

a vision for the future that has meaning and importance for very different people. Clarity, transparency and integrity, as we mentioned before, are also important components of communication, in order to elicit belief and avoid being second-guessed.

Trust (and therefore oxytocin) and self-management are likely to be key components of successful relationships, whether in business or in personal life. This again we explored in detail in a number of previous chapters. A leader who conveys no or little interest in others is unlikely to be trusted and perceived as inspirational or charismatic for long.[13] A leader who is charismatic but proves ineffective or uncontrolled is unlikely to remain influential (cults may be the exception here, as they are often ruled in the end by fear rather than attachment). Leaders who are practiced at self-management are more trusted and finding ways of helping others understand and practice self management is a way of reinforcing reciprocal trust. Appropriate delegation might seem a trite topic. It has been so overworked in management studies. But seen as a way of enabling others to learn to manage themselves with appropriate support, it is more akin to subsidiarity, a profound principle of Catholic social policy. It assumes "the autonomy and dignity of the human individual". A leader who trusts the ability of people to take decisions appropriate to their position is modeling the behavior they expect from others. A leader who takes decisions and responsibilities belonging to others is undermining their authority, credibility and confidence and inviting mistrust and bad performance.

Enabling lasting effects

If inspirational leadership indeed leads to improved performance, the question arises of how that might be maintained over time. Does an inspirational leader need constantly to inspire, to create new and ever bigger and better visions, and does that work or lead to "vision fatigue"? In our experience, inspirational leaders who inspire and then create environments in which people can develop intrinsic motivation and find rewards in the work itself are more effective. The experience of pleasure, fulfillment, even happiness, that comes as an intrinsic result of working optimally, reinforces inspiration by releasing the energy needed to persist and achieve beyond your own expectations. We have spoken of flow already (see also Box 10.2), but the question we address here is not how an inspirational leader, working flat out on a transformational business plan to achieve their vision, experiences flow themselves – but how they enable others also to experience flow in playing their part to achieve that vision.

BOX 10.2 FLOW

We assume that most if not all our readers have at some point in their lives, experienced what Mihaly Csikszentmihalyi calls Flow, a state of optimal experience, when attention is freely – and fully – focused on pursuing one's goals. Almost impossible to describe, it feels effortless, like floating or flowing, although the brain and body are deeply engaged in action, and because it can cause a person to lose their sense of self in the process, it is, most often, recognized retrospectively. Creative people of all kinds, from artists through musicians to scientists, leaders and writers experience flow in the process of creation.

The conditions for flow, according to Csikszentmihalyi[14] are that:

- The tasks people engage in must be just beyond their current reach – but not their potential, so that discovery, creativity, innovation and personal growth might be elicited.
- The tasks must have clear goals, which can be pursued within a system where there are rules which enable timely, appropriate, feedback on progress, whether from others or preferably oneself.
- The individual must be capable of focusing attention (certain conditions such as acute anxiety might prevent attention being focused).
- There must be an element of freedom in the choice of the activity.
- There must be an absence of threats which distract attention and elicit avoidance emotions and behaviors.

Looking at these conditions carefully, you can see that it is possible for leaders to create environments in which they are met more often than not. It might not be possible in a crisis, such as a turnaround to avoid bankruptcy, when choice has to make way for direct orders, but otherwise, these conditions can be built into a working environment. Placing people at the right levels in organizations so that they are stretched and supported in their growth is difficult, but largely, albeit imperfectly, achievable.[15] Managers and leaders who adopt a coaching style and actively encourage and support learning and independence are contributing significantly to individuals' ability to find inspiration and flow in their work. We have spoken before about the need for clarity in goal setting and allowing considerable autonomy in how people achieve common goals. Creating systems in which feedback is swift, appropriate and relevant is harder, and depends on the nature of the work, but is always helped by making goals and values explicit and clear.

This is also where a strong culture can be helpful. If I understand and accept (internalize) what is "good" and "bad" behavior in my organization, because the culture makes those absolutely clear, I can monitor my own work to a great extent.[16] Setting goals and allowing people to find their own way to achieving them, within clearly defined boundaries, is a great way of not only allowing for choice, but also innovation. A small software company that followed that approach in meeting the customer's goals managed to cut costs and grow their business exponentially within a couple of years. Their bright people found innovative solutions in every part of the business, including sourcing some kit that was both lower cost and more robust from the high street, rather than conventional trade suppliers.

Avoiding putting people who cannot handle stress in stressful roles is a no brainer. Taking threats and fear out of the working environment is more easily done when markets are growing and competition is low, but harder in volatile environments when whole industries are threatened by global competition and disruptive, incredibly fast growing new technologies. As we have already said, this is where leaders need to find a way of "managing the future". Creating a strategy which acknowledges and addresses reality, but doesn't overstate the negative environmental aspects, setting short-, medium- and long-term targets, remaining realistically positive and confident, demonstrated by words, actions, stance and mood, all help create a buffer to fear.

A whole greater than the sum of its parts?

Finally, there are certain experiences which enable people to feel profoundly part of a whole which is greater than the sum of its parts, to take part in something with others which takes them outside and beyond themselves and helps them grow and develop, which gives them a sense of value, and to feel an inner harmony and deep connectedness. Some see this as one of the great benefits offered by organized religions, others recognize these experiences as part of spirituality, of the essence of what it means to be human, yet others see them as the by-products of evolution, where they might support group and community cooperation and cohesion.

Communal rites, dancing and choral singing can evoke similar feelings. The interconnectedness of brain and body, emphasized in the physicality bubble of Chapter 8, is a key part of the explanation. One of us remembers a training program where all participants were given drumsticks and taught to drum in rhythm, starting with just one person and building into an exhilarating, chest-vibrating, whole of dozens "marching to the same tune".[17] It served as a great example of the power of a common vision and coherence.[18]

Science has not yet clarified how these effects might work. It is however worth bearing in mind that although some communal activities indeed arouse strong emotions which promote affiliation and bonding between people, these are best carefully targeted and not overused. They can be great for new teams and organizations, or to create a sense of belonging to one group. Our experience is that, in the corporate context at least, unless these are underpinned by fair systems which treat people equitably and unless leaders and managers implement transparently fair behavior, the effects are rarely lasting, and might even have adverse consequences by raising expectations which are then not met.

In addition, psychologists have identified a tension in human beings between a need to feel individual, a unique person, and simultaneously a valued member of a community. Culture plays a role, with Eastern civilizations tending more to the communal and Western towards the individual. Interestingly economists in the US also found a strong positive correlation between a country's individualism and its measures of innovation.[19] Inspirational leaders who seek to create a conforming group of followers around them may need to be reminded that a balanced approach might better serve to grow both their people, and their organizations. In order to maintain motivation, organizations need a systems approach which enables people to identify with common goals, but also to understand clearly how their own individual talents, skills, knowledge and work contribute to their achievement and have appropriate feedback on their progress towards them (Box 10.3). They need opportunities to work in teams and also to shine as individuals.

BOX 10.3 CUI BONO?

Daniel Goleman, in an April 2014 post on Linked-In, quoted the Dalai Lama at an MIT conference on global systems. "He suggested that when we are making decisions or considering courses of action, we should ask ourselves: Who benefits? Is it just ourselves, or a group? Just one group, or everyone? And just for the present, or also for the future?"

Innovation

Inspiration is wonderful but it is not enough. When we speak about being inspired ourselves it is usually a precursor to action involving major change and achievement in our lives. It is not enough for a leader to have new, inspirational, transformational ideas and ways of thinking and acting, those who work with and for that leader need to be inspired in turn to create new ideas, new ways of thinking and working that will ensure the sustainability of the transformation.

For individuals, organizations and nations to fulfill their potential and thrive, inspiration must lead to action. For leaders to create sustainable success a significant part of that action needs to contribute to innovation. This is one of the greatest leadership challenges: how to ensure that transformation does not stagnate, that it does not lead to a continuation of the same old thinking leading to same old behaviors leading to the same products resulting in not the same but declining profits. Innovation drives economic growth and prosperity. New ideas must emerge and be made real so that they serve society and organizational and systemic barriers to their success must be reduced. Innovation must be nurtured not just for new things but for improved, more enabling, social structures, institutions, processes and services.

We have taken a definition of innovation, derived from an unpublished paper by John Chisholm,[20] that it is the creation of something new which makes a positive difference to society, or to a part of society.

Our definition assumes that creativity is part of innovation, but that innovation has the social purpose.[21] Not everyone is capable of the same levels of creativity, but most people have experienced a moment of discovery.

Processes of innovation

Innovation starts with discovery, the creation of a new idea or concept. Neuroscience has given us some insights into the creation of new ideas and the processes and conditions that can turn them into innovations. A new idea – or concept – is a new pattern of wiring between neurons in the brain, the creation of a new network. These are sometimes called maps or schemata. That new pattern might come from new knowledge being adapted into existing patterns which are then changed, or by joining a number of existing ones to create something new.

We have already spoken about the role of the potentiator emotions, surprise and startle, in creating optimum conditions for change, and they are indeed often implicated in discovery. Leaders create unexpected changes in an organizational environment (whether in structure, process or goals) in order to achieve a startle effect which can elicit new ideas. New concepts often arise from interaction with other people whose experiences and knowledge are very – sometimes surprisingly – different. In a report by Credit Suisse on diversity published in August 2012,[22] a strong correlation (but not causation) was found between companies with diverse boards and senior management and better performance in bottom line results and innovation. Some of the reasons why that might be are outlined in Chapter 11.

It is also likely that existing brain connections need to be changed significantly (and across a wider number of brain areas than are usually engaged in dealing with particular types of knowledge and problems) in order to assimilate very different new concepts which challenge long held assumptions, and a diverse group of people is more likely to generate such challenges. One of the most innovative organizations in the US, DARPA, has a number of rules to ensure that people are constantly challenged. Projects are chosen by competition, no one is allowed to stay working in DARPA for more than five years, no matter how successful, and problems are opened up as competitions or challenges to engage the widest possible community outside the organization.

We have spoken of the brain as being action and goal driven and also mentioned the extent to which it operates by using past experience to "predict", to make assumptions about what is going to happen next, whether that is about the next step down a staircase or how the markets will move. Solving a hard problem is a process which creates the conditions for new ideas. Existing patterns are tested against the problem and if they fail to predict or provide the next step in a solution the brain experiences some dissonance. Avoiding that discomfort can provoke the brain to find new ways of reaching the desired goal motivated again by the emotional "values gauge". Indeed some scientists have found that for some people stress and adversity can be the springboards for creative growth.[23] As in flow, putting people in challenging situations which are just outside their current capacity but most likely within their potential helps them to exercise this ability to seek new patterns for solving hard problems.

The power of persistence

This is also where a tolerance of risk and failure are helpful. Alison Mowbray in her quest for an Olympic medal embodied a quote often attributed to Winston Churchill: "success is the ability to move from failure to failure without losing enthusiasm".

Praising and rewarding persistence and hard work for young children is now being recommended as a way of motivating them to work for their success, instead of praising anything they do as good. Recognizing that failure is a step towards learning what it takes to succeed is often used to compare the extraordinary innovation culture of the US in places such as Silicon Valley and the Boston corridor, with that of the UK and other countries in the EU. Leaders who tolerate failure and accept a reasonable level of risk in organizations as an inevitable part of testing out new concepts, indeed of innovation, can help motivate people to try and try again. Leaders need also to recognize that some people need more support than others to deal with failure and develop resilience. Gender and culture may also have some effect; for example, women often have less confidence and have less tolerance of risk in certain conditions, and there are some cultures where shame is a very strong motivator and public knowledge of failure or error is seen as a significant threat (see further Chapter 11).

Expertise

In order to generate new ideas that have a good chance of delivering value to society the people involved need to have expertise in the relevant domain, an openness to new experience, flexibility of thinking, have appropriate goals and encounter challenges which are stretching.

Being in touch with a network of people working in similar or contingent fields is generally held to be useful: clusters are good examples of this. Working at the interstices of domains of knowledge can also create dissonance, and being engaged and interested in a wider range of activities than just one's own domain is also often a mark of exceptionally creative people.[24] Leaders can make sure they involve a diverse range of people in key teams. They can encourage learning from peers outside the organization and support exchanges through conferences, online networks and communities of practice. They can actively campaign against the "not invented here" attitude that many market leaders acquire when the environment is stable. They can remind staff of the value that solving problems will bring to others, to their customers and to society in order to inspire and motivate persistence in solving problems, such as creating something that will help customers even more than a current service.

AHA!

Sometimes simply working on a problem, even with great skill and expertise, is not enough. A familiar way of generating new concepts, ideas or breakthroughs is the strategy of stopping work and doing something different, such as a walk in the woods, which serves to take attention away from the conscious efforts and allows more energy for activity under our conscious awareness, with much greater capacity and access to a greater number of stored patterns or memories in different parts of the brain. The moment of insight that often comes as a result is well known and familiar – the "aha!" moment.

Scientists using EEG saw different types of activity in the brains of those who struggled to find a solution, who had come to an impasse, from those who solved problems suddenly and apparently intuitively. The impasse was correlated with gamma waves in the right parietal occipital regions, indicating strongly focused attention and theta waves, suggesting memory related activity. Moments of insight were preceded by increased activity in the right prefrontal cortex, with strong alpha waves indicating that attention had been relaxed.[25]

It appears that the relaxation of attention enabled the brain to create a new pattern by restructuring of existing and/or new ones. Another study looked at possible neurobiological indicators and found that low levels of arousal, (and possibly low noradrenalin) were correlated to "creative innovation".[26] A more recent study, using transcranial direct current stimulation demonstrated that suppressing activity in the left prefrontal cortex made it easier to think of unusual uses for tools and common objects such as tissues![27] As Alison Gopnik memorably phrased it in her online *Wall Street Journal* article headline, "For Innovation, Dodge the Prefrontal Police".[28]

A number of steps are now understood to be part of the process of discovery. In her article "The AHA! moment" Nessa Victoria Bryce listed five:[29]

- Explore
- Focus
- Incubate
- Insight
- Follow-through.

Other researchers have different accounts, but they roughly all follow the same pattern:

- Acquisition of knowledge.
- Focusing attention on a relevant issue.
- Relaxing attention through a variety of means.
- The aha! moment.
- Working hard to turn that insight into a practical solution.

Leaders need to understand these processes and hence see the value in exchanges "over the water cooler", spaces in which people can interact or sit quietly away from their desks, and in flexible working that allows for taking a walk or going to the gym, just when the pressure to solve a problem is greatest. Relieving excessive stress allows emotions on the attachment end of the spectrum to emerge and thus releases creative energies into generating new ideas.

A leader who creates a spark and lights the fire of inspiration and innovation needs to be capable of working at a number of levels which interact in complex patterns. Allowing for creating great motivation, releasing energy and the generation of new ideas is not enough. The goals set must involve the application of these ideas towards a common purpose. Although original ideas are generated by individuals it takes groups or teams, sometimes many teams of varied disciplines and skills over many years, to put them into action and rigorous processes need to be in place to ensure that the ideas and their outcomes are rigorously tested. Finding appropriate ways to feedback to teams and reward group efforts is often neglected but is as crucial in the innovation process.

Summary

What then does success look like for an inspirational leader? The organization *feels* uplifting, fresh, full of promise (see Box 10.4).

BOX 10.4 A WALK IN THE WOODS

In the words of Sumantra Ghosal, a famous professor of management at INSEAD, the difference between a creative, vibrant organizational context and one in which innovation and ideas are stifled is like the difference between a walk in the woods of Fontainebleau in the spring and a summer afternoon in downtown Calcutta. He used to say he could always tell within the first few minutes of walking into the reception area which of these two paradigms best matched the company.

> ## BOX 10.5   CHRIS: A CASE STUDY
>
> Chris, a very experienced senior investment banker, kind and wise and with a stellar track record, also said he could *feel* the difference between a good or bad potential investment opportunity within minutes of walking in the door. These intuitions, as we now know, when based on experience and tested with more analytical thinking, can be good indicators as they take account of a much larger range of parameters than working memory alone can handle.

Inspiration and creative innovation depend on the energies stimulated by emotions, so leaders need to keep asking themselves – and others – how the organization makes them feel (see Box 10.5). After inspiring individuals to be motivated and innovatory, leaders need to find ways of enabling them to act sustainably, to behave in ways that they might not have predicted, to take control of their work and environment in ways which may even be threatening to a centralized leadership. And that is the hardest challenge of all – finding and making clear the boundaries between rules and freedoms, between what works for the individuals, the teams and the organization, what will enable people to continue to behave in ways which invigorate the organization as a whole.

Having taught people to fly, if they are stifled, not allowed to exercise their potential, if they are not acknowledged and rewarded for the value they bring, if they are not heard when they propose changes or allowed to make significant changes within their own authority, if, in other words, they are not given an environment in which they too can exercise leadership, they will leave and take their wonderful talents and ideas with them.

Actions and reflections

• Practice focusing your attention on whoever you are engaging with. Try to understand as much as you can about them and what motivates or demotivates them about their work.

- Develop your passion about what you do in your organization into a short "story" which you can tell in different ways in under a minute.
- Ask yourself how you feel when you go to work in the morning. Reflect on your own feelings and try to understand why you feel as you do.
- Listen for words related to feelings when hearing from close colleagues and other staff. What are they telling you and why?
- Examine the structures and processes in your organization. To what extent do they support people in working autonomously and also across departments and disciplines? Do they support risk tolerance and learning from mistakes?
- Are people appropriately challenged and are there adequate resources to meet those challenges? Are feedback and rewards systems swift, transparent and fair?

chapter 11

Difference, Diversity and Gender

"…. the only way in which a human being can make some approach to knowing the whole of a subject, is by hearing what can be said about it by persons of every variety of opinion, and studying all modes in which it can be looked at by every character of mind. No wise man ever acquired his wisdom in any mode but this; nor is it in the nature of human intellect to become wise in any other manner."

John Stuart Mill, On Liberty

A growing body of research links economic performance to diversity. There is now considerable evidence from the US and Europe that having a gender-diverse board is strongly correlated[1] with bottom line success. A research report by Credit Suisse, after testing the performance of 2,360 companies globally, concluded that "it would on average have been better to have invested in corporates with women on their management boards than in those without".[2]

A recent study, looking at 7,600 companies in London between 2005 and 2007, found a small but significant "diversity bonus" for all types of London firms. Diverse management was linked to more product innovation, a diverse workforce was better at reaching diverse markets and there were positive links between a migrant population and entrepreneurship.[3]

A study in the US, surveying 1,800 individuals as well as looking at 40 case studies, also showed significant benefits for innovation and market growth. The researchers found that these were correlated with a *combination* of differences that are inherent (those that one is born with) and also those acquired through experience.[4] Although recently the emphasis has been on gender diversity – about which more later – evidence for the benefits of wider social diversity (gender, color, socioeconomic, age, nationality, disability) has been around for some time.[5] In Chapter 5 we saw how individual differences, in terms of how each brain creates its own world, can be challenging in communication. In this chapter we will see the other side of that coin. One of the most powerful benefits of a diverse workforce and inclusive and diverse leadership appears to be increased innovation and better flow from ideas to market. A number of reasons have been put forward as to why diversity should be so useful, notably that it improves decision making. Can neuroscience help us understand what difference and diversity mean, how they might play out between men and women and why that might be valuable for organizations?

Plasticity and epigenetics: the engines of difference

The evidence for brain plasticity even into old age (see Chapters 2 and 9), added to our emerging knowledge of epigenetics, the science of environmental changes to the "behavior" or expression of genes, means we must change the language around nature versus nurture, genetic code versus environment. As ever, the more we know, the more we see the complex intimacy of the interrelationships between the two. We have already discussed, throughout this book, some of the ways in which our environment, primarily relationships with other people, as well as our own decisions and actions, shape our brain. We are now seeing that our genetic code is not just an immutable blueprint, or hardwired system, but a working plan adaptable, or vulnerable, to changing internal and external circumstances.

In the womb, the different experiences and environments are already beginning to shape our brains, our bodies and who we are as people, into entirely unique entities. Identical twins with an identical genetic code are still born with differences and acquire even more of them throughout life. Although transgenerational transmission of genetic changes is much rarer, it appears that, in some circumstances, the lives lived by our parents and grandparents shape some of our attributes by contributing to the degree to which some of our genes can be switched on or off, just as ours will contribute to those of our children and grandchildren.

During the Second World War, in the winter of 1944–5, the west of Holland experienced a period of extreme food shortage, which became known as the Hunger Winter. Because the war created what were, in effect, forced, horrible, experimental conditions for a very large number of people, many researchers have been able to follow the effects.

Researchers from Leiden University Medical Center and Columbia University in the US published a paper in 2008 in the *Proceedings of the National Academy of Sciences*, showing how the near starvation conditions of pregnant mothers caused changes in how genes in their babies would be expressed later in life, with observable effects up to 60 years later.[6]

For example, when babies were born to mothers who were starved in the first three months of pregnancy, but had access to better food in the later months, they were born with normal weights but had a tendency to obesity in later life, and their children in turn were more likely to be heavier than average at birth.[7] The epigenetic transmission from generation to generation was not completely stable and thus could not provide accurate predictions at individual level, but over a large population it was possible to see predictable results.

So our genomes, our physical, social and cultural environments, as well as our thoughts, actions, habitual behaviors AND heritable genetic changes, contribute to shaping who we are: our bodies, identities, our non-conscious and conscious assumptions, our perspectives and attitudes, the frame to our world view, the breadth and depth of our knowledge and expertise, what others see as our character and nature and what we experience as our self. Such is the ability of the brain to change itself or be sculpted by every encounter, that your physical brain will be different by the time you finish reading this.

The diversity bonus

In Chapter 6 we saw that biases are so much a part of the way the brain normally operates that they are very difficult to counter. One of the most important ways leaders have to protect against bias and fallacious thinking, not only in themselves but also in their teams and organizations, is the introduction of diverse and challenging thinking and experiences in decision making, planning and teamwork. Diverse people bring not only diverse views but different sets of knowledge and ignorance too. How often has a new recruit asked the question that no-one else dared to ask and set a team on a different path? Or someone who is an "outsider" has asked to see the evidence, or has been able to provide comparative market data from a different field. Diversity comes from life experiences as well as culture, race and gender. A challenging personality can also bring valuable skepticism or provoke new thinking. The surprise/startle effect of hearing from someone with an entirely different world view can motivate a broader search for relevant information and stimulate creativity, so avoiding stereotypical thinking or the availability bias – only seeing what is immediately in front of you.

A change in organizational structure in an IT services company which brought closer together sales and marketing and software development not only reduced project completion times but resulted in fewer subsequent call-outs. After the first shocks of trying to understand each other's language and attitudes everyone felt they had a better grasp of how to improve usability for the clients.

A 300-year-old charitable organization was facing a future when its charitable purpose was no longer viable. The board recognized it needed to change, but with members who shared a lot of experience, no fixed terms of office and whose average age was over 65, no change had been agreed over a two year period. A new director, coming from another sector, recruited a number of new trustees – some much younger, some from different fields – and enabled the board to have much more robust discussions and agree a new, bold, strategy within months.

Being faced with the unexpected and unpredictable might cause the brain to experience a certain amount of discomfort – sometimes called dissonance. If the environment is one in which exploration and mistakes are encouraged, rather than one where they might come with fear of punishment, discomfort might provoke curiosity, might be a cause for focusing attention and hence energy on understanding the cause and avoiding it in future – thus perhaps encouraging more openness and greater propensity to try new ideas.

We have also seen how creativity and innovation flourish in the interstices between different fields and even businesses. Clusters of businesses in fields which can feed off each other have developed close to universities and are now seen as a model for innovation. Leaders bring multidisciplinary teams together to spark new ideas and innovation.[8] In the UK the government funded Research Councils are now trying to encourage cross-disciplinary work. Understanding another expert's perspective, from a different field, is a challenge to be overcome, demanding a focus, effort and energy that, in some people, might also result in creativity (see Box 11.1). Many of you will recognize this scenario, a diverse team arguing loudly and passionately before creating a common understanding, if not always a commonly agreed plan!

BOX 11.1   CREATIVITY FROM ADVERSITY

Challenge, adversity and even trauma appear to provoke creativity in some people, especially those with the "openness to experience" personality trait and a high need for individuality. One explanation offered is that this kind of experience shakes up previous beliefs and opens thinking to new ways. Kaufman, S B, 2014, "From contretemps to creativity", in Erb, H-P and Gebert, S, "Who am I?", *Scientific American Mind*, March-April.

This fits well with the surprise/startle emotion being a potentiator, enabling brain change.

Every individual will have a different perspective, but perhaps, in some cases, not different enough to avoid some of the biases we have described. It might be easier to align and conform if you value being part of the "same tribe",[9] also if you share a large proportion of experience and context: your environment, culture and assumptions. For example, people who have worked in the same company all their working lives, always lived in the same town, or those who have very similar educations in some elite institutions that draw candidates from similar backgrounds might be more susceptible to conformity of thinking.

People with different expertise, experiences, skills, from different cultures, backgrounds and types of education working together towards common goals, but with sufficient freedom to find their own way to those goals, might have a better chance to improve the quality of organizational decision making and be more likely to be creative.

A brain of two halves: gender and difference

Looking rather like a walnut, the brain is divided into two halves by a midline, central fissure extending from the back to the front of the brain. What the two halves are for, and why evolution has created such a division, has intrigued neuroscientists for at least the past 200 years. Now some tentative answers are beginning to appear. These are far from clear cut so we have taken a range of perspectives to give you some idea of the complexities and nuances involved in looking at how structure may play out in capacities and behaviors.

In *Why Humans Like to Cry: Tragedy, Evolution and the Brain*,[10] Michael Trimble simplifies matters by saying that the left side of the brain is for doing things that are pointing and propositional: the right side is concerned with urging and yearning. Another way of saying that would be that the left brain stores and uses what is known: the right brain is all the time on the look-out for what is new and engaging. From the right brain, once something that was new becomes familiar through use, it gets passed across into the left brain as something that is known, even "routinized" and which requires less conscious effort to use.

The two halves – hemispheres – are connected by a bridge of nerve fibers that together are called the *corpus callosum*. Women's brains are rather better endowed than men's in this area of the brain, with up to four times as many fibers in the corpus callosum. In shifting information between the two halves the female corpus callosum has been likened to a well-maintained motorway with excellent traffic flow, while the male system can sometimes be like an overgrown weedy country lane. Things move with much more difficulty and much more slowly.

The right brain deals with emotional information much more than the left brain, which likes facts. Sometimes the left brain is referred to as "the male brain" and the right brain as "the female brain" but it is a misleading over-simplification to describe them so. It is still not completely clear how the structural differences in male and female brains affect their function, but it is most likely through the way that men and women process information, use energy and manage relationships. Men's brains are about 10 per cent bigger and contain about 4 per cent more cells, but women's brains contain more neurons and more cellular connections, so they can be seen as more compact and efficient. In terms of performance, the largest difference is in visuo-spatial rotation (more women than men prefer to turn maps around rather than read them upside down), and any other differences are minor.

The other major structural difference is the size of the limbic system – this is larger in the female brain, increasing women's ability to connect and bond with others. Some scientists using MRI have found that the prefrontal cortex is also larger.[11] Most recently, in 2013, scientists from the University of Pennsylvania in the US reported finding significant differences in the way men and women's brains tend to build their connections, using diffusion tensor imaging (DTI).[12] Whereas women's brains had many more connections *between* hemispheres, men's brains had more connections *within* hemispheres. Men however had more connections between the right and left halves of the cerebellum. These studies might provide support for previous research in gender based differences in behavior, fit

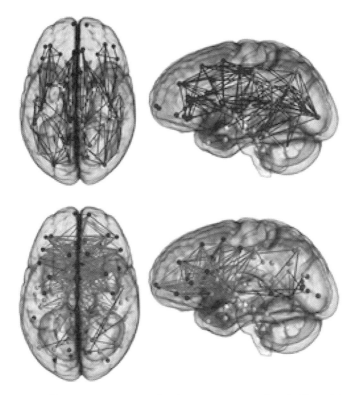

FIGURE 11.1 / Differential wiring of male (upper) versus female (lower) brains

Source: Verma, R et al, 2014, "Sex differences in the structural connectome of the human brain", *Proceedings of the National Academy of Sciences*, 111(2): 823–8 (reproduced with permission).

well with the earlier findings about women's larger corpus callosum, and begin to show possible explanations for men's superior coordination in movement, and women's superiority in articulating their own emotions and understanding others'.

Two halves make a whole?

A great synthesizing of modern knowledge about the two halves of the brain has been accomplished by Iain McGilchrist, literary scholar, neuropsychiatrist and fellow of All Souls, Oxford.[13] In *The Master and his Emissary:*

The Divided Brain and the Making of the Western World, McGilchrist starts from an understanding that the brain is the place where "mind meets matter".[14] The two halves of the brain, he suggests, deal with information differently. The left half likes to deal with pieces of information in isolation; the right half with something as a whole – the *gestalt* as it is often called. So the right brain might understand metaphor, while the left brain does not.

McGilchrist is clear that the most fundamental difference between the hemispheres is in the type of attention they give to the world.[15] That is important because if we are defined by what we see through what we attend to, then how we attend to and see things will have a huge effect upon who we are and what we do. Western education especially values routes to becoming experts – specific ways of seeing the world. But being expert is also about the risk of becoming limited in vision.

The critical nature of the shift from being expert achiever to becoming a synthesizing leader is Bill Torbert's view of the developmental journey involved in becoming a leader. Recently awarded the Center for Creative Leadership's Career Contribution to Applied Leadership Award, Torbert has created a most useful developmental theory and metric about becoming a leader who, to succeed, must necessarily become a strategist. He has especially explored the paradox that expert achievers (who have been trained to be intolerant of ambiguity) tend to be the people who are spotted for leadership roles, whereas it is only through being comfortable with the uncertainties of understanding other people well that ambiguity and complexity can be made manageable. The shift from being expert achiever into becoming a real strategist is an uncomfortable journey, however exciting: and it may be that part of the discomfort is that the right hand side of the brain has to come into use a good deal more, and that takes time and serious effort (remember Chapter 4 on testosterone, risk and entrepreneurship).

The brain is not just a decision-making organ: not just the organ of relationships; not just a specialized kind of hardware or wetware. It is what makes the world. The world has no meaning except the meaning that we assign to it. To do that well, both halves of the brain have to be integrated effectively: and that is not an easy task.

Structure is not the only way in which men and women's brains differ, although it is the best studied. There are chemical differences too: some major neurotransmitter receptors are distributed differently. Finally, there are functional differences: for example, the amygdala responds differently to acute and chronic stress in men and women, and also processes emotional memories in different ways.[16] What we can say is that, notwithstanding these gender based differences, men and women are still more similar as to their brains than their height.

The brain works by interconnection across several axes. We have concentrated on the horizontal axis in this chapter and mentioned the vertical (cortex, limbic, brainstem) axis in Chapter 2 where information moves from logical to emotional to physical – and this can also differ based on gender or other forms of diversity. In Chapter 8 we looked at agility across six functions of the brain. Generally speaking, women tend to have a richer vocabulary for emotions and men tend to push emotions into their bodies such that things like muscular tension, redness of the skin or raising of the voice are better indicators of mood. Women may cry more easily or their voice may become higher pitched but they are also more likely to be understanding and articulating what is destabilizing them. So to a large extent, understanding others means understanding how emotions are processed and expressed differently.

We have focused here on gender diversity as this is where we have the greatest amount of evidence from neuroscience and psychology, but we are mindful of guarding against stereotypes and brandishing them across the board. Traits like empathy vary with situations, and under certain circumstances, gender differences can disappear. We do know some differences are innate: one-day-old female babies focus more on faces than males, and even baby boy monkeys prefer cars and trucks to dolls. Both brain imaging and psychological research are leading to greater understanding of the differences between the sexes, but certainly in terms of function, the overlap between men's and women's brains is greater than any difference.

Women at work

How might this apply to what we see in the workplace? Looking at financial risk taking as applied neuroscientists, we would say this is a physical activity, just like kicking a ball. Every thought that you have is accompanied by some changes in your body through your autonomic nervous system, partially related to adrenalin release; for example, breathing, blood pressure, sweating or clenching your fists. These often work through feedback loops so that changes in your body can also affect your thoughts and decisions. Testosterone is a classic example. Men have more of it than women. Younger men have more of it than older men (it seems to drop significantly over the age of 30). Men are more motivated by competition. Although a large number of studies have concluded that women are more risk averse, the evidence is far from clear cut (see Box 11.2).

BOX 11.2 ATTITUDES TO UNCERTAINTY

It would appear that where the outcome is dependent on the individuals' own perception of competence or likelihood of success, men's higher levels of confidence and greater propensity towards over-optimism is a critical factor: "Due to lower confidence in their knowledge and information, women perceive more 'uncertainty about uncertainty' than men".

Schubert, R, Gysler, M, Brown, M and Brachinger, H-W, 2000, "Gender specific attitudes towards risk and ambiguity: An experimental investigation", paper, July, Center of Economic Research, Swiss Federal Institute of Technology, Zurich.

See also Trautmann, S T, Vielder, F M, and Wakker, PP, 2008, "Causes of ambiguity aversion: Known versus unknown preferences, *Journal of Risk and Uncertainty*, 36: 225–43;

Wieland, A. and Sarin, R, 2012, "Gender differences in risk aversion: A theory of when and why, working paper, UCLA Anderson School of Management; Borghans,L, Golsteyn, B H H, Heckman, J J and Meijers, H, "Gender differences in risk aversion and ambiguity aversion", IZA discussion papers no. 3985; Dreber A and Hoffman M, 2010, "Biological basis of sex differences in risk aversion and competitiveness", paper, UCLA.

The ramifications of this in sport, warfare and financial services are interesting, to say the least. Now, after a global financial crisis where male traders and bankers have been portrayed as driven by emotions such as greed and macho bravado, women's sensitivity to context in relation to risk and (perhaps also) their discomfort with ambiguity may serve them well. We have already noted calls for more women in top banking positions and overall the proportion of women on boards is growing in the US and UK. However, with the exception of Ana Botin at Santander, major global banking organizations have male chairs and CEOs.

The issue of women in leadership has become acute. Rhetoric and equal recruitment have proved ineffective at creating significant changes in gender balance at senior management and board levels in business and in government. Although North America, some Scandinavian countries and some emergent economies are showing real progress – and in the UK in June 2014 the last male only FTSE 100 board appointed its first woman non-executive director – women still feel blocked, and a critical mass has not yet been achieved. Or put another way; is it that women's careers are still almost entirely defined by "masculine" systems? If differences within the brain (hemispheres) and between brains are being shown to be of immense importance, how might that play in how we create and run organizations to enable greater diversity?

Research conducted by Dr Shaheena Janjuha-Jivraj in the UK in 2011 amongst all kinds and sizes of organizations, from small family firms to large multinationals, including charities and government departments and agencies, showed what women themselves perceive to be the barriers for their career progression and not just in the financial sector.[17] The findings were remarkable for their coherence across all the 500 women respondents and debunked the myth that women were choosing to spend their energies on family over achieving senior, board-level positions.

Women acknowledged some responsibility for their lack of progression: nearly 80 per cent recognized that they had to be more assertive and take more ownership of their career. About 70 per cent said they lacked a sponsor. They were made uncomfortable by the lack of clarity and transparency in promotion and recruitment processes for the most senior posts and about 50 per cent said they felt invisible. The 2012 CTI report[18] of a major research study led by Sylvia-Ann Hewlett demonstrated emphatically that lack of sponsorship was a key differentiator of success between men

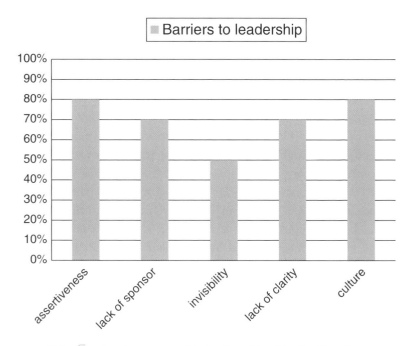

FIGURE 11.2 / Barriers to women achieving board-level leadership roles

Source: © Dr Shaheena Janjuha-Jivraj, 2012.

and women. Some women also said they found the culture at the top unwelcoming and uncomfortable and that this made them question the changes – and exchanges – they had to make to stay there.

The confidence gap

Underlying most of these barriers is the confidence gap between men and women. Commercial organizations (and financial ones might again be a prime example here) are geared for succeeding in highly competitive environments and are premised on harnessing the attention and energy of confident, competitive, staff to achieve their goals. The assumptions built into many of these organizational structures seem to be that individuals will find their own place, will take the initiative to compete for dominance and attention internally as well as externally. This appears to hold for many governmental organizations, charities and educational organizations too.

Three books have shed light on how this kind of organizational environment, which might be seen as male oriented, appears to disadvantage women in two ways. Firstly, Sheryl Sandberg's *Lean In*[19] is a great guide on how to succeed as a woman in man's world. Her account of how differently women are perceived when they do assert themselves however is a stark warning that acting like a man doesn't work, because the assumptions of many organizational environments are still that women will be nice, not compete aggressively for dominance but support others to the disadvantage of their own progress, and go make the coffee when asked. Otherwise they are deemed to be harridans or hard (the language is ours not Ms Sandberg's). Sylvia-Ann Hewlett's *Forget a Mentor, Get a Sponsor*,[20] shows that men appear to be better at networking and being spotted for talent development. Men appear to find promoting themselves and their achievements easier than women.

As coaches we so often come across very able, high powered women, who are very uncomfortable with self-promotion and believe that the excellence of their work and their loyalty will be recognized and justly rewarded, without additional trumpet blowing or networking effort on their part. This behavior, described as being a "Secret Cinderella",[21] works on the following assumption: "If I do a great job, the prince will turn up on my doorstep and try my foot with the glass slipper of senior management". And to stretch the metaphor even further, forgetting that it took a sponsoring fairy godmother to get you to the attention of the prince in the first place!

The third book, *The Confidence Code*, by Katty Kay and Claire Shipman, published in 2014,[22] analyzes confidence from a number of perspectives and puts it at the heart of women's progress towards leadership and the gender parity issue.

The issue of confidence is not just about how or whether women can reach the top: it is also about how they feel and perform when they are there. One of the most eminent women scientists in the UK, if not the world, physicist Professor Dame Athene Donald, Fellow of the Royal Society and Master of Churchill College Cambridge, has written a blog about so called "imposter syndrome".[23] It makes for sobering reading (see Box 11.3).

BOX 11.3   IMPOSTER SYNDROME

Imposter syndrome (also called fraud syndrome) is not a true psychological syndrome but a name for feeling that one isn't sufficiently competent or expert enough to be in the position one is, and/or that one does not deserve being appointed to a higher post. One's successes are often self attributed to luck or mistakes by others, rather than one's skill, hard work or expertise.

See further the work of Peggy McIntosh on Fraud Syndrome, Wellesley Center for Women and of Hugh Kearns of Flinders University in Australia.

Donald acknowledges feeling like that herself sometimes, and having informally explored the issue with other senior female scientists, she found that on the whole, they do too. In subsequent discussions she discovered that men also admit to similar feelings. Anecdotally, we have seen this again and again, in business, academia and government, across nations and cultures: both men and women experience these feelings, but women seem to be more held back by them.

We have already seen in Chapters 3, 4 and 9, how testosterone is correlated with confidence, and have looked at the likely effects that confidence in one's chances of success and knowledge might have on risk and ambiguity tolerance.

We have seen in Chapters 3 and 9 how confidence can be increased (or reduced) through changing behaviors and stance, through self-control, persistence through failure and through developing a sense of efficacy. We also noted that appearing confident is a valuable trait for a leader in managing uncertainty and fear of the future. What does the confidence gap mean for women as leaders?

In April 2014 a story hit the UK media to the effect that women CEOs were fired more often than men. One reason given was that companies under pressure to diversify their senior management were making riskier appointments; another that boardroom culture was still predominantly male and an uncomfortable fit for women CEOs. We have heard anecdotally that some boards are reluctant to appoint women CEOs because they feel that their higher propensity to risk aversion and the chance of lower confidence will lead to fatal hesitancy when fast decisions need to be taken.

There are some possible gaps in that kind of reasoning. The implication that pressure to appoint women leads to risky appointments is that choice is limited: we have often heard that there are not enough women out there both capable and willing – but that is contradicted by our research, and the work of organizations such as the 30% Club and Global Board Ready Women (GBRW). Through lack of sponsorship and women's own reluctance to shout about their achievements many who are both remain invisible, even in their own organizations. Better and earlier talent management can help address this, as can very open, unambiguous and positively encouraging recruitment processes.

There needs to be a better understanding of how diversity, both innate and from experience, adds value, to motivate wider searches. We know that there are highly qualified women looking for opportunities who are under the radar of many search firms because their experience does not fit a traditional mould – women with long-term leadership success from family businesses and other entrepreneurial organizations, for example. So a broader perspective and a mindset that is more open to diverse experience also helps.

We understand that culture change takes a long time and that impact depends on having critical mass. Having one woman on a board or senior management team will make a difference, but a 2006 study indicated that it takes three or more women on a board to create critical mass and deliver the diversity bonus through more fundamental change.[24]

Women can be great leaders

Neuroscience has given us understanding of the differences between individuals – of all kinds – due to the plasticity of their brains and the effect of environment on them, and of the value that diversity of thinking brings to organizations. This points to the need for women to stay true to their own values and styles of leadership, to be authentic. Trying to behave like a male leader will not help bring diverse views and experience to the table. Trying to behave like a male leader will only work if that is a genuine expression of who you are – and there are many women who are indeed quite "masculine" in the way their brain works, just as there are men who are highly tuned into their right hemisphere and are seen as having a strong "feminine side". Otherwise it will cause internal conflict, which will be felt by others and undermine trust and impact. You can fake it until you are it, but not if that does not change you and continues to conflict with your profound beliefs, core values and the actual effects and impact of your behaviors.

Neuroscience is also showing some directions towards new models of leadership, from the systems approach of Chapter 2 to the brain-based leadership in Chapters 3 and 9. Self-awareness and self-control, the balance between intuition and consciously rational, logical thinking, the ability to communicate profoundly and understand the role of emotions, to manage stress, are all critical to effective leadership. Human beings can learn those skills.

We have learned that testosterone alone in humans is not a sufficient marker of leadership, but that the balance of testosterone and cortisol is. We have seen how women can raise their testosterone levels and both men and women can learn to manage their responses to stress. We have seen how trust can be built and mutually maintained. We have understood that leaders who empower and develop their people are more likely to be successful and more likely to be followed by self-motivated staff. We have also seen how confidence can be built up and enhanced. All of these are pointers to women being as able to be leaders, and indeed great leaders, as men, with the caveat that they will, certainly, lead differently – or many of them will!

There is a small but increasing pool of great women leaders. Angela Merkel of Germany, Ellen Sirleaf of Liberia, Marjorie Scardino in the UK, Christine Lagarde of the IMF, Kathryn Wilde of New York City Partnership, Indra Moovi of PepsiCo, Sheryl Sandberg of Facebook and Angela Ahrendts (who moved from Burberry to Apple) are all examples. Many of the political women leaders (Thatcher, Gandhi, Meir) have been too controversial but have achieved changes with significant impact. Aung San Suu Kyi has become an icon for many, leading a movement for democratization in Myanmar from house arrest. The acceptance of women as leaders is changing, albeit slowly. In 2014, Glencore appointed its first female director, Patrice Merrin, ending its status as the last bastion of all-male boards in the FTSE 100.

Summary

Understanding the dynamic way the two hemispheres work together unlocks the possibility of understanding male–female differences and seeing the analogy of how both are utterly essential to the effectiveness of the organization as a whole. Understanding how diversity more widely contributes to better decisions and innovation may enable recruitment processes which are more open to different experiences and backgrounds, still totally focused on finding the right individual for the role but more aware of how that individual role fits the organization as a whole. Achieving a "critical mass of diversity" will allow us to see the impact of a new era of integration.

Actions and reflections

- When conducting skills audits for senior management or boards include measures for difference and diversity.
- Test your internal promotion and external recruitment processes for transparency and ambiguity. How easy do you make it for a wide variety of people to put themselves forward? How widely do you identify talent and potential?
- Ensure that you elicit, welcome and show gratitude for diverse views that challenge your thinking, especially when you disagree with them!
- Share your understanding of the benefits of diversity.

chapter 12

Whole Person, Vibrant Organization

"En ma fin gitmon commencement [in my end is my beginning]."

Mary, Queen of Scots

The final chapter of most books pulls everything together and comes to conclusions. This one is different.

In the spirit of the applied brain sciences this chapter is designed to leave you with an opening up of new possibilities and beginning to see options that are the basis for new answers or, if not necessarily new, answers that feel more firmly grounded in fact.

Let's start out with the fact that the brain is continuously bombarded with information as leaders are too. For the brain, five senses are pouring in millions of bits of information every day – and even staying on guard when we are asleep.

Strange noise in the night? *Wake up!* Cold toes? *Snuggle up.* Anxious about early-morning flight? *Wake up and get up!* It's too early. *I'll keep you half-awake, just in case.* I need my sleep. *You also need to get up.* Who's in charge round here? *Good question!*

Among the many remarkable accomplishments in its evolutionary development, the brain has pulled off two very clever tricks. The first is to get highly differentiated systems working together completely non-consciously. The second is to find economical ways of processing huge amounts of information to extract maximum output value.

"Differentiated systems" is just another way of saying "different departments". What the brain manages to do is organize the outputs from each of its functional departments, in milliseconds, and present them to the outside world as if it were a single system operating in there.

On the whole, people operate as consistent and complete personalities, as integrated entities. We are perhaps more conscious of the complexities, contradictions and inconsistencies of our own self, but we manage these so as to behave in a functional and effective way, more often than not. What a joy it would be if organizational departments, in what these days are dignified as complex systems, operated as easily across boundaries. The self, defined for these purposes as "personality" – the brain's own individual culture system – acts as the central integrator to make separate parts present as a whole. That's the job of "culture" inside organizations and why it is of such great importance.

Not only is culture a huge brand differentiator, it has the capacity to organize why and how people act both inside and outside the organization. So it is a critical part of the leader's capability to understand and manage the culture very well indeed. Like personality it gets the neurochemistry of the organization flowing and, done well, flowing in the direction that the organization wants.

How does culture work?

An update from the British Neuroscience Association (22 January 2011) reports that a team of scientists at the University of Rochester, Washington University in St. Louis and Baylor College of Medicine has unraveled how the brain manages to process the millions of complex, rapidly changing and often conflicting sensory signals to make sense of our world. Single cells in the brain establish which signals to give what weights to as being more or less important. That's what experience does for us. It's called "knowing". When millions of cells assign the same weights simultane-ously – a simple operation performed by many hundreds of thousands of neurons – the result is effective decision making.

A good leader gets others around him or her to know, "intuitively", how he or she would assign weights to critical issues. In this way the mind of the leader usefully invades the minds of subordinates. The brain cells of subordinates do what the leader wants. That's culture. It's not just saying "yes". It's knowing what "yes" would look like, feel like, be like.

Effective transmission of culture occurs through memes – the social equivalent of genes. *The Success Virus, a practical guide to using memes in corporate decision-making* by Dr Martin Farncombe shows how cultural transmission really works.[1]

BOX 12.1 MEMES

A meme is "a unit of cultural transmission or a unit of imitation", conveying almost everything that we share with our fellows: language, national characteristics, odd social customs, music, fashions, beliefs, our scientific and technological structures, the side of the road we drive on, religions, political and legal systems, and economic structures. There is no "inherent" or "self-evident" truth anywhere, not in politics, religion, society or business. All of these structures are made up of evolving and competing sets of memes. Memes also transmit the reasons that organizations exist and absolutely everything about the way that they work.

Now, not everyone absorbs memes readily, and mismatches between what individuals believe and what the corporation believes help explain why some people will succeed in organiza-tions while others, equally able, will fail.

The hardware of the human meme machine is the brain; the memes themselves act as application software, and the non-conscious elements of the brain are the operating system that decides what memes to store, load and run.

(See http://www.practicalmemetics.com/)

Like genes, memes act as replicators and, at best, are copied faithfully from one generation to the next (Box 12.2). If variations occur then diversity takes place. Where they are stored in the brain is not yet known but, as Farncombe points out, Mendel had worked out the nature of genetics 100 years before Watson and Crick were able to picture the double helix.

With the speed at which connectomics is re-shaping our understanding of the way the brain works, it won't be long before modern neuroscience has the beginnings of a fix on how memes work in the brain. For certain they are part of the emotional system, though, which is itself diffused throughout the pathways of the brain.

As a way of embedding these thoughts about memes, think of brain cells as being voters: or customers. How could the culture of a political party or of the organization so engage the voters or the customers that they really attached to the party or the product or the service? Steve Jobs seems to have got as close as anyone to working that out pragmatically.

The threat of change and the need for trust

Getting people to change their perceptions of the world is not easy however. The best bet for the brain is to stay the same. The brain that got us "here" is likely to be the best brain to get us "there", the brain says. It prefers continuity.

In the 10 January 2012 issue of *Scientific American* Christoph Korn (a neuroscientist interested in the neural mechanisms of decision making) observes that a bride walking down the aisle is unlikely to agree, in the remote event of her progress being interrupted for discussion, that there is almost a 50 percent chance that she will, in due course, divorce.[2] We humans, he says, underestimate the probabilities of adverse events and overestimate the probabilities of welcome events. Change or difference is most easily assessed by the brain as an adverse event.

Why is that? There is a major neurotransmitter chemical involved in decision making and what is called error prediction/correction. That chemical is dopamine. It is heavily involved in motivational processes and reward, pleasure and addiction. It is triggered and floods the brain to a greater or lesser extent when an event happens that produces desired outcomes and subsequently when the same event or the expectation of it happens again. If the expectation is unfulfilled then it starts learning not to switch on. This is what makes error correction possible, which in turn sets up internalized probabilities.

The particular trouble with big events, though, like the actuarial prospects of marriage failure, the possibility of a major accident or a nuclear disaster, is that for most people there is no first-hand experience on which to draw: so no predictive bases have been built up. We can think about them but not feel them. In consequence such situations have no real meaning. It is why scare tactics through advertising to change people's behavior, as on cigarette packets, rarely work.

Mature individuals trust what their own brains tell them from their own experience in preference to what any authority, however august, says. That is what makes shifting policy into social action so difficult.

People trust their own brains rather than someone else's unless they have been taught to trust others' in preference to their own: or, like children, have still-developing brains that can be molded to become the takers of, say, the anti-smoking message to their parents: or there are well-established trust-based relationships that have been tested and found functional, as in the best teams where trust resonates.

The nature of trust is also very closely connected with an individual's sense of self based on the eight basic emotions. Five of the eight, you will recall – fear, anger, disgust, shame and sadness – underpin escape/avoidance/survival behaviors such as politicking, presenteeism, fudging data, making compensation claims and anything else that preserves the wellbeing of the individual as against the organization.

Then there is the one emotion – surprise/startle – that sets up expectations at a high level. It is a potentiator. Disney World, Alton Towers and stand-up comedians know all about the way that surprise and startle can be profitable, especially when surprise/startle swings into the first of the two emotions that are the great drivers producing sustainable human energy – excitement/joy and trust/love. With those in play, anything is possible. Without them, it's a hard grind.

Oddly enough most organizations still think mobilizing the escape/avoidance emotions will get results. After a fashion it does, but at a very high cost in terms of effort, money and exhaustion. But nothing new or creative will happen that way. To achieve great organizational goals management has to create the conditions under which individuals actively want to be doing what they are doing and stretch themselves far more. The basis of that is active trust, which only the leader can generate.

Box 12.2 gives some of Farncombe's memetic rules for getting the messages as right as possible in managing whatever it is that a leader has to manage.

BOX 12.2 MAKING MEMES VIRULENT

The test of the ideas in Farncombe's book is whether or not it is possible to identify the factors that will allow us to construct a better meme. Compare a memeplex (a collection of memes) to a stealth bomber, and that the wings, camouflage, guns, bombs, engines and so on are useless by themselves but powerful when combined. Now make a clear distinction between the payload (the message you are trying to get across) and the container the payload is packaged into.

Farncombe extends the metaphor to a very useful list of criteria for both "container" and "payload". See if you can think of what they might be, write them down and then check yours against his book.

So if a trust-based culture is very central to an organization's effectiveness and memes are the mechanism of transmission of all its central ideas and precepts, we can get back to one of the core ideas underlying this book: which is that energy – human energy, managed by the brain managing its own energy in the first place, as Chapter 1 described – is central to an organization's effectiveness.

energy – human energy, managed by the brain managing its own energy in the first place – is central to an organization's effectiveness.

A new organizational paradigm

Profit is a way of expressing in monetary terms how human energy has been applied to the strategic and operational goals of the organization. Profit is also a measure of the extent to which a leader has been able to see how energy should be applied and have that made effective throughout the whole organization.

But we all know that profit is a historical process and balance sheets can be variously constructed – which is not to say that profit is not crucial or that balance sheets are not useful. Profit is the way energy is put back into the system, after all, through shareholders via sales and the way all outputs arising from sales have been managed.

Yet profit does not of itself have either a relational or an ethical component attached to it. And after the banking catastrophes of 2008 onwards there is a sense that a new sustainable organizational paradigm needs to emerge that is good for individuals and good for society as a whole.

We are of the view that the brain sciences will make a big contribution to that process by showing just how crucial effective relationship is to the way energy is managed in organizations. Such a view requires that there be a way of understanding the organization as a dynamic energy management task and being able to see – map and track – what is happening to energy flow in as close to real time as possible.

The science of understanding this organizational task now lags well behind the direction of travel in which the modern brain sciences are taking us. Organizational theory is as fragmented in its understanding of what the organization "is" as psychological theory was about "people" before the new brain sciences started creating the real prospect of a unifying understanding which takes the whole system into account.

One potentially powerful answer to this has been proposed by a husband and wife consulting team that originally started work together under Professor Chris Argyris at Harvard. More than 20 years ago Philip Cousins and Diane Downs set out to crack the question: What *is* an organization? With help from others on the way, they eventually developed a model that began to resemble the vital organs of the body. They have created the idea, built upon stratified systems theory, that it is possible to make visual the interconnectedness of any organization or any part of it: in other words, to see how energy flows around the organizational system and where it is effective and where it is blocked. This is a whole systems view with a visual metric attached to it.[3]

Think for a moment about your body and its vital organs as an energy system; and the way the brain focuses all the efforts of your body, including itself, into what it attends to. Remember that where attention goes energy flows. And then consider that there is less than very little in management theory and practice that makes human energy management a conscious choice or skill.

there is less than very little in management theory and practice that makes human energy management a conscious choice or skill.

This is largely because organizational theory has not resolved the question of "What is an organization?" But if we ask: "What are the vital organs of any organization or any part of it?" it becomes possible to see that there are some elements, as in the body, that are necessary and sufficient for effective life and without which we could not exist. Then there are other elements that, though intensely useful, are not in the same sense vital. There are many parts of the body – legs, arms, eyes, ears and so on – with which it is possible to do without: though having them all and well coordinated makes everything much easier. But they would have no value at all without the vital organs that energize them.

Inherent in the idea is that the same vital elements are replicated in any part of the organization – just in the way that DNA runs through the whole of the body. The vital elements for the whole organization are 11 in number – leadership, strategy, communications, operations, culture, finance, systems and structure, development (of people, processes and products), sales, staff and customers. They are equally applicable to the marketing department as they are to the finance department or IT. Each main department needs to have leadership that links into the leadership of the whole, a culture that contributes effectively to the whole, development that fits with strategic and operational objectives, and so on.

Moreover, the same principles can be applied to every individual within the organization. Each person has to be a leader to him- or herself, needs a personal strategy for focusing their energy into the strategic objectives of the organization, creates an interpersonal culture, and so on and so on. In such a way individuals within a corporate system are exactly like neurons or cells throughout the body. They are part of the whole and need to have elements in them that fit into the whole if the whole is to be as effective as possible.

Part of the departmental struggle that pervades so many organizations arises from the fact that individuals get highly identified with the bit of the system they know rather than the whole system. It's where they belong. In consequence anything outside the department is seen as threatening and creates defensive behavior or a kind of passive resistance to difference. As our brains evolved within tribal systems that is still their default mode of action.

Contributing to inter-departmental struggling is the further fact that different departments typically attract different kinds of individuals. Sales types tend not to be accountants: marketing and external affairs people do not usually have a background in quality control or complex project management. People's personalities define their choice of jobs just as their jobs also shape their personalities.

Engineers know that all contacting surfaces need lubricants if the available energy is to be deployed for maximum performance. But when the parts of the human system have friction between them time and energy get wasted and performance goals get lost. In the managing of human energy that concept is hardly understood at all. And what is it, this lubricant? It is relationship – one of the key elements that together with information and energy create the working mind.

Of course people intuitively know when things are working well or badly. They can feel it. Our tribal brain is highly tuned to the perception of inter-personal effect. Yet those self-directing energy systems called "people" who bring their central integrator systems (the self) to work every day are the only source of organizational effectiveness. The quality of relationship within which they work via the limbic (emotional) system of the brain is the key lubricant to that effectiveness.

Over the last two centuries the science behind medicine has made more possible a common understanding of what is happening within the whole system of the body. This is now becoming possible organizationally. Comparisons may now be made between and within organizations based upon linkages between the elements of the whole model that define how human energy is (or is not) flowing around the organization.

So from a leader's point of view it is beginning to be possible to map and track in almost real-time, world-wide, what is happening within the brain-based complexity of a networked organization. As with fMRI scans of the brain, what had previously looked like soft stuff that X-rays could not focus on and so had not been possible to image whilst working is being brought into visual consciousness.

If leaders are to lead they need this kind of information to see what is happening across all elements of the whole system for which they carry responsibility. That is the difference between eighteenth-century medicine that had no understanding of the madness of King George and twenty-first-century neuroscience that, with regard to madness, is getting some grip on how the neurochemistry of the brain becomes disturbed and is beginning to grasp some of what can be done about it. Management science is getting there too, now that there is a scientific system for imaging the networks of any organization within a definition of its vital organs. That gives some hope of knowing where to apply the lubricant of limbic leadership for lowering the friction across departmental boundaries.

So a properly networked organization is a place where attention, energy and relationships are in harmony, managing the information flow that is the lifeblood of all organization.

Structuring organizations around "networks" is an idea that has been around for 20 years or more, but there is yet to be an organization that has built its organizational chart to show how its networks work. Organograms generally still default to single-line, hierarchical descriptions – dotted lines sometimes for a bit of complexity or to obscure uncertainty – or there are matrix structures in which no-one truly comfortably lives.

a properly networked organization is a place where attention, energy and relationships are in harmony, managing the information flow that is the lifeblood of all organization.

The trouble with networks is that it is hard to track what is happening in them. This makes it all the more remarkable that the brain can manage its 86 billion neurons[4] in an amazing set of parallel systems without one interfering too much with another. In *Nature Neuroscience* for 6 May 2014, and using a correlation technique devised and patented for the purpose, Joerg Hipp and colleagues from the University Medical Center, Hamburg-Eppendorf and the Center for Integrative Neuroscience, University of Tübingen tracked how the brain manages the electrical part of its energy system to keep things in order. They found, reports Brian Hung in *The Atlantic* for 11 May, that:

"different areas of the brain, often far apart from each other within the geographic space of the brain, are communicating through a fast-paced synchronized set of brain signals. These networks can be considered preferred pathways for sending signals back and forth to perform a specific set of cognitive or motor behaviors. And they do this by using different frequencies within the signaling system, ranging from 5 to 45 hertz".

Fascinating to an applied neuroscientist though that may be, what are its implications for the design of organizations? Well, they are at the same time both very far-reaching and very simple. Take the quotation from Hung and substitute "organization" or "department" for "brain": and substitute "achieve goals" for "perform a specific set of cognitive or motor behaviors".

Then think what the efficiency gains would be for an organization that was being so described.

The effectiveness of any organization is an accumulation of those expensive things called brains that generally walk in on two legs each day. So brains can begin to be seen as bundles of energy and are the only source of profit, focus, performance or anything else that fascinates the organization. Organizationally there is no other source of anything.

The individual brain manages its own effectiveness, how it uses its energy supply, through the control of its emotional system. In organizations the emotional system of any individual is largely dependent upon the relationship network within which each and every individual exists. A leader at whatever level has the key task of creating the interpersonal emotional framework and through that framework the way each brain in the system is working and delivering on the organization's goals.

Underpinning all energy and all relationships and the way attention gets focused on information is the specificity of any one person's neurochemistry. Our individuality and diversity gives us great strengths. Corporately much of that strength is at risk of being wasted because the management of energy flow in organizations as the primary source of profit is not yet properly understood. When it is, less energy may create greater rewards and certainly much more individual satisfaction.

Moving forward

Everything in this book is intended to give you knowledge, practices and tools to support you in developing your leadership capacity to your full potential and then discovering you have yet more potential, and so on, and to enable you in turn to support others in developing theirs.

You will have seen that leadership is about who you are as a person, and what you do: how you manage your brain and its energy, how you relate to other people, and how you inspire and motivate them to use their brains and energy to innovate and achieve common organizational goals.

In reading the book you will perhaps have got to know yourself better, in terms of understanding how your brain works. You will understand how being a leader is a dynamic process of continuous change and development for yourself and the people you work with.

We hope that your appetite for that development has increased and that your sense of what it means to be in control of change has strengthened through some of the actions and reflections at the end of each chapter.

What can you do now to make the best use of the material in the book and the ideas it has stimulated for you?

Revisit the models regularly, especially when you feel under pressure:

- The Neural Tethering Model© in Chapter 4 for resilience.
- The Leadership Brain Agility© model and brain Olympics concept from Chapter 8 to boost your performance.
- The emotions spectrum in Chapter 1 to engage others.
- The new leadership model in Chapter 3 to help your focus on self-awareness and self-management as the basis for developing your PFC.

Each time you think about applying neuroscience to business, consider:

- One thing you could do to work on yourself as a leader.
- Something you could do or help someone with to enable growth in your team.
- What the broader implications are of applying this more widely to create a learning organization with diverse and creative thinking.
- How to innovate moving forward into an uncertain future full of possibilities.

And remember:

"Fortune favors the prepared mind".

Louis Pasteur

Glossary

Adrenal gland   Endocrine gland, above the kidneys, which releases the hormone adrenalin (q.v.).

Adrenalin   A hormone, released by the adrenal medulla and the brain, that acts with noradrenalin to activate the sympathetic division of the autonomic nervous system. Sometimes called epinephrine.

Alzheimer's   A common cause of dementia (q.v.) the most notable symptom of which is loss of memory; other symptoms, such as confusion, decline in reasoning, changes in personality, apathy or irritability and aggression are also often present. Physical symptoms are protein tangles and plaques in the brain.

Amygdala/e   There are two amygdalae, small almond shaped structures deep in the brain, on the inner surfaces of the temporal lobes, one in each hemisphere, crucial to continuously monitor the emotional significance of external and internal stimuli. The amygdalae are also much involved in learning and memory.

Anabolic   A process that tends towards building up organs and tissues.

Antioxidants   Man-made or natural substances that may prevent or delay some types of cell damage.

Autonomic Nervous System (ANS)   A system of both peripheral and central nerves that serves the internal organs and the cardiovascular system, and which largely serves functions outside conscious control, such as heart rate, digestion, respiration, salivation. It includes the sympathetic and parasympathetic nervous systems.

Axon   A protrusion from the cell body, specialized to conduct signals towards a dendritic connection with another neuron.

Basal ganglia   Clusters of neurons, which include the caudate nucleus, putamen, globus pallidus and substantia nigra, that are located deep in the brain and play an important role in movement.

Biomarker or biological marker   Measurable biological parameters, such as levels of neurotransmitters, hormones, or electrical activity, or the presence or absence of certain kinds of cell that can be used as indicators of certain biological states, conditions, effects or behaviors.

Brainstem   The major route by which the forebrain sends information to, and receives information from, the spinal cord and peripheral nerves. It controls, among other things, respiration and regulation of heart rhythms.

Catabolic   A process that tends towards the breakdown in living organisms of more complex substances to simpler ones with the release of energy.

Central nervous system   The brain and spinal cord.

Cerebral hemispheres   The two specialized halves of the brain. The left hemisphere is specialized for speech, writing, language and calculation; the right hemisphere is specialized for spatial abilities, face recognition in vision and some aspects of music perception and production.

Cerebrospinal fluid (CSF)   A liquid found within the ventricles of the brain and the central canal of the spinal cord.

Chromosome   Structure found in the nucleus of a cell, which contains the genes. Chromosomes come in pairs, and a normal human cell contains 46 chromosomes.

Chunking   A term used to denote the brain's ability to use grouping together to enable working memory to hold more elements, so for example, chunking numbers by grouping them in 3s and 4s, e.g. 0203 555 9678, as we often do to remember telephone numbers.

Cingulate Cortex   A part of the brain surrounding the corpus callosum, involved in emotional processing.

Cognitive   The process or processes by which an organism gains knowledge of or becomes aware of events or objects in its environment and uses that knowledge for comprehension and problem-solving.

Connectomics   The study of connectomes or neural connections in the brain.

Corpus Callosum   A broad bundle of neural fibers which connects the two hemispheres in the brain, under the cortex and enables communication between them.

Cortex   The outermost layer of the cerebral hemispheres of the brain. It is responsible for all forms of conscious experience, including perception, emotion, thought and planning.

Cortisol   A steroid hormone (specifically a glucocorticoid) produced by the adrenal gland, in response to stress and low blood glucocorticoid. Cortisol effectively prepares the organism for fight or flight; it affects the immune system, amongst other effects. In humans, it is secreted in greatest quantities before dawn, readying the body for the activities of the coming day. It is also important in focusing attention. If stress persists unduly cortisol has adverse effects on brain function and can destroy brain cells.

Dementia   This is an umbrella term used to describe impaired mental functioning, with symptoms including loss of memory and reasoning capacity, which can also affect the ability to speak and understand. Dementia is often associated with mental decline in old age, but can also be caused by illness or physical damage. Alzheimer's is the best known form of dementia.

Dendrite   From the Greek dendron, tree: a tree-like extension of the neuron cell body. Along with the cell body, it receives information from other neurons.

Dopamine   A catecholamine neurotransmitter known to have multiple functions depending on where it acts. Dopamine-containing neurons in the substantia nigra of the brainstem project to the caudate nucleus and are destroyed in Parkinson's victims. Dopamine is thought to regulate emotional responses, and play a role in schizophrenia and cocaine abuse.

DTI   Diffusion tensor imaging is an MRI (q.v.) process which enables the tracking of movement of molecules (mainly of water) in the brain.

EEG   Electroencephalogram, or electroencephalography, a technology or process for recording changes in voltage across the scalp generated by activity within the brain.

Emotions   Emotions are thought to be related to activity in the brain areas that direct our attention, motivate our behavior and determine the significance of what is going on around us.

Endocrine   Pertaining to the glands that secrete hormones into the bloodstream which circulate around the body. This system includes estrogen, testosterone, growth hormones, adrenalin and insulin amongst others. Glands include the thyroid, parathyroid, pancreas, pineal and gonads.

Endorphins   Neurotransmitters produced in the brain that generate cellular and behavioral effects like those of morphine.

Epigenetics   An emerging science looking at how environmental effects might influence the way genes are expressed.

Episodic memory   Autobiographical memory, including events, actions, contexts – including time and place.

EQ   Emotional Quotient; tests designed to measure emotional intelligence.

Estrogen   A group of sex hormones found more abundantly in females than males. They are responsible for female sexual maturation and other functions.

Executive functions   Also known as cognitive control and supervisory attentional system, this is an umbrella term for the management of cognitive processes including working memory, reasoning, task flexibility, and problem solving as well as planning and execution.

Explicit memory   That which can be consciously recalled, and consists of autobiographical or episodic memory and semantic memory.

Flow   A term used by Mihaly Csikszentmihalyi to denote the state of being totally immersed in what you are doing, to the point of losing self-awareness, but with enhanced effectiveness.

fMRI   Functional magnetic resonance imaging; an imaging technique using technology that measures changes in blood flow in the brain when the subject is performing a task, using the changes in magnetism between oxygenated and deoxygenated blood.

Frontal lobes   The part of the brain, in each hemisphere, which is located primarily behind the forehead, roughly to the mid line of the skull. One of the four divisions (the others are: parietal, temporal, occipital) of each hemisphere of the cerebral cortex. It has a role in controlling movement and associating the functions of other cortical areas.

Gestalt   A psychological theory and school of practice which looks at the whole rather than just the parts with particular importance on the relationship between the parts.

Glymphatic   The system or process by which cerebrospinal fluid moves through channels formed by glia, cleansing the mammalian brain of harmful waste.

Growth hormone   Growth hormone, also known as somatotropin or somatropin, is a peptide hormone that stimulates growth, cell reproduction and regeneration in humans and other animals. It is also a stress hormone.

Gyrification   Cortical folding or convolution is the process and the extent of folding of the cerebral cortex in mammals as a consequence of brain growth.

Gyrus   In large mammals the surface of the cerebral cortex is folded, giving a much greater surface area in a confined space as in the skull. A fold or ridge in the cortex is termed a gyrus (plural gyri).

Hebbian principle   A theory, first described by Donald Hebb in 1949 and later proved correct, that the frequent stimulation of firing of another cell increases the efficiency of the stimulus transmission. Frequently summarized as "Cells that fire together wire together". The implication of hard wiring is inaccurate, as cells that regularly fire together are not physically connected together, but their concerted firing is simply made more certain.

Heuristic   From the Greek, to find techniques or strategies based on experience for solving problems and making judgments.

Hippocampus/i   A brain structure shaped something like a sea-horse, located under the cerebral cortex. There are two hippocampi, one in each hemisphere. It plays a number of significant roles in brain function, notably in learning, memory and emotional processing. The hippocampus is one of the structures mentioned as part of the "limbic system" (q.v.).

Homeostasis   The state of a system when regulated so as to be balanced and stable, normally within a narrow range of parameters; used of physiological systems, such as body temperature.

Homunculus   A term, literally meaning "little man" commonly used in neuroscience as a teaching or memory tool to describe the distorted scale model of a human drawn or sculpted to reflect the relative space human body parts occupy on the somatosensory cortex (sensory homunculus) and the motor cortex (motor homunculus).

Hormone/s   Biochemicals secreted by glands in the body and transmitted via the blood which regulate various states and processes; hormones are chemical messengers that affect functions such as sleep, growth, mood, digestion and many others.

Hypothalamus   A complex brain structure with a wide variety of functions, including monitoring the autonomic nervous system and regulating the pituitary gland.

Insulin   Insulin is a peptide hormone, produced by beta cells in the pancreas, and is central to regulating carbohydrate and fat metabolism in the body. It causes cells in the skeletal muscles and fat tissue to absorb glucose from the blood.

Interoception   The sense of the physiological condition of the body relating to, or being aware of, stimuli arising within the body and especially in the viscera.

IQ   Intelligence Quotient; a way of measuring general intelligence through a set of tests.

Limbic system   This term is often used to represent those parts of the brain involved in emotional processing and expression, and normally is held to include the cingulate cortex, the hippocampus, the hypothalamus, the amygdala and some parts of the neocortex. The concept of a single "emotional processing and expression system" has been questioned more recently, and indeed it is more likely that a number of brain systems or networks are involved, but the term limbic system is still often used as shorthand for those parts of the brain involved in emotion. NB remember that these networks and their component structures will also have other functions.

Locus coeruleus   The locus coeruleus is a nucleus in the brainstem involved with physiological responses to stress and panic. It is the principal site for brain synthesis of noradrenalin.

Loss aversion   The tendency (bias) of the human brain to assign a greater value to a loss than to a gain of the same value.

Melatonin   Produced from serotonin, melatonin is released by the pineal gland into the bloodstream. It affects physiological changes related to time and lighting cycles.

Meme   An idea, behavior, or style that spreads from person to person within a culture.

Mentalize   See Theory of Mind.

Mindfulness   A form of meditation, derived from Buddhism, involving the practice of focusing attention on what you are experiencing, in the present, non-judgmentally.

Mindset   An established set of attitudes held by an individual or a group.

Mirror Neurons   These neurons, in the brain's motor cortex, fire when some animals (primates and humans) observe another performing a goal directed action. Their function is hotly debated, some scientists seeing them as being a crucial part of the human ability to empathize, others as simply one part of the system which interprets meaning in others' actions.

Mirroring   The tendency of humans to imitate, involuntarily, the physical behavior of another person with whom they are deeply involved; partners are frequently observed matching each other's movements as if in a mirror, over a drink or a meal, for example.

Motor cortex   That part of the brain which regulates movement and is a sub-structure of the frontal lobes.

MRI   Magnetic resonance imaging, see also fMRI.

Myelin, or myelin sheath   The fatty substance that surrounds axons and insulates them, thus increasing the speed of the signals they carry.

Myelination   The process by which a fatty layer, called myelin, accumulates around nerve cells. Myelination enables nerve cells to transmit information faster and allows for more complex brain processes.

Neocortex   The convoluted, "grey matter" outer surface of the mammalian brain, consisting of 6 layers of neurons.

Neural   Pertaining to neurons or the nervous system.

Neurons   Cells in the brain and nervous systems, which process electrical and chemical signals.   Neurons have extensions which look like long filaments with branches, the dendrites, and an axon, which can have many branches.

Neuropeptide   Small protein-like molecules (peptides) used by neurons to communicate with each other.

Neuroplasticity   The ability of neurons to forge new connections or make new pathways.

Neurotoxins   Neurotoxins are an extensive class of substances such as alcohol which can adversely affect function in both developing and mature nerve tissue.

Neurotransmitters   The chemicals that flow between neurons in synapses (q.v.), to enable communication of signals. These brain chemicals communicate information throughout our brain and body. The brain uses neurotransmitters to tell your heart to beat, your lungs to breathe, and your stomach to digest. They can also affect mood, sleep, concentration, weight, and can cause adverse symptoms when they are out of balance. Neurotransmitter levels can be depleted in many ways. Stress, poor diet, neurotoxins, genetic predisposition, drugs (prescription and recreational), alcohol and caffeine usage can cause these levels to be out of optimal range.

Noradrenalin   A catecholamine neurotransmitter, produced both in the brain and in the peripheral nervous system. It seems to be involved in arousal, reward and regulation of sleep and mood, and the regulation of blood pressure.

Occipital Lobe   One of the four divisions (the others are: frontal, parietal, temporal) of each hemisphere of the cerebral cortex, which includes much of the brain's visual processing system.

Opioids   Any psychoactive chemical that resembles morphine or other opiates in its pharmacological effects. Opioids work by binding to opioid receptors, which are found principally in the central and peripheral nervous system and the gastrointestinal tract.

Oxytocin   Produced by the hypothalamus and stored and secreted by the posterior pituitary gland, oxytocin acts primarily as a neuromodulator in the brain and is known as the bonding hormone.

Parasympathetic nervous system   A branch of the autonomic nervous system concerned with the conservation of the body's energy and resources during relaxed states.

Parietal lobes   The part of the brain, in each hemisphere, which is located behind the frontal lobe, forming a saddle shape under the middle and partly the back part of the skull.

Perceptions   The processing of sensory stimuli through the brain.

Peripheral nervous system   A division of the nervous system consisting of all nerves not part of the brain or spinal cord.

Pineal gland   An endocrine organ found in the brain. In some animals, it seems to serve as a light-influenced biological clock.

Pituitary Gland   A small structure at the base of the brain with two lobes, the pituitary is an endocrine organ closely linked with the hypothalamus. It triggers a number of hormones that regulate a number of crucial activities, such as growth, reproduction, and lactation and it plays a key role in ensuring the body stays within safe limits of temperature, hydration, energy resources.

Plasticity, plastic   When used in relation to the brain, meaning capable of change.

Pre-frontal Cortex (PFC)   A part of the neocortex (q.v.), covering the frontal lobes, behind the forehead, where in humans, the higher executive functions of the brain are held to be located.

Pruning   A term used to describe the loss of neuronal connections when unused.

Reticular formation   A region in the brainstem that is involved in multiple tasks such as regulating the sleep-wake cycle and filtering incoming stimuli to discriminate irrelevant background stimuli. It is essential for governing some of the basic functions, and is one of the oldest parts of the brain.

Right ventrolateral pre-frontal cortex   The part of the pre-frontal cortex that is located on the inner aspect of the right hemisphere and is active during the updating of action plans and in responding to decision uncertainty.

Semantic memory   Semantic memory is that which can be consciously recalled and which consists of facts, data and other non-autobiographical information.

Serotonin   A monoamine neurotransmitter believed to play many roles including, but not limited to, temperature regulation, sensory perception and the onset of sleep. Neurons using serotonin as a transmitter are found in the brain and in the gut. A number of antidepressant drugs are targeted to brain serotonin systems.

Steroid   A type of organic compound that contains a characteristic chemical arrangement. Examples of steroids include cholesterol, the sex hormones estrogen and testosterone, and steroid drugs such as anti-inflammatory agents.

Stimulus/i   Anything in the environment capable of being perceived by one or more of our senses and eliciting a response.

Sympathetic nervous system   A branch of the autonomic nervous system responsible for mobilizing the body's energy and resources during times of stress and anxious arousal.

Synapse/synaptic connection   The space between the protrusions of two neurons where chemical and electrical signals are exchanged, normally between the axon of one neuron and the dendrite of another.

Testosterone   A steroid hormone from the androgen group. In mammals, testosterone is secreted primarily by the testicles of males and the ovaries of females, although small amounts are also secreted by the adrenal glands. It is the principal male sex hormone and an anabolic steroid.

Theory of Mind (ToM)   The ability to conceive of another entity as having a mind and a perspective different to one's own and to attempt to interpret it, also known as mentalizing.

Vagus nerve   The cranial nerve responsible for such varied tasks as heart rate, gastrointestinal peristalsis, sweating, and quite a few muscle movements in the mouth and throat, including for speech and breathing.

von Economo Neurons   Also known as spindle cells, neurons that have an elongated shape of the main body and only one dendrite, found only – so far – in the brains of higher mammals – apes and humans. Scientists have assumed that they play a role in social interactions.

Working memory   A term used to denote that part of memory which acts as temporary storage, a 'holding tank' for information that we need to have or manipulate in order to perform a current activity. A well known example is holding a telephone number in your mind while you dial it. Working memory has very limited capacity.

Zeigarnik effect   Named after the psychologist who first described it, a psychological term used for the brain's tendency to remember unfinished tasks more than finished ones.

Notes

Preface

1. The scientific study of nervous systems, including the brain.
2. Greene, J and Cohen, J, 2004, "For the law, neuroscience changes nothing and everything", Philos. Trans R SocLond B Biol Sci. Nov 29, 359(1451): 1775–85.
3. Brown, P T, Meyler, J and Swart, T, 2009, "Emotional intelligence and the amygdala: towards the concept of the limbic leader in executive coaching", *NeuroLeadership Journal*, 2, 67–77.

1 There is Chemistry and Then There is *Chemistry*

1. Salerian, A J, 2003, *Viagra for Your Brain*, Abe Books, Salerian Products.
2. http://www.washingtonian.com/blogs/capitalcomment/local-news/alen-salerian-declared-unfit-to-stand-trial.php.
3. See www.richannel.org.
4. "How We Learn – Synapses and Neural Pathways" https://www.youtube.com/watch?v=BEwg8TeipfQ&feature=kp.
5. Circulatory, digestive, endocrine, excretory, integumentary (skin, hair, nails), lymphatic, muscular, nervous, reproductive, respiratory and skeletal.
6. Goleman, D, 1996, *Emotional Intelligence, Why It Can Matter More Than IQ*, Bloomsbury.
7. For a more detailed discussion see: Brown, P T, Swart, T and Meyler, J, 2009, "Emotional intelligence and the amygdala: towards the development of the concept of the limbic leader in executive coaching", *NeuroLeadership Journal*, 2: 1–11.

2   Brains, Bodies and Businesses: A Systems Approach

1. Dutton, J E and Ragins, B R, 2006, *Exploring Positive Relationships at Work Building a Theoretical and Research Foundation*, Psychology Press.
2. Chisholm, C A, 2012, "Developing a science-based rational for coaching", MSc thesis.
3. Carol Dweck, 2007, *Mindset: The New Psychology of Success*, Ballantine Books.
4. http://hbr.org/2013/07/your-brain-at-work/ar/1.
5. http://www.nytimes.com/2013/07/21/opinion/sunday/fast-time-and-the-aging-mind.html?_r=0.
6. Ellen Langer, 2009, *Counter Clockwise: Mindful Health and the Power of Possibility*, Ballatine Books.
7. Daniel Kahneman, 2012, *Thinking Fast and Slow*, Penguin.
8. Steve Peters, 2012, *The Chimp Paradox*, Vermilion.
9. https://www.youtube.com/watch?v=I5Tw0PGcyN0.
10. A D Craig, 2002, "How do you feel? Interoception: the sense of the physiological condition of the body", *Nature Reviews Neuroscience* 3 (August): 655–66, doi:10.1038/nrn894.
11. http://www.mckinsey.com/insights/organization/increasing_the_meaning_quotient_of_work.

3   The New Model Leader

1. "Work Stress Health", The Whitehall II Study, Cabinet Office, CCSU, UCL 2004.
2. Sherman, G D, Lee, J J, Cuddy, A J C, Renshon, J, Oveis, C, Gross, J J and Lerner, J S, 2010, "Leadership is associated with lower levels of stress" and Mehta, P H and Josephs, R A, 2010, "Testosterone and cortisol jointly regulate dominance: evidence for a dual-hormone hypothesis", Hormones and Behaviour, ScienceDirect.com, Elsevier, doi 10.1016/j.yhbeh2010.08.020.
3. Sapolsky, R M, 2005, "The influence of social hierarchy on primate health", *Science*, 308(5722): 648–52.
4. Mehta, P H and Josephs, R A, 2010, "Testosterone and cortisol jointly regulate dominance: Evidence for a dual-hormone hypothesis".
5. Andrew Lawrence, Luke Clark, Jamie Nicole Labuzetta and Barbara Sahakian, MRC/Wellcome Trust Behavioural and Clinical Neuroscience Institute, and Shai Vyakarnum, Judge Business School, University of Cambridge, UK.

Research referred to in article titled "The innovative brain", *nature*, 456/13, November 2008.

6. Lieberman, M D, 2013, *Social: Why Our Brains are Wired to Connect*, Oxford University Press, pp. 223 ff.
7. http://www.ted.com/talks/amy_cuddy_your_body_language_shapes_who_you_are.html.
8. Lieberman, M D, 2013, *Social: Why Our Brains are Wired to Connect*, p. 217.
9. Inaugural lecture by Professor A Mark Williams, Brunel University, September 2013.
10. Inaugural lecture by Professor A Mark Williams, Brunel University, September 2013.
11. Experiments have shown that normally socialized people anthropomorphize even abstract shapes moving around a computer screen, so that they describe them as if having purposeful actions (the small triangle is chasing the large one, but the large one manages to escape).
12. Maslow, A, 1954, *Motivation and Personality*, Harper.
13. Although we have sometimes used it; we would welcome your suggestions for alternatives!
14. Righetti, F and Finkenauer, L, 2011 If you are able to control yourself, I will trust you, *Journal of Personality and Social Psychology*, Vol 100(5) 874–86.

4 Testosterone, Risk and Entrepreneurship

1. http://www.pnas.org/content/105/16/6167.short.
2. Lamb, D, 2002, *The Arabs: Journeys Beyond the Mirage*, Vintage Books, 2nd edition, p. 274.
3. "Cultural neuroscience" is beginning to emerge as a discipline. See, for example, Chiao, J Y and Ambady, N, 2007, "Cultural Neuroscience: parsing universality and diversity across levels of analysis", in Ktayama, S and Cohen, D, *Handbook of Cultural Psychology*, Guilford Press, Chapter 9, pp. 237–41.
4. Ormerod, P, 1994, *The Death of Economics*, Faber & Faber.
5. Dixon, N, 1976, *On the Psychology of Military Incompetence*, Jonathan Cape.
6. Zhong, S, Israel, S, Xue, H, Sham, P C, Ebstein, R P and Chew, S H, 2009, *A Neurochemical Approach to Valuation Sensitivity Over Gains and Losses*, Proceedings of the Royal Society B, *Biological Sciences* 276 (1676): 4181–8.
7. Zak, P, 2012, *The Moral Molecule: The New Science of What Makes Us Good or Evil*, Bantam Press.
8. Braynov, S, 2013, "What human trust is and is not: on the biology of human trust", a paper at the 2013 Spring Symposium of the Association for the Advancement of Artificial Intelligence, pp. 10–15.
9. http://citeseerx.ist.psu.edu/viewdoc/download?doi=10.1.1.360.3908&rep=rep1&type=pdf.

10. The gyri (singular gyrus) are the folds on the surface of the brain, and increased folding in the cortex has been shown not only in Buddhist monks but also in other people who practice meditation for 30 minutes, three times a week for three months. This physical change correlates to better regulatory ability of the PFC, which governs executive functions including impulse control, detecting bias signals and being able to switch tasks.
11. Begley, S, 2007, *Train Your Mind, Change Your Brain*, Ballantine Books.
12. http://blogs.hbr.org/2013/12/entrepreneurs-brains-are-wired-differently/.
13. Pratt, L A and Brody D J, 2008, "Depression in the United States household population, 2005–2006", *NCHS Data Brief*, (7):1–8.

5 Why is the Soft Stuff so Hard?

1. There are even programs offering accreditation in EI development and training.
2. 2 March 2012, see http://www.strategy-business.com/article/ac00034?gko= f5243.
3. Frith, C, 2007, *Making up the Mind*, Blackwell.
4. ToM is what appears to be missing from some people on the autistic spectrum, who cannot conceive that another person might have a mind which is different to theirs, with literally a different point of view.
5. Lieberman, M D, 2013, *Social: Why Our Brains are Wired to Connect*, Oxford University Press.
6. Gallagher H and Frith C, 2003, "Functional Imaging of 'Theory of Mind'", *TRENDS in Cognitive Sciences*, 7(2), February.
7. McCabe et al in Gallagher H and Frith C, 2003, "Functional Imaging of 'Theory of Mind'".
8. Cf Lieberman, M D, 2013, *Social*.
9. This does not imply that it is necessarily the mirror neurons that are both responsible for imitating actions and deriving meaning about intent. It is likely that a great number of other brain areas are involved, and that mirror neurons play a key part in this process. See further Ben Thomas, 2012, "What's so special about mirror neurons", *Scientific American* guest blog, 6 November.
10. Gallese, V, 2007, "Before and below 'theory of mind': embodied simulation and the neural correlates of social cognition", *Phil. Trans. R. Soc.* B 29 April, 362, doi: 10.1098/rstb.2006.2002.
11. Goleman D and Boyatzis, R, 2008, "Social intelligence and the biology of leadership", *Harvard Business Review*, 86(9), 74–81.
12. A recent study at Concordia University in Canada showed that infants as young as 18 months could tell the difference between justified and

unjustified emotional reactions. See http://www.concordia.ca/cunews/main/releases/2013/10/16/babies-know.html.

13. Frith, C op cit pp. 169–60.

14. Sy, T, Cote, S and Saavedra, R, 2005, "The contagious leader: impact of the leader's mood on the mood of group members, group affective tone, and group processes", *Journal of Applied Psychology*, 90(2): 295–305 and Goleman, D, Boyatzis R and McKee A, 2001, "Primal leadership: the hidden driver of great performance", *Harvard Business Review*, 79(11): 42–51. There is some contradictory evidence, see Hsee, C K, Hatfield, E, Carlson, J G and Chemtob, C, 1990, "The effect of power on susceptibility to emotional contagion", *Cognition & Emotion*, 4(4): 327–40.

15. Kahneman, D, 2012, *Thinking Fast and Slow*, Kindle edition, Penguin, p. 387.

16. Mar, R A, 2011, "The neural bases of social cognition and story comprehension", *Annual Review of Psychology*, 62: 103–34; Mar, R A, Oatley, K, Djikic, M and Mullin J, 2011, "Emotion and narrative fiction, interactive influences before, during and after reading", *Cognition and Emotion*, 25: 818–33; Mar, R A, Oatley, K and Peterson, J B, 2009, "Exploring the link between reading fiction and empathy: Ruling out individual differences and examining outcomes", *Communications*, 34, 407–28; Oatley, K, 2011, *Such Stuff as Dreams: The Psychology of Fiction*, John Wiley & Sons.

17. A famous example is the "woman in the gorilla suit" experiment, where more than 50 per cent of the audience of a short film could not recall seeing "a gorilla" walking behind a group of people playing ball, having been asked to count the number of times the ball was thrown.

18. Mintzberg, H, "Rebuilding companies as communities", *Harvard Business Review*, July–August, pp. 140ff.

19. Indeed several studies have reinforced how strong this feeling is by demonstrating that people feel pleasure in punishing cheats and "takers".

20. Brown, P T and Brown V, 2012, *Neuropsychology for Coaches*, Open University Press and McGraw-Hill Education.

21. Cranston S and Keller S, 2013, "Increasing the 'meaning quotient' of work", *McKinsey Quarterly*, January.

22. Csikszentmihalyi, M, 2008, *Flow: The Psychology of Optimal Experience*, Harper Perennial, Rider.

6 The Challenge of Decisions

1. Goldberg, E, 2009, *The New Executive Brain: Frontal Lobes in a Complex World*, Oxford University Press.

2. The adult brain is 2 per cent of our body mass, but consumes more than 20 per cent of its energy: Baumeister, R and Tierney, J, *Willpower: Rediscovering our Greatest Strength*, Penguin, p. 15 (Kindle edition).
3. Kahneman, D, 2012, *Thinking Fast and Slow*, Penguin.
4. Emotions are crucial even in economic decision making, as indicated by an experiment using fMRI to examine the brains of 19 players engaged in the Ultimatum Game: Sanfey, A G et al, 2003, "The neural basis of economic decision-making in the ultimatum game", *Science*, New Series, 300(5626) (June): 1755–8. Although a small scale experiment, it confirms other findings, see for example, Bechara A, Damasio H and Damasio A R, 2000, "Emotion, decision making and the orbitofrontal cortex", *Cerebral Cortex*, 10: 295–307.
5. Baumeister and Tierney, *Willpower*, pp. 30 ff (Kindle edition). It appears that the anterior cingulate cortex is involved in recognizing mismatches between actions and intentions, acting as some kind of error detection system. It is in this part of the brain that signals are weaker after a lot of decisions or exercise of will power.
6. See further Bazerman, M H and Moore, D A, 2009, "The escalation of commitment", in *Judgement in Managerial Decision Making*, John Wiley & Sons, Chapter 6.
7. Baumeister and Tierney, *Willpower*, p. 80.
8. More and fuller examples can be found in Daniel Kahneman's best-selling book, *Thinking Fast and Slow* and in Bazerman and Moore's *Judgement in Managerial Decision Making*. Kahneman's book is a wonderful read, Bazerman and Moore's is denser, but well worth exploring.
9. However it might be less surprising if compared with the assumptions with which the brain interprets what we see, for example, that something smaller is further away. Optical illusions take advantage of these assumptions.
10. Although there has been some doubt thrown recently on the power of priming, which is similar to anchoring, but using words, there is enough evidence to suggest that there is an effect, although not always as strong or even direct as some of the experiments might claim.

7 Changing Yourself – Changing Others

1. Aarts, H and Dijksterhuis, A, 2000, "Habits as knowledge structures: Automaticity in goal-directed behavior", *Journal of Personality and Social Psychology*, 78(1): 53–63.
2. That does not apply when walking is more challenging than usual, for example hill walking on holiday, or has to be relearned after an accident or stroke.

3. Klingberg, T, 2009, *The Overflowing Brain*, Oxford University Press.
4. Siegel, D, 1999, *The Developing Mind*, Guilford Press, pp. 136 ff.
5. Klingberg, T, 2009, *The Overflowing Brain*, Oxford University Press, pp. 99 ff.
6. Dijksterhuis, A and Aarts, H, 2010, "Goals, attention and (un) consciousness", *Annual Review of Psychology*, 61: 467–90; and Carter, R *Consciousness*, 2002, Weidenfeld and Nicholson, pp. 193 ff.
7. Doidge, N, 2008, *The Brain that Changes itself*, Penguin, p. 78.
8. Siegel, D J, 1999, *The Developing Mind,* Guilford Press, pp. 137 ff.
9. Siegel, *The Developing Mind*, p. 36.
10. Simons, D J and Chabris, C F, 1999, "Gorillas in our midst: sustained inattentional blindness for dynamic events", *Perception*, 28: 1059–74.
11. Bishop, S R, 2004, "Mindfulness: A proposed operational definition", *Clinical Psychology: Science and Practice*, 11: 3; Health Module.
12. Doidge, *The Brain that Changes itself*, p. 63.
13. Gerhardt, S, 2009, *Why Love Matters*, Routledge, p. 45.
14. Evidence for the principle that, given appropriate practice, humans improve on essentially every task, is prevalent throughout the psychology literature, ranging from the domain of perceptual learning (Fahle and Poggio, 2002) to that of motor learning (Karni et al, 1998) and cognitive training (Willis et al, 2006). An important distinction in the field concerns the time course of the learning. Many researchers have differentiated between an early, fast stage of learning that occurs on the order of minutes as the participant becomes familiar with the task and stimulus set and a much slower stage of learning triggered by practice but which requires hours and sometime days to become effective. This distinction is observed in both the perceptual (Karni and Sagi, 1993) and the motor (Karni et al, 1998) learning domains (but see Karni and Bertini, 1997, for examples of "slow" learning in purportedly "fast-learning only" paradigms and vice versa). Quoted from C. S. Green and D. Bavelier, 2008, "Exercising your brain: A review of human brain plasticity and training-induced learning", *Psychological Aging*, 23(4): 692–701. Author manuscript available in PMC 2010, 5 July.
15. Schwartz, J M and Begley, S, 2002, *The Mind and The Brain: Neuroplasticity and the Power of Mental Force*, Harper Collins; Doidge, N, 2008, *The Brain that Changes itself*, Penguin, p. 62; Klingberg, T, 2009, *The Overflowing Brain*, Oxford University Press, p. 12.
16. Schwartz and Begley, *The Mind and The Brain*, p. 335.
17. Schwartz and Begley, *The Mind and The Brain*, 217 ff.; Frith, C, 2007, *Making up the Mind: how the Brain Creates our Mental World*, Wiley-Blackwell, p. 106.
18. The well known example of London black cab drivers is also relevant here. When it was found that they had a larger hippocampus than other drivers, some scientists questioned whether that might be because people with a

better developed sense of space and direction were both attracted and more suited to this profession. But more recent studies showed both that the right posterior hippocampus grew with the amount of time spent learning the Knowledge and driving (Maguire, Woollett and Spiers, 2006) and shrank after retirement (Maguire, Woollett and Spiers, 2009).

19. Goldberg, E, 2009, *The New Executive Brain*, Oxford University Press, pp. 65 ff.
20. See further Brown, P, Chisholm, K and Swart, T, 2013, "Understanding emotions", *Developing Leaders*, 12: 11–12 and Brown, PT, Swart, T and Meyler J, 2009, "Emotional intelligence and the amygdala: towards the development of the limbic leader in executive coaching", *NeuroLeadership Journal*, 2: 1–11.
21. See note 5 and also *Future Leaders and the Trouble with Testosterone*, Tara Swart blog in IEDP Ideas for Leaders 13 October 2013.
22. Gailliot, M T, Baumeister, R F, DeWall, C N, Maner, J K, Plant, E A, Tice, D M, Brewer, L E (Florida State University) and Schmeichel, B J (Texas A&M University), 2007, "Self-control relies on glucose as a limited energy source: Willpower is more than a metaphor", *Journal of Personality and Social Psychology*, 92(2): 325–36; the famous and now controversial Mischel "Marshmallow Test" is also often cited and a more recent longitudinal study in New Zealand also shows that evidence of the ability to exercise will power in childhood has strong correlation with success in later life.
23. And indeed in many articles you could substitute will power for self control and vice versa without much seeming to change the content!
24. Note that this does not imply that this is the only part of the brain involved!
25. Cohen J R , Lieberman, M D "The common neural basis of exerting self-control in multiple domains", in Hassin, R, Ochsner, K and Trope, Y (eds), *Self Control in Society, Mind, and Brain*, Oxford University Press, Chapter 8.
26. Muraven, M, Baumeister, R F and Tice D M, 1999, "Longitudinal improvement of self-regulation through practice: Building self-control strength through repeated exercise", *Journal of Social Psychology*, 139(4): 446–58; Muraven, M and Baumeister, R F (Case Western Reserve University), 2000, "Self-regulation and depletion of limited resources: Does self-control resemble a muscle?, *Psychological Bulletin*, 126(2): 247–59.
27. Boksem, M A S, Meijman, T F and Lorist, M M, 2005, *Mental fatigue, motivation and action monitoring*, University of Groningen, The Netherlands, 4 August.
28. If lack of self-control is due to a deficit in fuel, it is a lack of capacity, not of motivation although increasing motivation can increase the amount of effort before capacity is totally exhausted.
29. Gailliot, M T et al, 2007, "Self-control relies on glucose as a limited energy source" (note 22).

30. Muraven, M and Slessareva, E, 2003, "Mechanisms of self-control failure: Motivation and limited resources", Personality and *Social Psychology* Bulletin, 29(7): 894–906.

8   Elite Performance, Brain Agility and Engagement

1. http://www.pnas.org/content/early/2013/12/26/1321664111.full.pdf.
2. Xie, L, Kang, H, Xu, Q, Chen, M J, Liao, Y, Thiyagarajan, M, O'Donnell, J, Christensen, D J, Nicholson, C, Iliff J J, Takano, T, Deane, R and Nedergaard, M, 2013, "Sleep drives metabolite clearance from the adult brain", *Science*, 342 (6156): 373–7.
3. http://www.academia.edu/2504976/Mirror_Neurons_From_Origin_to_Function.
4. http://www.sciencedirect.com/science/article/pii/S1053811910009584.

9   Stress, Resilience and Confidence

1. http://www.hse.gov.uk/statistics/causdis/stress/index.htm.
2. http://www.huffingtonpost.co.uk/natasha-shearer/work-related-stress-business_b_3545476.html.
3. Hammerfald, K, Eberle C, Grau M, Kinsperger A, Zimmermann A, Ehlert U and Gaab J. 2006, "Persistent effects of cognitive-behavioral stress management on cortisol responses to acute stress in healthy subjects--a randomized controlled trial", *Psychoneuroendocrinology*, 31 (3): 333–9.
4. Hamill, P, 2013, *Embodied Leadership*, Kogan Page.
5. Burnout is a process that has different elements to it, some clearly negative but some, according to certain schools of thought could be linked in a more positive way to finding or reconnecting with personal identity, ultimate meaning and purpose.
6. Resilience is often mentioned as a positive attribute of organizations and their leaders. There is no simple definition, but, in the context of leadership, it is generally accepted as the ability to manage stress effectively, to be ready for anything and to "bounce back" returning quickly to high performance through adversity, change and challenging situations – real or perceived.
7. Southwick, S M and Charney, D S, 2013, "Ready for anything", *Scientific American Mind*, 24(3): 32–41. Sapolsky, R M, 1989, "Hypercortisolism among socially subordinate wild baboons originates at the CNS level", *Arch Gen Psychiatry*, 46: 1047–51, quoted in Sherman et al, 2012 (note 8).

8. Sherman, G D, Lee, A J, Cuddy, A J C, Renshon, J, Oveis, C, Gross, J J and Lerner, J S, 2012 "Leadership is associated with lower levels of stress", in *Proceedings of the National Academy of Sciences, 109*: 17903–7.
9. Weiss, J M, 1968 *Effects of coping responses on stress* Journal of Comp Physiological Psychology 65:251-260
10. Gerhardt, S. (2004) *Why Love Matters: How Affection Shapes a Baby's Brain*, Routledge, Chapter 3.
11. Mullainathan, S, 2013, *Scarcity: Why Having too Little Means so Much*, Allen Lane.
12. Rusbridger, A, 2013, *Play it Again: An Amateur against the Impossible*, Vintage.
13. Published by Marshall Cavendish Business.
14. http://www.nytimes.com/2014/01/19/magazine/breathing-in-vs-spacing-out.html?_r=2.

10   Creating the Spark, Lighting the Fire

1. For Daniel Siegel, the mind is an emergent property of the brain's activity, perhaps that which is our subjective experience of that activity, our sense of being an agent and having a self.
2. Mowbray, A, 2013, *Gold Medal Flapjack, Silver Medal Life*, Matador.
3. Even in cases where it was thought that there were finite windows of opportunity for change, such as in the perception of phonemes, new research is showing that with the right kind of attention, feedback and practice the brain can learn to perceive the difference between l and r, for example, in adulthood; see Wyner, G, 2014, "How to teach old ears new tricks", *Scientific American Mind*, 25(4): 24.
4. Siegel, D, 1999, *The Developing Mind*, Guilford Press, p. 4.
5. Goleman, D, 2000, "Leadership that gets results", *Harvard Business Review*, March–April: 78–90.
6. Goleman, D, 2000, "Leadership that gets results". The main thrust of the article was that one style will not suit every circumstance and leaders benefit from being able to deploy a number of them.
7. Waldman, D A, Balthazar, P A and Peterson, S J, 2011, "Leadership and neuroscience: Can we revolutionise the way that inspirational leaders are identified and developed?", *Academy of Management, Perspectives*, February.
8. For an inspirational account of the power of emotion to generate motivational energy see Brown, P, 2012, *Neuropsychology for Coaches: Understanding the Basics*, Open University Press.

9. Goleman D and Boyatzis R, 2008, "Social intelligence and the biology of leadership", *Harvard Business Review*, September: 74–81.
10. See Young, E, 2012, "The X Factor", *New Scientist*, 23 June: 38–41.
11. Waldman et al, 2011, "Leadership and neuroscience" (note 7).
12. See also Brown, P, 2012, *Neuropsychology for Coaches*, p 107 on relationship management, and Chapter 8 affective interaction, passim.
13. Waldman et al, 2011 (note 7).
14. Csikszentmihalyi, M, 2008, *Flow: The Psychology of Optimal Experience*, Harper Perennial.
15. Some leaders follow the principles of Elliott Jaques' and Wilfred Brown's Career Path Appreciation process to help them place people at the right level of authority and decision making within organizations according to an assessment about their ability to deal with uncertainty. A caveat is that there may be an underlying assumption that people's potential and abilities are relatively fixed.
16. There is a wonderful section on how cultures are created from mythologies based on values in Macdonald, I, Burke, C and Stewart, K, 2008, *Systems Leadership: Creating Positive Organizations*, 3rd edition, Gower.
17. These experiences have sometimes been compared to the ecstatic state that some sufferers of epilepsy report on – like Dostoyevsky in *The Idiot*. A small number of studies have reported increased activity in certain brain areas (temporal lobes, insula, amygdala, limbic regions have all been mentioned) when people experience such feelings, and also that stimulation of specific parts of the brain can cause people to experience religious visions. Ananthaswamy, A, 2014, "Fits of rapture", *New Scientist*, 25 January, 221(2953): 44.
18. The dangers of the "dark side" of some kinds of leadership, through which people lose their autonomy, are ruled by fear for the benefit of a leader, sometimes with a small inner group, have been explored in depth by Professor Dennis Tourish: Tourish, D, 2013, *The Dark Side of Transformational Leadership*, Routledge.
19. Erb, H P and Gerbert, S, 2014, "Uniquely you", *Scientific American Mind*, March–April, 25(2).
20. Chisholm, J, 2013, "A general theory of innovation", unpublished paper.
21. Creativity is a very similar process, but its purpose may also be self expression or self fulfillment, rather than a wider benefit to society, although art can bring a combination of both.
22. https://www.credit-suisse.com/newsletter/doc/gender_diversity.pdf.
23. Kaufman, S B, 2014, "From contretemps to creativity", *Scientific American Mind,* March–April 25(2).

24. Simonton, D K, 2012, "The science of genius", *Scientific American Mind*, November–December, 23(5).
25. Sandkühler, S and Bhattacharya, J, 2008, "Deconstructing insight: EEG correlates of insightful problem solving", *PLOS One* 23 January, 3(1): e1459. doi: 10.1371/journal.pone.0001459.
26. Heilman, K M, Nadeau, S E and Beversdorf, D O, 2003, "Creative Innovation: Possible Brain Mechanisms", *Neurocase*, 9(5): 369–79.
27. Chrysikou, E G, Hamilton, R H, Coslett, H B, Datta, A, Bikson, M and Thompson-Schill, S L, 2013, "Noninvasive transcranial direct current stimulation over the left prefrontal cortex facilitates cognitive flexibility in tool use", *Cognitive Neuroscience*, 4(2): 81–9.
28. *Wall Street Journal* online 5 April 2013.
29. Bryce, V, 2014, "The AHA! moment", *Scientific American Mind*, July–August.

11   Difference, Diversity and Gender

1. Remember that correlation doesn't imply causation, just that the two factors are more often found together. It may be that more successful, innovative organizations are forward looking enough to recruit, retain and promote diverse talent at senior levels. Or it might mean that diversity is a contributing factor to that success.
2. Credit Suisse, August 2012. The research also found 'that companies with one or more women on the board have delivered higher average returns on equity, lower gearing, better average growth and higher price/book, value multiples over the course of the last six years.
3. Nathan, M and Lee, N, 2013, "Cultural diversity, innovation, and entrepreneurship: Firm-level evidence from London", *Economic Geography*, 89: 367–94. doi: 10.1111/ecge.12016.
4. Sylvia Ann Hewlett, et al, 2013, "How diversity can drive innovation, *Harvard Business Review*, December, accessed April 2014.
5. See, for example, the Kellogg Insight Report, *Better Decisions Through Diversity*, October 2010 and the more recent CTI report *Innovation, Diversity, and Market Growth*, 2012.
6. See, Heijmans, B T, et al, "Persistent epigenetic differences associated with prenatal exposure to famine in humans", *Proceedings of the National Academy of Sciences*, 105(44): 17046–9.
7. Research by Lumey et al, quoted in Carey, N, 2012, *The Epigenetics Revolution*, Icon Books.

8. David Feitler *The Case for Team Diversity Gets Even Better*, HBR blog, 12:00 PM 27 March 2014.

9. Erb, H-P and Gebert, S, 2014, "Who am I?", *Scientific American Mind*, March/ April. These authors indicate the tension between wanting to be an individual and wanting to be part of a group.

10. Trimble, M, 2012, *Why Humans Like to Cry: Tragedy, Evolution and the Brain*, Oxford University Press.

11. Goldstein, J M et al (Harvard Medical School), 2012, "His brain, her brain", *Scientific American Mind*, Special Edition, Summer.

12. Verma, R et al (University of Pennsylvania), 2013, "Sex differences in the structural connectome of the human brain", *Proceedings of the National Academy of Sciences,* 111(2): 823–8; published ahead of print December 2, 2013, doi:10.1073/pnas.1316909110.

13. The quotation marked passages that follow come from McGilchrist's Introduction and first chapter of his book, McGilchrist, I, 2009, *The Master and his Emissary: The Divided Brain and the Making of the Western World*, Yale University Press.

14. McGilchrist, I, 2009, *The Master and his Emissary*.

15. McGilchrist, I, 2009, *The Master and his Emissary*, pp.

16. See Goldstein, J M et al, 2012, "His brain, her brain", pp. 8 ff.

17. Janjuha-Jivraj, S, 2011, "Moving forward, women's views on board recruitment", report prepared for Women in Public Policy, House of Lords, UK, 14 December. http://www.womeninpublicpolicy.org.uk/women-leading-business-write-up/.

18. CTI Research Report 11 January 2012, "Sponsor effect 2.0: Road maps for sponsors and protégés".

19. Sandberg, S, 2013, *Lean In: Women, Work, and the Will to Lead*, W H Allen.

20. Hewlett, S-A, 2013, Forget a Mentor, *Find a Sponsor: The New Way to Fast-Track Your Career*, Harvard Business Review Press.

21. Chisholm, C. and Janjuha-Jivraj, S, 2014, "Scaling the heights", *Private Life*, Arbuthnot Latham Client Magazine, Spring.

22. Kay, K and Shipman, C, 2014, *The Confidence Code: The Science and Art of Self-Assurance – What Women Should Know*, HarperBusiness.

23. Occamstypewriter.org – "What am I doing here?", 27 January 2013, followed by "Getting away with it", 12 February 2014.

24. Kramer, V W, Konrad, A M and Erkut, S, The Critical Mass Project 2006–8, Wellesley Centers for Women; see also Torchia, M, Calabro, A and Huse, M, 2011, "Women directors on corporate boards: From Tokenism to critical mass", *Journal of Business Ethics*, August, 102(2): 299–317 and Vinnicombe, S, 2008, *Women on Corporate Boards of Directors: International Research and Practice*, Edward Elgar.

12   Whole Person, Vibrant Organization

1. Published by Martin Farncombe as a series of articles at http://www.practicalmemetics.com/.

2. Korn, C, 2010, "The neuroscience of looking on the bright side", *Scientific American,* available at http://www.livescience.com/17848-neuroscience-optimism-human-brain.html.

3. For an example of this visual metric in use, see Brown, PT, 2010, "Synergy in buildings: towards developing an understanding of the human interface", *Proceedings of the International Solar Energy Society,* Freiburg, Germany, 23–4 June, pp. 149–54.

4. At the latest count. For many years, estimates were of approximately 100 billion neurons.

Index

Aboriginal Australians, 10–11
absenteeism, 152, 153
adaptability, 26
adaptive decisions, 93–4
addiction, 64, 69, 70, 71, 215
adrenal gland, 35, 61, 63, 154, 224, 232
adrenalin, 2–3, 5, 154, 156, 202,
  224, 226
affect heuristic, 101–2
affect network, 27, 30–7
aggression, 55, 62
agility
  across brain functions, 161
  Leadership Brain Agility model, 35,
    136–43
  of thinking, 26
aging, 21
"aha!" moments, 187–9
Ahrendts, Angela, 209
alcohol, 5, 70, 132, 152, 157, 230
altruism, 89, 90, 167
Alzheimer's disease, 88, 103, 133, 135,
  224, 226
ambiguity, tolerance of, 26, 73, 200, 207
  see also uncertainty
amygdala, 72, 224, 228
  emotions, 143
  first impressions, 146
  gender differences, 201
  mentalization, 80

anabolic steroid hormones, 61, 232
anchoring, 105
anger, 9, 12, 13, 122, 170, 215
ANS, see autonomic nervous system
antioxidants, 134, 135, 224
Apple, 48, 57
Argyris, Chris, 218
Ariely, Dan, 148
attachment emotions, 9–10, 12–13, 90,
  92, 119, 163, 170, 176–7, 189
attention, 20, 29, 111
  emotions and, 95
  relaxation of, 188
  selective, 19, 27, 86
  see also focused attention
attitudes, 83–4
Aung San Suu Kyi, 209
autonomic nervous system (ANS), 12,
  154, 202, 224, 228, 230
availability heuristic, 87, 103–5, 107
avoidance emotions, 90, 119, 170, 180,
  215, 216
  see also survival emotions
awareness, 22, 32
  see also body awareness;
    self-awareness
axons, 111, 224, 229, 230

Bandura, Albert, 91
basal ganglia, 139, 142, 143, 224

Baumeister, R., 94, 121
Bazerman, M. H., 238n8
behavior, 4, 58
    changing, 22, 32, 63–4, 112–13,
        121, 135, 171
    cognitive behavioral stress
        management, 159
    stress impact on, 152
behavioral economics, 65
bias, 24, 87, 92, 101, 109, 195
    cognitive bias modification, 165
    confirmation bias, 87, 106–7
    detection of, 236n10
    instinctive, 32
bilingualism, 39
body awareness, 35–6, 39, 138, 228
body language, 46, 167, 171
    see also non-verbal communication
body scan exercise, 35–6
bonding, 13, 15, 57, 182, 198, 230
Botin, Ana, 203
Boyatzis, R., 83
brain
    "aha!" moments, 187–8
    body relationship, 158, 159
    cerebral hemispheres, 113, 118, 127,
        137, 197–201, 225
    changing the, 114–16, 123, 214
    chemistry of the, 2–6, 16
    communication of intent, 78–80
    development of the, 13, 174
    differences between brains, 65, 193–4
    differentiated systems, 211–12
    emotional system, 222
    executive functions, 18, 19–21, 38,
        45, 58, 114, 227, 231, 236n10
    focused attention, 116–17
    gender differences, 198–9, 201
    goal driven actions, 49
    guesswork by the, 78, 104, 107
    heuristics, 86–7, 101

information processing, 83–4
innovation, 184, 185
Leadership Brain Agility model, 35,
    136–43
meditation impact on the, 72
neuronal connections, 111–12, 113,
    114–15, 176
potential, 173
reading out loud, 131
reality created by the, 77, 78
response to fairness, 14
risk taking, 66–7
signaling system, 221
sleep impact on the, 132–3
stories, 85, 86, 107
systems perspective, 7
threat perception, 39
wetware, 1
    see also neurons; neuroplasticity;
        neuroscience; pre-frontal cortex
brain cells, 1, 6, 22–3, 37, 212–13,
    214, 227
brain networks, 26, 27–38, 81
brain scanning, 26, 27, 29, 30, 146, 220
brainstem, 31, 32, 138, 142, 225, 229, 231
Broca's area, 131
bromodeoxyuridine (BrdU), 23
Brown, Wilfred, 243n15
Bryant, Peter, 73
Bryce, Nessa Victoria, 188
burnout, 38, 44, 160, 241n5

caffeine, 5, 132, 135, 157, 230
Campbell Soups, 76
Career Path Appreciation process,
    243n15
catabolic steroid hormones, 61
catechins, 135
CBM, see cognitive bias modification
CBSM, see cognitive behavioral stress
    management

central nervous system, 25, 225, 230
CEOs, *see* chief executive officers
cerebral hemispheres, 113, 118, 127,
    137, 197–201, 225
cerebrospinal fluid (CSF), 133, 225, 227
change, 111–25, 135, 214
    agility across brain functions, 161
    environment, 116, 122–3
    focused attention, 114–15, 116–17
    habitual behaviors, 112–13
    motivation and self-control, 115,
        119–22
    repetition and practice, 115, 117–19
    streamlining of change processes, 38
    see also neuroplasticity
charisma, 177, 179
Charney, Dennis, 162, 165
chemistry, *see* neurochemistry
chief executive officers (CEOs), 146,
    207
Chisholm, John, 184
chromosomes, 60, 225
"chunking" of information, 51, 96–7,
    109, 225
Churchill, Winston, 186
cingulate cortex, 225, 228, 238n5
Clinton, Bill, 130
clusters, 187, 196
coaching, 33–4, 37, 53, 123, 158, 181
    brain-based, 148, 161
    intuition, 32
    stress management, 44
cognitive behavioral stress
    management (CBSM), 158–9
cognitive bias modification (CBM), 165
cognitive control, 19, 45–6
cognitive enhancers, 135
cognitive processes, 225
    see also executive functions;
        information processing
commitment, 14, 49

communication, 81, 92
    communication skills, 48, 178
    embodied, 82, 84
    empathy, 83
    feeling systems, 171
    of intent, 78–80
    non-verbal, 17, 32, 81, 171
compassionate meditation, 89, 165
competence, 50–2
Conant, Douglas R., 76
confidence, 46–7, 58, 91, 166, 168–71
    body language, 167
    gender differences, 202, 205–7
    risk taking, 63
confirmation bias, 87, 106–7
conflict processing, 39
conformity, 197
Confucius, 11
connectomics, 214, 225
contagion, 82–3, 145, 157–8, 177
control network, 27, 37–8
conversational capital, 85
cooperation, 89, 91
corpus callosum, 198, 199, 225
cortex, 31, 32, 138, 146, 225
    see also motor cortex; pre-frontal
        cortex
cortisol, 5, 61, 65, 68, 75, 161, 209, 225–6
    body posture, 167
    contagion, 157–8
    engagement, 147
    heart attacks caused by, 30
    leaders, 43, 44, 58
    mindfulness training, 63
    physical exercise, 156
    stress, 154–5
    suppressed by oxytocin, 167
    survival emotions, 12
    testosterone impact on, 46
Cousins, Philip, 218
Craig, A. D., 36

creativity, 59, 89, 133, 142, 243n21
   attachment emotions, 170
   design thinking, 143
   diversity, 196
   evolutionary responses, 29
   executive functions, 20
   innovation, 184
   Leadership Brain Agility model,
      137, 138
   restriction of, 13, 90
   trust as enabler of, 16
Credit Suisse, 185, 192, 244n2
Crowther, Geoffrey, 173
CSF, see cerebrospinal fluid
Csikszentmihalyi, Mihaly, 91, 180, 227
Cuddy, Amy J., 46, 167
culture, 183, 186, 204, 205, 212–14, 219
customers, 9–10

Dalai Lama, 174, 183
Damasio, Antonio, 96, 159
DARPA, 185
Darwin, Charles, 111
decision making, 13, 33, 65, 67–8,
      93–110, 133, 213
   affect network, 31
   checks and balances, 97–8
   decision fatigue and will power, 94–5
   delaying a decision, 99–100
   delegation of, 179
   diversity impact on, 193, 197
   emotions, 95–6, 238n4
   entrepreneurs, 73
   executive functions, 20, 114
   heuristics and fallacies, 101–8
   intuition, 96–7
   leadership skills, 52
   learning from mistakes, 98–9
default network, 27, 28, 37–8, 81
delayed gratification, 47, 72
delegation, 88, 91, 110, 166, 179

dementia, 98, 135, 224, 226
dendrites, 111, 226, 230
depression, 4, 75
design thinking, 136, 143
diet, 5, 134, 135, 157, 230
diffusion tensor imaging (DTI), 198, 226
digital media, 132
disgust, 9, 12, 69, 80, 176, 215
disruptive innovation, 136, 144
dissonance, 196
distractions, 29, 47, 124, 170
   cognitive resources, 135
   goal setting, 50, 123
   work environments, 122
diversity, 54, 185, 192–3, 195–7, 208,
      209–10, 222, 244n1
Dixon, N., 66
dominance, 42, 44, 55
Donald, Athene, 206
Donne, John, 76
dopamine, 5, 63, 66, 161, 226
   attachment emotions, 12
   engagement, 147
   error prediction/correction, 215
   reward network, 30
Downs, Diane, 218
Drucker, Peter, 27
drugs, 5, 69, 70, 135, 152, 230, 231
d.School, 143
DTI, see diffusion tensor imaging
Dunant, Henri, 174
Dweck, Carol, 25

economic decision making, 238n4
economics, 65
EEG, 95, 187, 226
EGCG, 135
Einstein, Albert, 174
electrical signaling, 3, 61
Elizabeth I, Queen of England, 168
emotional intelligence, 13, 17, 36

empathy, 139, 143
EQ, 76, 226
evolutionary responses, 29
    lack of, 83
emotions, 2, 9–13, 77, 82, 168–70,
    215–16
    affect heuristic, 101–2
    affective interaction, 176–7
    affect network, 27, 30–1
    attachment, 9–10, 12–13, 90, 92,
        119, 163, 170, 176–7, 189
    bodily maps of, 129–30
    contagion, 82–3, 177
    decision making, 95–6, 99, 238n4
    definition of, 226
    focusing of resources, 119–20
    focus on, 91–2
    gender differences, 199, 201
    halo effect, 102–3
    incentives, 121–2
    influencing attitudes, 84
    inspirational leadership, 178
    intent shaped by, 80
    interoception, 36
    Leadership Brain Agility model,
        137, 139
    limbic system, 228
    mirror neurons, 145
    motivation, 90, 91, 120
    naming, 109
    Neural Tethering Model, 70
    neurotransmitters, 6
    parenting, 16–17
    regulation of, 46, 51, 55, 114, 121,
        133, 165, 226
    stories, 85
    stress impact on, 151
    survival, 9, 12, 156, 170, 215
    tuning into others', 158
    understanding, 171, 209
empathy, 17, 46, 52, 80, 83

coaching, 158
design thinking, 143
emotional intelligence, 139, 143
gender differences, 201
mirror neurons, 145, 229
stories, 86
endocrine system, 2–3, 6, 154, 226
endorphins, 156, 226
energy, 4, 51, 217–22, 238n2
    decision making, 67
    interoception, 36
    parasympathetic nervous system, 230
    sympathetic nervous system, 231
engagement, 144–7, 172
entrepreneurs, 45, 46, 73–4
environment, 116, 122–3, 124–5, 181
epigenetics, 193–4, 226
episodic memory, 85, 103, 117,
    226, 227
EQ (Emotional Quotient), 76, 226
equality, 54
error correction, 20, 215
estrogen, 5, 158, 226, 231
ethics, 55–6
evolutionary responses, 20, 29, 88
excitement, 9, 12, 147, 170, 216
executive functions, 18, 19–21, 38, 45,
    58, 114, 227, 231, 236n10
exercise, see physical exercise/training
expertise, 50–2, 58, 59, 97, 125,
    186–7, 200
explicit memory, 117, 227
eye contact, 32, 81, 130, 142, 147

facial expressions, 17, 82
failure, 186, 207
fairness, 14, 52, 88, 92
    corporate systems, 182–3
    dopamine, 30
    evolutionary benefits, 90
    values, 54

fallacies, 101, 108, 109, 195
Farncombe, Martin, 213, 214, 216
fasting, 64, 166
fear, 9, 12, 90, 123, 161, 170, 215
    buffer to, 182
    impact on decision making, 96
    lack of trust, 14
    limbic system, 143
    mentalization, 80
    rejection, 176
    systems based on, 10
feedback, 91, 124, 181, 183, 191
    facial expressions, 82
    flow, 180
    non-verbal communication, 17
    openness to, 59
    teams, 189
feelings, 169, 170, 171, 191
"fight, fright, flight" responses, 62, 69,
    154, 225
financial gain and loss, 69, 70
first impressions, 102, 104, 145–6
flexibility, 20, 45, 46, 52, 133
flow, 91, 180–1, 227
fMRI (functional magnetic resonance
    imaging), 146, 220, 227, 238n4
focused attention, 22, 32, 51, 59,
    134, 190
    "aha!" moments, 188
    changing the brain, 114–15, 116–17
    decision making, 100–1, 104
    environmental factors, 116
    flow, 180
    goals, 49, 124
    improving, 173
    Neural Tethering Model, 68
    pre-frontal cortex, 45, 46
    self-control, 122
framing, 106, 110
    see also reframing

Franklin, Benjamin, 93
Frankl, Victor, 33
free will, 33, 120
Frisén, Jonas, 23
Frith, Chris, 79–80
Frith, Uta, 79
frontal cortex, 143, 178
frontal lobes, 21, 118, 227, 231
    see also pre-frontal cortex

Gallagher, Helen, 79–80
Gallese, V., 81
Gandhi, Mahatma, 40, 174
gender
    confidence, 47, 186, 202, 205–7
    decision making, 94
    differences between male and
        female brains, 138, 198–9, 201
    embryo development, 60
    women in the workplace, 202–5
    see also women
genes, 6, 67, 77, 193–4, 225, 226
gestalt, 200, 227
gestures, 17
Ghosal, Sumantra, 189
Gifford, Jonathan, 168, 171
glands, 6, 61
Glencore, 209
glucose, 95, 114, 134, 228
"glymphatic" system, 133, 227
goals, 37, 49–50, 58, 59, 122–3, 216
    behavior change, 121
    common, 181, 183, 189, 197, 222
    control network, 38
    flow, 180
    focused attention, 116, 124
    habitual behaviors, 112
    motivation, 90–1
    reading out loud, 131
    stretch, 110

Goldberg, E., 93–4
golden circle concept, 31–2
Goleman, Daniel, 12, 175, 183
Google, 29
Gopnik, Alison, 188
"gorilla suit" experiment, 117, 237n17
gratitude list, 172
green tea, 135–6
growth hormone, 61, 226, 227
"gut feeling", 34, 142, 146, 158
    affect network, 30–1
    decision making, 96–7
    Leadership Brain Agility model, 137,
        139
gyrification, 72, 227
gyrus, 227, 236n10

habitual behaviors, 112–13
halo effect, 102–3
Hamill, Peter, 159
health, 42–3, 44, 51, 153–4, 155, 172
hearing, 128, 131, 141, 169
heart disease, 43, 153
Hebbian theory, 31, 117–18, 227
heuristics, 86–7, 101–8, 109, 228
Hewlett, Sylvia-Ann, 204, 205
Hipp, Joerg, 221
hippocampus, 31, 128, 228
    damaged by cortisol, 43
    stress impact on, 154
    taxi drivers, 23, 25, 112, 115,
        239n18
Hirst, Tara and Peter, 18
homeostasis, 6, 228
homunculus, 129, 228
Hood, Bruce, 6
hormones, 5–6, 61, 114, 145, 147,
    228, 231
    see also adrenalin; cortisol;
        estrogen; testosterone

Hung, Brian, 221
hydration, 134
hypothalamus, 15, 154, 228, 230, 231

immune system, 154–5, 225
"imposter syndrome", 206
impulse control, 20, 27, 45, 236n10
incentives, 121–2, 123, 124
individualism, 183
influence, 20, 42, 48, 55, 58–9, 83–4
information processing, 51, 83–4,
    96–7, 212
inhibitory control, 39
innovation, 13, 89, 136, 144, 172,
    183–6
    creative, 188, 190
    default network, 28
    diversity, 192–3, 196, 244n1
    goal setting, 181
    individualism linked to, 183
    restriction of, 90
    trust as enabler of, 16
    Type 1 and Type 2 mindsets, 25
inspiration, 175–9, 180, 181, 183–4,
    189–90
instinct, 32, 33, 51, 110
insulin, 61, 226, 228
integrative thinking, 143
integrity, 82, 84, 92, 139, 143, 179
interoception, 35–6, 39, 138, 228
introspection, 27, 39
intuition, 32–5, 39, 59, 142, 190, 209
    coaching, 158
    debate around, 30
    decision making, 96–7, 109, 213
    leaders, 51
    speed of, 83
    see also "gut feeling"
IQ (Intelligence Quotient), 47, 76, 133,
    174, 228

Janjuha-Jivraj, Shaheena, 203–4
Jaques, Elliott, 243n15
jealousy, 13
Jha, Amishi, 169
job control, 42–3
Jobs, Steve, 48, 57, 92, 214
journaling, 34, 156
joy, 9, 12, 170, 216

Kahneman, Daniel, 72, 86, 104, 238n8
Kay, Katty, 206
Klingberg, T., 118
knowledge, 58, 187, 188, 225
Korn, Christopher, 214

Lagarde, Christine, 209
Lamb, David, 64
Langer, Ellen, 28
language, 78–9, 131, 145, 178
lavender, 128
leadership, 7, 26, 219, 222–3
    communication, 81, 84
    confident, 46–7, 168–71
    "dark side" of, 243n18
    definition of, 41–2
    developmental theory, 200
    engagement, 144–7
    executive functions, 19
    expertise, 50–2
    goals, 49–50
    Goleman's research, 175
    influence, 48
    innovation, 184
    inspirational, 175–9, 180, 181,
        183–4, 189–90
    leadership training, 40
    learning, 52–3
    model leaders, 40–1
    neuroscience-based model of, 58–9
    pre-frontal cortex, 45–6
    risk tolerance, 45
    storytelling, 48–9, 84–6

stress, 42–4, 162–3
trust and, 13–14
values and ethics, 54–6
what we need from leaders, 56–7
women, 203–5, 207, 208–9
Leadership Brain Agility model, 35,
    136–43
Leahy, Terry, 9–10
learned helplessness, 64
learning
    amygdala, 224
    different ways of, 178
    hippocampus, 228
    from mistakes, 98–9, 108, 166
    "spiral learning", 141
    time course of, 239n14
    workplace trust, 13
Lee, Robert E., 18
Leeson, Nick, 67
left brain hemisphere, 113, 118, 127,
    137, 197–8, 225
Leone, Alvar Pascual, 118
Libet, Benjamin, 120
Liebermann, Matthew, 81
limbic system, 31–2, 128, 138, 139,
    170, 198, 228
Lincoln, Abraham, 126, 174
listening, 142, 147, 178
Liu Ji, 8
Lo, Andrew, 69
locus coeruleus, 62, 229
logic, 137–8, 141–2
loss aversion, 24, 90, 229
love, 9, 12, 13, 15, 170, 216
loyalty, 49, 59, 77
l-theanine, 135–6
lubricant analogy, 219–20

Madoff, Bernie, 55
Mandela, Nelson, 168, 174
maps, 184
Martin, Roger, 143

Mary, Queen of Scots, 211
Maslow, Abraham, 54
Mason, Malia, 26, 27
Mayo, Charles Horace, 150
McGilchrist, Iain, 199–200
McKinsey, 37
meaning, 53–4, 57, 77–8, 86, 92, 171
"meaning quotient", 37
meditation, 39, 53, 123, 236n10
   compassionate, 89, 165
   focused attention, 117, 124
   gut instinct, 142
   gyrification, 72
   as stress relief, 44, 157, 165
melatonin, 63, 229
memes, 213–14, 216–17, 229
memory
   amygdala, 224
   episodic, 85, 103, 117, 226, 227
   focused attention, 117
   gender differences, 201
   Hebbian theory, 31
   hippocampus, 25, 228
   loss of, 224, 226
   neurons, 118
   semantic, 103, 117, 227, 231
   smells, 128
   see also working memory
mentalization, 80, 232
mental toughness, 69, 71, 73
Merkel, Angela, 209
Merrin, Patrice, 209
Merzenich, Michael, 116
metacognition, 72
Mill, John Stuart, 192
mindfulness, 29, 53, 59, 63, 123, 129
   cognitive resources, 135
   definition of, 229
   focused attention, 117, 124
   gyrification, 72
   interoception, 36
   intuition, 34

as stress relief, 157, 165
   US military, 169
mindset, 25–6, 229
Mintzberg, Henry, 88
mirroring, 86, 177, 229
mirror neurons, 79, 85, 145, 177,
   229, 236n9
Mischel Marshmallow Test, 46–7, 240n22
mistakes, learning from, 98–9, 108, 166
MIT Sloan School of Management, 136
mobile devices, 132
money, 30
Montgomery of Alamein, 168
mood, 5, 16, 168, 170, 171
   interoception, 36
   noradrenalin, 230
   regulation of, 51
Moore, D. A., 238n8
Moovi, Indra, 209
morale, 40, 168
motivation, 20, 81, 89–91, 143, 172,
   189, 190
   changing the brain, 115, 119–22
   common goals, 183
   dopamine, 30, 215
   inspirational leadership, 175, 179
   lack of self-control, 240n28
   Leadership Brain Agility model,
   137, 139
   Neural Tethering Model, 69, 70, 71
   self-motivation, 59
   simplistic motivational systems, 9
   stories, 49, 86
   to win, 49–50
motor cortex, 118, 228, 229
Mowbray, Alison, 173, 186
Moynier, Gustave, 174
MRI (magnetic resonance imaging),
   198, 229
   see also fMRI
multitasking, 124, 133
music, 131, 147

Myatt, Mike, 81
myelination, 24, 229
myelin sheath, 111–12, 229

narrative fallacy, 107–8
Nelson, Horatio, 9
neocortex, 228, 229
nerves, 61
network maps, 167
networks, organizational, 221
neural networks, 118
Neural Tethering Model, 68–73, 75
neurochemistry, 2, 4–5, 16, 68,
    220, 222
neuroeconomics, 65
neuroendocrines, 2–3, 61, 63
neurogenesis, 23, 24, 25, 37, 135
neurons, 3, 221, 230
    basal ganglia, 224
    creation of new, 23, 25, 135
    damaged by cortisol, 43
    decision making, 95
    dendrites, 226
    gender differences, 198
    Hebbian theory, 31, 117–18
    mirror neurons, 79, 85, 145, 177,
        229, 236n9
    neuronal connections, 111–12, 113
    plasticity, 22, 37
    sensory, 129
    synaptic connections, 24–5, 232
    von Economo neurons, 79, 232
neuropeptides, 15, 230
neuroplasticity, 22–5, 136, 148, 166,
    193, 208
    "attention intensive" exercises, 140
    brain-based coaching, 161
    definition of, 230
    Hebbian theory, 31
    interoception, 36
    volition, 37

neuroscience, 18–19, 21, 26, 30, 41,
    74, 176
    see also brain
neurotoxins, 5, 132–3, 230
neurotransmitters, 5–6, 111, 226, 230
    contagion, 145
    decision making, 95
    gender differences, 201
Newton, Isaac, 174
Nightingale, Florence, 144
non-verbal communication, 17, 32,
    81, 171
    see also body language
noradrenalin, 5, 62, 63, 230
    attachment emotions, 12
    creative innovation, 188
    engagement, 147
    locus coeruleus, 229
nutrition, 134, 135, 157

occipital lobe, 187, 230
olfactory bulb, 23
O'Mara, Shane, 133
opioids, 147, 230
optimism, 163
organizational change, 119, 160
organizational culture, 9, 181, 204,
    205, 212–14, 219
organizational structure, 221
organizational theory, 218
Ormerod, P., 65
oxygen, 114, 134
oxytocin, 5, 62, 65, 75, 179, 230
    attachment emotions, 12
    engagement, 147
    reward network, 30
    trust, 15, 57, 68, 161
    warm relationships, 167

parasympathetic nervous system, 230
parenting, 16–17

parietal lobes, 118, 187, 230
Pasteur, Louis, 223
perceptions, 77, 86, 119, 146, 154, 230
peripheral nervous system, 25, 154, 230, 231
persistence, 121, 174, 186, 187, 207
personality, 21, 58, 164, 212
Pert, Candace, 159
Peters, Steve, 72
PFC, see pre-frontal cortex
physical exercise/training, 63, 75, 133–4, 156
physicality, 17, 137, 138, 142, 172, 182
pineal gland, 132, 226, 229, 231
Pistorius, Oscar, 126–7
pituitary gland, 15, 154, 228, 230, 231
planning, 20, 29, 45, 114, 227
plasticity, 22–5, 136, 148, 166, 193, 208
  "attention intensive" exercises, 140
  brain-based coaching, 161
  definition of, 231
  Hebbian theory, 31
  interoception, 36
  volition, 37
pleasure, 27, 29–30, 179–80, 215
posture, 167
power, 42
practice, 32, 52–3, 124, 141, 173, 239n14
  changing the brain, 22, 115, 117–19
  expertise, 51
  Neural Tethering Model, 68–9
  resilience, 165
  will power, 121
pre-frontal cortex (PFC), 38, 45–6, 55, 58, 231
  "aha!" moments, 187–8
  decision making, 95
  development of the, 52
  executive functions, 21, 114
  focused attention, 100

gender differences, 198
goals, 49
  limitations of the, 56
  meditation impact on the, 72, 236n10
  pre-frontal regulation, 33
  priming effect, 105–6, 110, 238n10
  problem solving, 114, 133, 185, 186
  executive functions, 227
  persistence, 187
  restriction of, 90
profit, 217
progesterone, 5
pruning, 113, 114–15, 118, 231

rapport, 130, 145
readiness potential, 120
receptors, 6, 12, 201
reflection, 34, 109, 110
  see also self-reflection
reframing, 44, 45–6, 55, 110, 163, 164, 165
  see also framing
relationships, 8, 56, 57, 58, 64, 76–92
  building, 20
  decision making, 67–8
  lubricant analogy, 219–20
  Neural Tethering Model, 73
  neuronal connections, 176
  power of, 84
  supportive, 163, 167
religion, 182
repetition, 115, 117–19
  see also practice
Research Councils, 196
reservation wages, 148
resilience, 64, 73, 90, 161–7, 172, 174
  confidence, 168
  definition of, 241n6
  leaders, 52, 58
  Neural Tethering Model, 69, 71
  physical training, 75

resilience – *continued*
  sleep, 132–3
  to stress, 156
  US military, 169
resonance, 82–3
reticular formation, 143, 231
reward network, 27, 29–30
reward systems, 91, 122, 123, 191
right brain hemisphere, 113, 118, 127,
  197–8, 200, 208, 225
right ventrolateral pre-frontal cortex
  (RVLPFC), 45, 67, 121, 231
risk, 64–8
  adrenal glands, 63
  management of, 51
  Neural Tethering Model, 69, 70
  risk taking, 34, 46, 63, 66–7
  tolerance of, 45, 55, 174, 186, 207
Rusbridger, Alan, 166

sadness, 9, 12, 170, 215
Sahakian, Barbara, 45
Salerian, Alen, 3–4
Sandberg, Sheryl, 205, 209
Santander, 203
Saudi Arabia, 64
scarcity effect, 164
Scardino, Marjorie, 209
schemata, 184
selective attention, 19, 27, 86
self-actualization, 53–4
self-awareness, 36, 127, 173, 208–9
  change, 123
  emotions, 139
  leaders, 55, 83, 96
  mindfulness meditation, 53
  Neural Tethering Model, 68
  see also body awareness
self-control, 45–7, 53, 57, 173, 208–9,
  240n23
  changing the brain, 115, 119, 121

confidence, 207
energy intensity, 114, 117
incentives, 122
lack of, 240n28
see also will power
self-efficacy, 81, 91, 207
self-esteem, 151
self-management, 52, 55, 58, 121, 123,
  174, 179
self-reflection, 82, 114, 173
  decision making, 104–5, 109
  language as tool for, 78
  leaders, 51, 52, 55, 58
semantic memory, 103, 117, 227, 231
senses, 32–3, 127–31, 169
serotonin, 5, 62, 66, 75, 161, 231
  engagement, 147
  exercise, 134
  melatonin produced from, 229
  physical exercise, 156
Shakespeare, William, 60, 73, 161
shame, 9, 12, 122, 170, 176,
  186, 215
Shipman, Claire, 206
Siegel, Dan, 174, 242n1
Sinek, Simon, 31
Sirleaf, Ellen, 209
skills, 58, 125, 172
sleep, 5, 132–3, 157, 230, 231
smell, 32–3, 85, 127, 128, 169
social affiliation, 14, 15
"social approach", 44
social interaction, 53, 55, 232
social life, 44
social networks, 43, 52, 88
Southwick, Steven, 162, 165
speech, 138, 141
spindle cells, 79, 232
"spiral learning", 141
spirituality, 182
Stanford University, 143

startle response, 120, 147, 170, 185, 195, 196, 216
status, 42, 43, 44
steroids, 61, 231
stimuli, 33, 116, 119, 230, 231
storytelling, 48–9, 84–6, 107–8, 191
stress, 3, 4, 24, 145, 151–61
    chemicals related to, 154–5
    cortisol, 225–6
    costs of, 153, 156
    dealing with, 156–61
    gender differences, 201
    impact of, 151–2
    interoception, 36
    leadership, 42–4, 162–3
    neurotransmitters, 5, 230
    recovery, 64
    reducing, 90
    relieving, 189
    as springboard for creative growth, 185
    sympathetic nervous system, 231
stress inoculation, 166
subsidiarity, 179
suicide, 4
supervisory attentional system, 19
surprise, 12, 120, 147, 170, 185, 195, 196, 216
survival emotions, 9, 12, 156, 170, 215
    see also avoidance emotions
sympathetic nervous system, 231
synaptic connection, 24–5, 31, 232
systems perspective, 7, 136, 218

Tallis, Raymond, 159
task flexibility, 20, 227
task switching, 39, 236n10
taste, 32–3, 127, 129, 169
taxi drivers, 23, 25, 112, 115, 239n18
teams, 13, 189, 196
temporal lobe, 131, 141, 224

Teran, Elena Ortiz, 73
Tesco, 9–10
testosterone, 5, 60–2, 65, 161, 209, 231, 232
    body posture, 167
    confidence, 46, 47, 207
    endocrine system, 226
    impact on trust, 68
    leaders, 44, 58
    men, 202
    motivation to win, 49–50
    risk tolerance, 45
    testosterone-fuelled behavior, 62–3, 74, 75
Theory of Mind (ToM), 79, 80, 232, 236n4
therapeutic relationship, 22, 32, 44, 68–9
Thuret, Sandrine, 23
Tierney, J., 94
tiredness, 94–5, 110
Toffler, Alvin, 135
Torbert, Bill, 200
touch, 127, 129, 169
Tourish, Dennis, 243n18
transcendental meditation, 165
Trimble, Michael, 197
trust, 9, 12, 13–16, 84, 92, 170, 216
    brain reward systems, 161
    building, 20
    Confucius on, 11
    decision making, 68
    emotional intelligence, 143
    engagement, 147
    eye contact, 130
    leadership, 56–7, 58–9, 88
    mutual, 10
    openness to, 144–5
    relationships of, 123, 179
    sense of self, 215
    "turn to" list, 172
Type 1 and Type 2 mindsets, 25

uncertainty, 13, 34, 85–6, 231
  availability heuristic, 87
  Career Path Appreciation process,
    243n15
  entrepreneurs, 73
  gender differences in attitudes
    to, 202
  stress, 151
  see also ambiguity, tolerance of
US military, 169

vagus nerve, 155, 232
values, 54–6, 59, 82, 90, 92, 139, 143,
  169
veridical decisions, 93–4
vision (leadership), 20, 40, 49, 175,
  178–9, 182
vision (sight), 128, 130, 169, 230
volition, 36–7
von Economo neurons (VEN), 79, 232

Waytz, Adam, 26, 27
wearable technology, 22, 39,
  138, 166
weight loss, 33–4
Welch, Jack, 22, 76
Wellington, Duke of, 9
Wernicke's area, 131
wetware, 1
Whitehall studies, 42
Wilde, Kathryn, 209

will power, 94–5, 109, 174, 240n22,
  240n23
  changing the brain, 115, 119
  cingulate cortex, 238n5
  energy intensity, 114, 121
  see also self-control
"winner effect", 63
Winston, Lord, 6
women, 8, 60–1, 62
  confidence, 47, 186, 202, 205–7
  decision making, 94
  differences between male and
    female brains, 198–9, 201
  estrogen effect, 157, 158
  financial performance of companies,
    192, 244n2
  leadership, 203–5, 207, 208–9
  risk tolerance, 63, 186
  in the workplace, 202–5
working memory, 49, 92, 114, 190
  "chunking" of information, 51, 96,
    109, 225
  definition of, 232
  executive functions, 20, 227
  pre-frontal cortex, 45

yoga, 36, 39, 157

Zak, P., 68
Zeigarnik effect, 99, 232
Zhong, S., 66

Printed and bound by CPI Group (UK) Ltd, Croydon, CR0 4YY